Critical Essays on
THORNTON WILDER

CRITICAL ESSAYS
ON
AMERICAN LITERATURE

James Nagel, General Editor
University of Georgia, Athens

Critical Essays on
THORNTON WILDER

edited by

Martin Blank

G. K. Hall & Co.
An Imprint of Simon & Schuster Macmillan
New York

Prentice Hall International
London Mexico City New Delhi Singapore Sydney Toronto

G. K. Hall & Co.
An Imprint of Simon & Schuster Macmillan
866 Third Avenue
New York, New York 10022

Library of Congress Cataloging-in-Publication Data

Critical essays on Thornton Wilder / [edited by] Martin Blank.
     p.   cm.—(Critical essays on American literature)
     Includes bibliographical references and index.
     ISBN 0-7838-0020-7
     1. Wilder, Thornton, 1897–1975—Criticism and interpretation.
I. Blank, Martin (Martin Joseph) II. Series.
PS3545.I345Z645 1995
818'.5209—dc20
                                         95-2274
                                          CIP

The paper used in this publication meets the minimum requirements of the American National Standard for Information Sciences—Permanence of Paper for Printed Library Materials, ANSI Z39.48-1984. ∞™

10   9   8   7   6   5   4   3   2

Printed in the United States of America

for Harold Corn

Contents

◆

General Editor's Note

◆

The Critical Essays on American Literature series seeks to anthologize the most important criticism on a wide variety of topics and writers in American literature. Readers will find in various volumes not only a generous selection of reprinted articles and reviews but original essays, bibliographies, manuscript sections, and other materials brought to public attention for the first time. This volume, *Critical Essays on Thornton Wilder*, is the most comprehensive collection of essays ever published on one of the most important modern writers in the United States. It contains both a sizable gathering of early reviews and a broad selection of more modern scholarship. Among the authors of reprinted articles and reviews are Edmund Wilson, Malcolm Cowley, Granville Hicks, Francis Fergusson, Robert W. Corrigan, Megan Marshall, and Harry Levin. In addition to a substantial introduction by Martin Blank, readers will also find three original essays commissioned specifically for publication in this volume: new studies by Paul Lifton on the relationship of Wilder's plays to French symbolism, Donald Haberman on Wilder's influence on American and European drama since the 1940s, and Martin Blank on Wilder's use of Greek mythology in his play and opera *The Alcestiad*. We are confident that this book will make a permanent and significant contribution to the study of American literature.

JAMES NAGEL
University of Georgia

Publisher's Note

◆

Producing a volume that contains both newly commissioned and reprinted material presents the publisher with the challenge of balancing the desire to achieve stylistic consistency with the need to preserve the integrity of works first published elsewhere. In the Critical Essays series, essays commissioned especially for a particular volume are edited to be consistent with G. K. Hall's house style; reprinted essays appear in the style in which they were first published, with only typographical errors corrected. Consequently, shifts in style from one essay to another are the result of our efforts to be faithful to each text as it was originally published.

Chronology

♦

1897	Thornton Niven Wilder born 17 April in Madison, Wisconsin.
1906	Attends school in Hong Kong, where father, Amos Wilder, is consul general.
1906–1909	Attends school in Berkeley, California. First exposure to plays at the Greek Theatre.
1910	Returns to China; attends the China Inland Mission School at Chefoo.
1912	Attends the Thacher School in Ojai, California; acts in school plays.
1913–1915	Attends Berkeley High School. Begins writing his "three minute plays."
1915–1917	Attends Oberlin College.
1917	Attends Yale University.
1918	Serves in U.S. Coast Artillery Corps.
1919–1920	Returns to Yale and is awarded a B.A. Writes essays and drama criticism for the *Boston Evening Transcript. The Trumpet Shall Sound* published in *Yale Literary Magazine.*
1920–1921	Studies archaeology at the American Academy in Rome.
1922–1925, 1927–1928	Teaches at Lawrenceville School in New Jersey.

1925–1926   Studies French literature at Princeton; awarded an M.A.

1926   *The Cabala* published. *The Trumpet Shall Sound* produced off-Broadway.

1927   *The Bridge of San Luis Rey* published.

1928   *The Angel That Troubled the Waters* published. Awarded the Pulitzer Prize for *The Bridge of San Luis Rey*.

1930   *The Woman of Andros* published.

1930–1936   Teaches at the University of Chicago.

1931   *The Long Christmas Dinner and Other Plays* published.

1932   Translates André Obey's *Lucrèce* for Broadway production.

1933   *Lucrèce* published.

1935   *Heaven's My Destination* published.

1937   Adapts Ibsen's *A Doll's House* for a Broadway production.

1938   *Our Town* produced on Broadway; receives a second Pulitzer Prize. *The Merchant of Yonkers* produced on Broadway.

1942   *The Skin of Our Teeth* produced on Broadway.

1942–1945   Enlists in the U.S. Army Air Intelligence and serves in the United States, Africa and Italy.

1943   Awarded a third Pulitzer Prize for *The Skin of Our Teeth*.

1947   Receives Litt.D. from Yale.

1948   Translates Sartre's *Morts Sans Sepulture* as *The Victors*; play produced off-Broadway. *The Ides of March* published.

1950–1951   Holds the Charles Eliot Norton Professorship at Harvard; receives L.L.D. from Harvard.

1952   Awarded a Gold Medal by the National Institute of Arts and Letters.

1954   *The Matchmaker* produced at the Edinburgh Festival, tours Europe, and sustains successful run in London.

1955   *The Matchmaker* produced on Broadway. *The Alcestiad* (under the title *A Life in the Sun*) produced at the Edinburgh Festival with a satyr play, *The Drunken Sisters* (Gluttony).

1957   Two plays of *The Seven Deadly Sins*—*Bernice* (Pride) and *The Wreck on the Five-Twenty-Five* (Sloth)—produced at the Berlin Festival; receives German Booksellers' Peace Prize.

1961   Premiere of the opera *The Long Christmas Dinner*, with a libretto by Wilder and music by Paul Hindemith, in Mannheim, Germany.

1962   *Plays for Bleecker Street*, including *Infancy* and *Childhood* from *The Seven Ages of Man* and *Someone from Assisi* (Lust) from *The Seven Deadly Sins*, produced off-Broadway. Premiere of the opera *The Alcestiad*, with a libretto by Wilder and music by Louise Talma, in Frankfurt, Germany.

1963   Receives the Presidential Medal of Freedom.

1965   Receives the National Book Committee's Medal for Literature at the White House.

1967   *The Eighth Day* published; receives the National Book Award.

1973   *Theophilus North* published.

1975   Dies 7 December in Hamden, Connecticut.

1979   *"American Characteristics" and Other Essays* published.

1985   *The Journals of Thornton Wilder, 1939–1961*, published.

Introduction

◆

MARTIN BLANK

Thornton Wilder's body of work, the product of a career spanning more than 50 years, may be seen as relatively small. His career, however, represented many facets of the intellectual and artistic life, in addition to his achievements as novelist and dramatist. Wilder was the author of seven novels, five full-length and many one-act plays, adaptations-translations of four plays into English (including *The Sea Gull*, never produced), the librettos of two operas, and several film scripts written in collaboration. Wilder also pursued scholarly interests and wrote many critical essays.[1] He authored a multivolume journal and maintained a voluminous correspondence, writing thousands of letters during his lifetime. In addition, Wilder held posts as university professor and prep school master and was a frequent lecturer and actor in his own plays. Wilder's many creative interests suggest a greater achievement than is generally acknowledged. But it is for his work as novelist and dramatist that Wilder established his reputation and it is for this he will be remembered.[2]

In commenting on the work for which Wilder is best known, Leon Edel called him "our only great novelist who could be at the same time a supreme playwright."[3] When his achievements are considered by critics today, they are judged to be those of a dramatist rather than a novelist. In identifying the major American novelists of the first half of the twentieth century, critics tend to think first of Ernest Hemingway, F. Scott Fitzgerald, and William Faulkner. Other names would be considered, but Wilder's would not, even though he was originally thought of as part of the generation of novelists who first came to prominence in the 1920s. In drama Wilder's work is sometimes considered an addendum to the achievements of Eugene O'Neill, Tennessee Williams, and Arthur Miller.

Throughout his career Wilder was periodically honored but frequently ignored by the critics. Edmund Wilson, writing in 1928, shortly after the success of *The Bridge of San Luis Rey* catapulted Wilder to international celebrity, noted that there needed to be a good deal said about Wilder's art "which no one, so far as I know, has said."[4] Nearly 50 years later, in 1975, Malcolm Cowley stated that "in point of intelligent criticism, Wilder is the most neglected author of a brilliant generation."[5]

There are several reasons for Wilder's anomalous critical reception and his consequent standing in the literary community. First, his writing is markedly different from that of his contemporaries, and critics often did not know how to respond. Wilder frequently built his works on moral, religious, and metaphysical ideas, rather than focusing on social and psychological complexities, the predominant concerns of his contemporaries. Second, unlike many writers of his day, Wilder never revolted against the values and beliefs of nineteenth-century American Protestantism; after the first world war he never turned in despair to agnosticism or nihilism, but seeing man as flawed, Wilder retained his faith in man's capacity for goodness. Third, unlike the realists portraying idiosyncratic characters inhabiting a specific time and place, Wilder, as allegorist, portrayed characters behaving in ways to suggest the universality of all times and all places. Consequently, some critics were alienated or disoriented by the allegorical and moral resonances in Wilder's writing. Fourth, as a traditionalist Wilder never rebelled against the "genteel" or the beautifully embellished sentence in literature. Further, in his writing Wilder used several literary techniques, including the cliché and the purposeful use of banality and sentiment, techniques for which he was severely criticized. A small number of critics recognized the ways in which these literary devices advance Wilder's aesthetic and philosophical arguments.

Wilder found inspiration for his work not only from observation and experience but also from books and his knowledge of the past. Tyrone Guthrie, director of several of Wilder's plays, wrote of him, "I have never met anyone with so encyclopedic a knowledge of so wide a range of topics. . . . [H]e has been everywhere, has known—and knows—everyone."[6] Those ideas that are present in Wilder's work are not new; they appear in classical literature and philosophy of all ages. But one of Wilder's achievements was to communicate complex and sophisticated ideas found in the classics, making them available to audiences of great as well as little learning. His erudition and his knowledge of people, events, and ideas caused some critics to view Wilder's writing as lacking passion, with frequent charges made that he was "a pedagogue," "bookish," and "pretentious." In his writing Wilder alternated between the novel, drama, and essay; he portrayed the tragic, comic, and farcical, all with seeming ease. Wilder was difficult to categorize; some critics felt that he flaunted his knowledge and that his work reflected the dilettante.

Wilder's critical reputation was further compromised by his literary influences and his admitted appropriations from those sources. Wilder frequently drew on the past to expand the frame of reference of his novels and plays, to offer resonances beyond what he had written. For example, *The Trumpet Shall Sound* is indebted to Jonson's *The Alchemist. The Bridge of San Luis Rey* has portions based on Prosper Mérimeé's play *La Carosse du Saint-Sacrement.* Wilder also borrowed from the letters of Madame de Sévigné in creating the character of the Marquesa in *The Bridge. The Woman of Andros* is based on Terence's *Andria. Our Town* was inspired by the *Odyssey* (Emily's farewell to earth) and Dante's *Purgatory* (the patience of the waiting dead). *The Matchmaker*, along with its earlier incarnation, *The Merchant of Yonkers*, has its antecedents in a nineteenth-century Viennese play by Johann Nestroy, an earlier English play by John Oxenford, and significant borrowing from *The Miser*, which in turn is based partly on *Aulularia*, by Plautus. *The Skin of Our Teeth* is heavily indebted to *Finnegans Wake.* The second act of *The Alcestiad* is a virtual retelling of Euripides's version of the myth. Wilder's extensive knowledge and use of world literature help make his work difficult to place in a narrow frame of reference.

Wilder enjoyed popular appeal with readers and theatergoers both at home and abroad. This made him suspect of pandering to the middle class; as a result, some critics dismissed his art. His appeal, however, is based on a broad range of aesthetic and intellectual thought that many critics were unable to appreciate. Before Wilder there was no precedent in American literature for the synthesis of knowledge and artistry he represented. Despite the criticism leveled at Wilder, he was often praised as a graceful and ironic stylist, possessing a comic sensibility that masked a tragic view of life. In addition, he was acknowledged to be a pioneering and profoundly original dramatist.

To identify the extensive critical literature of Thornton Wilder's work, it is necessary to consult several bibliographies. These works list thousands of entries (through 1990) dealing with Wilder's life and work: biographies, dissertations and theses, book-length critical studies, portions of books, scholarly essays and monographs, periodical articles, and reviews of publications and productions of Wilder's plays. With continuous productions of his plays throughout the world, many additional articles and reviews have been written in the intervening years. Ever since the great success of *The Bridge of San Luis Rey*, Wilder has been written about, both in English and in many foreign languages, principally German, and for many years in countries where German is spoken Wilder was the most popular American author.

The first of these studies, *Thornton Wilder: A Bibliography* (1958),[7] was published by the U.S. Information Service in Germany, in answer to a need for information by interested citizens of that country. This was followed by publication in the United States of J. M. Edelstein's *A Bibliographical Checklist of the Writings of Thornton Wilder* (1959) and Heinz Kosok's "Thornton Wilder: A Bibliography of Criticism" (1963).[8] The following year Jackson R. Bryer's "Thornton Wilder and the Reviewers" (1964) appeared. It lists

critiques from magazines and newspapers, primarily in English, and covers
Wilder's work through 1962.[9] One of the two most comprehensive bibliogra-
phies is Michael Vincent Williams's doctoral dissertation "Thornton Wilder's
Anglo-American and German Critics: A Bibliography" (1979),[10] which doc-
uments more than 2,000 items. A useful supplement to Williams's work is
Richard H. Goldstone and Gary Anderson's *Thornton Wilder: An Annotated
Bibliography of Works by and about Thornton Wilder* (1982).[11] The most recent
bibliography—and, along with Williams's work, an invaluable study—is
Claudette Walsh's *Thornton Wilder: A Reference Guide, 1926–1990* (1993).[12]
In her work Walsh attempts to consolidate all literary criticism written in
English about the works of Thornton Wilder from 1926–1990.

Three biographical studies of Wilder have been published. First, Richard H. Goldstone's *Thornton Wilder: An Intimate Portrait* (1975)[13] is, in
Goldstone's words in his foreword, "not a formal biography. It is a portrait—
an *intimate* portrait because it presents impressions of its subject by a number
of persons who have stood close to Thornton Wilder." Goldstone's book
encompasses critical analysis of Wilder's work that relates to his biographical
portrait. This book was followed by Linda Simon's *Thornton Wilder: His
World* (1979),[14] a sympathetic study of her subject that provides useful
information on Wilder's life and work. The most comprehensive study to date
is Gilbert A. Harrison's *The Enthusiast: A Life of Thornton Wilder* (1983)[15], an
authorized biography that benefits from Harrison's access to Wilder's papers
and journals and the cooperation of the Wilder family.

Several critical studies of Wilder have been published. The first to
appear is Rex Burbank's *Thornton Wilder* (1961),[16] which examines Wilder's
work through *The Alcestiad* and attempts an overall assessment. Helmut
Papajewski's *Thornton Wilder*,[17] the first German monograph, was published
the same year and later translated into English by John Conway for American
publication (1968). Another German work, Hermann Stresau's *Thornton
Wilder* (1963), intended as a basic introduction to the novels and plays, was
translated into English by Frieda Schutz, in a somewhat altered version
(1971).[18] Bernard Grebanier's *Thornton Wilder* (1964)[19] is a pamphlet that
discusses Wilder's work through *The Alcestiad* and argues for his place in
American literature. Malcolm Goldstein's *The Art of Thornton Wilder* (1965)[20]
examines the novels and plays through *Plays for Bleecker Street*, views the
main theme in Wilder's work as "the joy the individual discovers in living"
and argues that Wilder has given "full treatment to the problems that occur
with never ending urgency in the life of each member of the race." Donald
Haberman's *The Plays of Thornton Wilder: A Critical Study* (1967)[21] examines
the forms of Wilder's plays and their relationship to his content. Haberman
finds that Wilder's work "has exhibited one direction which the new myths,
the new metaphors, and the new forms may take to illuminate man's new
position." M. C. Kuner's *Thornton Wilder: The Bright and the Dark* (1972)[22]
discusses the themes, techniques and influences through *The Eighth Day* and

finds Wilder a serious moralist and dedicated artist, intent on showing ordinary aspects of life often neglected in other writers' works. Mary Ellen Williams's *A Vast Landscape: Time in the Novels of Thornton Wilder* (1979)[23] focuses on the aspect of time in Wilder's work and contains a compelling introduction by Warren French, who argues that Wilder should have been awarded the Nobel Prize in literature. Amos Wilder's *Thornton Wilder and His Public* (1980)[24] argues that his brother's work is a "total humanistic outreach" and that even though he is a consistent defender of modernist achievement, he nevertheless questioned the "dogmas" of the age—iconoclasm and alienation. Americans have not received Wilder's work, Amos Wilder believes, with the same ardor as the Germans have. David Castronovo's *Thornton Wilder* (1986)[25] is a perceptive study in which he found that "we are hard pressed to think of a writer who combines irony and gentle acceptance of existence in Wilder's way. For almost fifty years he continued to show what he felt about isolation and torment, joy and wonder." Donald Haberman's *"Our Town": An American Play* (1989)[26] discusses major themes and ideas, the critical reception of the play, and several subsequent productions. Finally, Jackson R. Bryer's *Conversations with Thornton Wilder* (1992)[27] anthologizes several interviews the author gave between 1929 and 1975.

During the 1920s Wilder published two novels and a collection of plays; he also saw a play produced. *The Cabala* (1926), the first of Wilder's works to be reviewed, received generally favorable notices. Theodore Purdy, Jr., writing in the *Saturday Review of Literature*, found the novel "distinctly disorganized in structure and a great deal of the writing is frankly imitative" but also acknowledged that "in its total effect this novel often makes thoroughly good reading."[28] The critic for the *New York Times Book Review* praised it: "The appearance of Thornton Wilder's *The Cabala* marks the debut of a new American stylist. This first novel of a hitherto unknown writer is a literary event, because Mr. Wilder is the first of the postwar crop of American writers to consider prose as something more than a medium of expression. . . . Mr. Wilder's style is more mature than its content. Nevertheless, *The Cabala* is a work of art, both in form and design."[29]

The Trumpet Shall Sound was produced in 1926 and marked the first professional production of a Wilder play. But the realistic form Wilder chose was inappropriate to embody his Christian allegory of justice, mercy, and spiritual rebirth. The reviews were poor and the play failed. The reviewer for the *New York Herald Tribune* found the play "besprinkled with misty symbolism" and called it "sophomoric."[30] The *New York Times* reviewer thought the play "furnishes a rather murky evening among the better known symbols."[31] Because the play was so quickly dismissed by the critics and Wilder's reputation was not yet firmly established—little damage was done as a result of the production of the play.

The Bridge of San Luis Rey (1927) received almost universal praise from the critics and made Wilder an instant celebrity. Wilder's mastery of style and language, blending sparse, polished prose with his use of the ironic, was praised. Some critics hailed Wilder as a refreshing corrective to the verbal excesses of the naturalists, while others attached the label "Christian humanist" to him. Critics also singled out the novel's structure and its metaphysical qualities as noteworthy. Laurence Stallings of *McCall's* said the book is "the philosophical novel brought to perfection."[32] C., M. (assumed to be Malcolm Cowley), writing in the *New Republic*, found that the book "without pretense to greatness is perfect in itself. . . . [T]he texture is completely unified; nothing falls short of its mark; nothing exceeds it; and the book as a whole is like some faultless temple erected to a minor deity."[33] Clifton Fadiman, writing in the *Nation*, thought the book was proof "that an American, if he is willing to exercise rigorous selection and understatement and a measured observance of the prose style of the masters, can create a novel . . . with pure grace."[34] Finally, Isabel Patterson of the *New York Herald Tribune* hailed the novel as "a little masterpiece, fully confirming the promise implicit in Thornton Wilder's first novel, *The Cabala*, of the addition of a distinguished artist to the ranks of American writers."[35] Wilder was awarded his first Pulitzer Prize for *The Bridge of San Luis Rey*.

"The Angel That Troubled the Waters" and Other Plays (1928), a collection of "three minute plays for three persons," is designed to be played in the mind of the reader. The plays are fanciful treatments of platonic, literary, and religious themes. The critical reaction was mixed, essentially polite but indifferent. Some critics admired the unique form; others objected to the plays' brevity and preciosity. T. S. Matthews, writing in the *New Republic*, believed Wilder had capitalized on the success of *The Bridge of San Luis Rey*, concluding, "It is a pity that this notebook for what must be a more solidly considered achievement should have been ripped untimely from him."[36] Other critics also wondered whether the plays would have found a publisher without the success of the previous work. The collection seemed immature, slight, and too slim to be considered a major literary contribution.

During the 1930s Wilder published two novels and a collection of plays; he also had two plays produced. *The Woman of Andros* (1930) is set on an imaginary island in the Aegean, two centuries before the birth of Christ. The reviews were mixed. Henry Hazlitt, writing in the *Nation*, found Wilder's situations "patently arranged, the plot shopworn, and at no time . . . was I able to lose sight of Mr. Wilder in the act of being a fine stylist. The whole thing, in fact, seems to me primarily an exercise in style."[37] Edmund Wilson in the *New Republic* admired Wilder's technical skill but sensed a "broken-hearted Proustian sob which had welled up, all too unmistakable, from the peculiar sentimentality of our own time and not from any state of mind that one can associate with the Greeks." Wilson wrote that Wilder was becoming imitative, and "just because he is evidently a first-rate man, one would like to see him more at home."[38] However, Henry Seidel Canby, writing in the *Saturday Review of Literature*, praised the novel, finding Wilder's craftsmanship outstanding: "[T]here is not one self-conscious word or superfluous phrase in the book, but because with skill and a patience and an understanding of the lofty ideas in a beautiful setting with which he deals, Wilder has been willing to carry his writing over those leagues beyond impressionism which our journalist-novelists have never tried to follow, the pain of labor, or the haste of composition, being too great." Moreover, Canby linked Wilder and Hemingway as "the bellwethers of the oncoming generations. They are more alike than they seem. Each has powerful sentiment under the restraint of his form. Each stands mightily for an intense perfection of his expression. Hemingway has only one utterance—of the vernacular—and shapes that with an eloquent simplicity which seems to be the voice of yesterday but actually has some of the accent of all time in it. He is a journalist trying to make art out of intensity. Wilder is a scholar and a moralist in whose ears literature is always murmuring."[39] Carl Van Doren, writing in the *New York Herald Tribune*, called *The Woman of Andros* superior to both *The Cabala* and *The Bridge*.[40] The anonymous reviewer for the *New York Times Book Review* concurred, calling the novel "the best book we have had from him."[41]

The following year *The Long Christmas Dinner and Other Plays in One-Act* was published (1931). As a result of the Great Depression, which had brought about sweeping changes in America's cultural life, most critics were not impressed by Wilder's work. The six plays in the volume, while set in the United States, did not deal with contemporary social issues. Moreover, the theatricality of three of the plays—the title play, *The Happy Journey to Trenton and Camden*, and *Pullman Car Hiawatha*—was objected to by some critics. Walter Prichard Eaton of *New York Herald Tribune Books*, who did not object to the theatricality, believed the results of Wilder's work failed to do justice to the promise inherent in the style he chose.[42] An important exception to the prevailing opinion was expressed in the *New York Times Book Review* by Percy Hutchinson, who found that the three plays "may be regarded as being very near to miniature masterpieces."[43] While the volume was not a critical success, it marked Wilder's debut as a dramatist not only of promise but of substance as well. For the first time the theatricalism of the later plays, for which he would become well known, was introduced.

Heaven's My Destination (1935) is a comic picaresque set in the contemporary American Southwest. The critical response was mostly favorable but not enthusiastic. Several reviewers were puzzled and objected to the ambiguity of Wilder's treatment of his subject; other critics, such as Sidney Olson of the *Washington Post*, faulted the novel for having its central character portrayed as a "uniquely foul" religious bigot.[44] Edmund Wilson, writing in the *New Republic*, hailed the novel as Wilder's finest to date.[45] Henry Seidel Canby of the *Saturday Review of Literature* found Wilder's work "admirable story telling."[46] R. P. Blackmur in the *Nation* called the book "a lively, entertaining novel of picaresque incident." He wrote that Wilder was concerned with the representation of goodness and has always been concerned with it. While the time and place have been altered from his previous novels, Wilder's theme has not changed.[47] The novel was received by most critics as light satire, not to be taken seriously.

Our Town (1938) was to emerge as the work of dramatic literature to attract the greatest number of audiences and readers in this century. However, the immediate response of the reviewers was not overwhelmingly positive. Some were puzzled by the striking unconventionality of the theatrical style of *Our Town* but were surprised and delighted nonetheless. A few called the play a clever hoax. George Jean Nathan, writing in *Scribner's Magazine*, called the play "a stunt."[48] However, Mary McCarthy in the *Partisan Review* praised the play, calling it "an act of awareness, a demonstration of the fact that in a work of art, at least experience *can* be arrested, imprisoned and vicariously felt."[49] Brooks Atkinson of the *New York Times* expressed the majority view and called *Our Town* "hauntingly beautiful."[50] Similarly, John Mason Brown of the *New York Post* wrote that the play was "one of the sagest, warmest, and most deeply human scripts to have come out of our theatre."[51] Wilder received his second Pulitzer Prize for *Our Town*, becoming the only author to receive the honor for both the novel and the drama.

The Merchant of Yonkers (1938) was an overwhelming failure. The critics were not quite sure whom to blame, but there was little doubt that Wilder's new play was one of the major critical disappointments of that season. John Mason Brown wrote in the *New York Post* that never "to my knowledge have two brief and supposedly merry hours stretched themselves out into such an eternity."[52] A more moderate view was taken by Brooks Atkinson, who wrote in the *New York Times* that Wilder would be forgiven "for the intervals in which the fun does not flow freely."[53] John Anderson of *New York Journal American* found the work "coy" and "arch" and summed up his findings: "[W]hen a farce isn't funny, there is nothing to be done."[54] Richard Watts, Jr., held the majority view and wrote in the *New York Herald Tribune*: "*The Merchant of Yonkers* disappointed me sorely."[55]

During the 1940s Wilder wrote one play and one novel. *The Skin of Our Teeth* (1942) opened on Broadway to a generally favorable critical response. Howard Barnes, whose review appeared in the *New York Herald Tribune*, expressed the majority view when he called the play "a vital and wonderful piece of theatre."[56] The anonymous reviewer for *Newsweek* wrote, "[C]all it comedy, fantasy, allegory or cosmic vaudeville show, Wilder has contrived something provocative and stimulating."[57] Rosamond Gilder of *Theatre Arts* called the play "not only a tribute to the indestructibility of the human race . . . ; it is also a giddy proof of the theatre's own imperishable vitality."[58] A minority review was written by Wilella Waldorf of the *New York Post*, who criticized the play as "a stunt show."[59] Wilder received his third Pulitzer Prize for *The Skin of Our Teeth*.

With *The Ides of March* (1948) coming so soon after the war, critics were generally unsympathetic to Wilder's portrait of Caesar as existential man and tragic hero. Their reaction was respectful but unenthusiastic. Some were put off by Wilder's historical inventions and manipulation of time sequences, wishing the story to be told in chronological order. Richard Watts, Jr., reviewed the novel for the *New Republic* and saw that Wilder captured the greatness of Caesar but objected to what he believed was a sympathetic portrait of him.[60] Orville Prescott, writing in the *New York Times*, called the novel "cold, precise, artful and quite lacking in the divine fire that glows about a major work of art."[61] Paul Jordan-Smith, reviewing the novel for the *Los Angeles Times* wrote, "[T]hose who appreciate good writing and deep insight will . . . cherish it as one of this distinguished author's best novels."[62] Amy Loveman in the *Saturday Review of Literature* called *The Ides of March* ". . . perhaps Mr. Wilder's finest work. It is marked by high imagination, beauty of style, and richness of thought."[63] The book, however, was virtually ignored by the prestigious literary journals and the academic critics. The acclaim it did receive did not engender enthusiasm, and the novel was perceived as a curiosity. The book's reception in England was much more positive than that accorded it in the United States. The reviewer for the (London) *Times Literary Supplement* saw Caesar as a man of enormous stature and great tragedy, "and the tragedy is the more impressive because it is never stated. It arises from the total impression of this short, witty and extremely serious book."[64]

In the 1950s Wilder wrote two full-length plays, plus several of his cycle plays. Wilder's slightly revised version of his 1938 failure, *The Merchant of Yonkers*, now called *The Matchmaker*, opened in New York in 1955. It was enthusiastically received by most reviewers, and the play became Wilder's longest running success. Reviewing *The Matchmaker*, Robert Coleman of the *New York Daily Mirror* wrote, "If you expect to share the slaphappy shenanigans in West 45th Street, you'd better run, not walk to the box office. Otherwise, you're going to have to wait too long to enjoy this side-splitting mad-house of merriment."[65] William Hawkins of the *New York World-Telegram and Sun* concurred: "Better jump in front of a subway than miss *The Matchmaker*. [It] is so unusual and so rigorously uplifting, that to miss it is tantamount to starving yourself."[66] The play's success did little to raise Wilder's stature in the critical community. Its great commercial success made it suspect, as though popular appeal and artistic merit were mutually exclusive. Other critics, forgetting the ancient and honorable roots of the genre, viewed farce as somehow not worthy of serious critical analysis. The play was therefore not considered an enduring contribution to American drama. *The Alcestiad* (1955), Wilder's version of the Greek myth of Alcestis, was produced at the Edinburgh Festival. For that engagement the play's title was changed to *A Life in the Sun*, and Wilder's one-act satyr play *The Drunken Sisters* (Gluttony) was incorporated into the production. The critics were almost unanimously disappointed. In 1957–58 *The Alcestiad* was presented in several German-language productions in Europe, and it played much more successfully. (For a survey of the critical reception to the several productions, see my essay "*The Alcestiad*: The Play and Opera," appearing elsewhere in this volume.)

Wilder's final efforts as a dramatist are the two projected but never completed cycles of plays *The Seven Ages of Man* and *The Seven Deadly Sins* that he began writing in the 1950s.[67] Two of the plays from *The Seven Deadly Sins* cycle, *Bernice* (Pride) and the *The Wreck on the Five-Twenty-Five* (Sloth) were produced at the Berlin Festival in 1957.[68] Critical reaction ranged from favorable (with reservations) to enthusiastic. The simplicity of the plays and their productions surprised some critics and audiences. The reviewer for *Tag* called *Bernice* the high point of the evening; the reviewer for *Die Welt* thought *The Wreck on the Five-Twenty-Five* was "a little gem of psychological insight and secret love of mankind"; and the critic for the *Frankfurter Neue Presse* considered the two plays outwardly gray "but shining with the simple, dry poetry of everyday life."[69]

During the 1960s Wilder saw additional cycle plays produced and a novel published. *Plays for Bleecker Street* (1962) contained *Someone From Assisi* (Lust), *Infancy*, and *Childhood*. Critics generally found the first play to be poorly conceived but endorsed the latter two plays as dramatically worthy. Richard Watts, Jr., of the *New York Post* wrote, "I thought the most original and interesting of the plays was 'Infancy.'"[70] Walter Kerr, writing in the *New York Herald Tribune*, concluded, ". . . [L]et us simply be thankful for the curious memory called 'Childhood.' "[71] Howard Taubman, writing in the *New York Times*, stated that all three plays "are fresh in conception, differentiated in style and uncommonly compelling in performance. Taking advantage of the simplicity of approach of arena theatre, Mr. Wilder's *Plays for Bleecker Street* needs only a few chairs and bench to evoke worlds of deep reality and dewy imagination."[72] *The Eighth Day* (1967), Wilder's first novel in 19 years, is a murder mystery that explores the consequences of a miscarriage of justice in a small Illinois mining town of 1902. The initial reviews were favorable. Eliot Fremont-Smith of the *New York Times* called it Wilder's "best and most absorbing novel."[73] Melvin Maddocks of the *Christian Science Monitor* wrote that Wilder had raised the ultimate questions and "sent them whirling their deep spirals with a wit and learning and felt intelligence no other American novelist of the moment can match."[74] Malcolm Cowley, writing in the *Washington Post Book Week*, admired the broad sweep of the novel, the realistic evocation of a bygone era, and Wilder's thoughtful ruminations on time, history and the American people.[75] The negative reviews were exceedingly harsh. Benjamin DeMott in the *New York Times Book Review* called Wilder a "metaphysical nag, forever itching the enormous questions" and called the writing "frail in imaginative authority and passion."[76] Stanley Kaufmann in the *New Republic* wrote that the characters were flat and unbelievable, and the unconventional form of the novel disastrous.

Kaufmann denounced the book as "shockingly and unredeemingly bad." [77] The novel's appearance at the height of the Vietnam War, civil rights battles, and the burning and looting of American cities was seen as evidence that Wilder was out of touch and had nothing to say to his fellow Americans; he was considered irrelevant to his time. Nevertheless, the novel was chosen winner of the National Book Award in fiction for 1967.

In the 1970s Wilder's final novel was published. *Theophilus North* (1973) is a semiautobiographical picaresque set in Newport, Rhode Island, in 1926 and recounts a series of separate stories that are held together by Theophilus's involvement with the lives of the many people he encounters. The reviews were mixed, but more favorable than not. Some reviewers realized that *Theophilus North* would be Wilder's final work. While it was ignored by some critics, as *The Ides of March* had been, it was not subject to the scorn and derision that had greeted *The Eighth Day*. Peter S. Prescott in *Newsweek* called the book "mannered, romantic and sentimental." [78] The anonymous reviewer of the (London) *Times Literary Supplement* wrote that the novel should be prized for its subtlety and its blend of different literary forms: "a social satire in the best Edith Wharton manner, an epic, a fable and a romance." [79] Geoffrey Wagner in the *National Review* praised the novel for its "sunny disposition at the end of a long and distinguished career" and said it "can only be matched, of late, by Thomas Mann's *Felix Krull*." [80]

In the years after Wilder's death in 1975, two of his works, *"American Characteristics" and Other Essays* (1979) and *The Journals of Thornton Wilder, 1939–1961* (1985), were published. [81] They were not widely reviewed. Those reviews they did receive were thoughtful and acknowledged Wilder's contributions as essayist and journalist. The importance of these books in illuminating Wilder's literary concerns, as well as his objectives and achievements in his own writing, were noted by the critics. Writing of *"American Characteristics" and Other Essays* in *Columbia*, Riley Hughes found that Wilder has "fresh and pertinent things to say when he discusses the effect that American 'disconnection' from places and objects has had on the national psychology." [82] Victor White in the *Dallas Morning News* wrote that the essays "provide an exciting overview of literary life in the U.S. and perhaps of life everywhere in the past 40 years." [83] Reviewing the *Journals*, Earl Rovit wrote in the *Library Journal* that Wilder "demonstrates his capacity for first-rate scholarship . . . cultural criticism . . . and exploration of esthetic theory." [84] Gilbert A. Harrison reviewed the book for the *Washington Post Book World* and argued that Wilder had "the best informed literary intellect of his generation of American writers of fiction." [85]

Several sympathetic critics have championed Wilder's work over the years in both periodicals and journals: Edmund Wilson, Granville Hicks, Malcolm Cowley, John Gassner, and Brooks Atkinson. Among the first to recognize Wilder's achievements and to lend strong support is Wilson, whose 1928 essay "Thornton Wilder: The Influence of Proust" is included in this volume. His 1930s essays, "Dahlberg, Dos Passos, and Wilder," "The Economic Interpretation of Wilder," "The Literary Class War: I," and "Mr. Wilder in the Middle West"[86] all lent credibility and strong support to Wilder's claim as a major writer.

Other important critical articles of the 1930s include Michael Gold's "Wilder: Prophet of the Genteel Christ," a devastating personal attack; Robert McNamara's "Phases of American Religion in Thornton Wilder and Willa Cather"; and E. K. Brown's "A Christian Humanist: Thornton Wilder."[87] Vernon Loggins's "Cleaving to the Dream" shows that Wilder is "more faithful to his sense of the beautiful than any American writing today."[88] Ross Parmenter in "Novelist into Playwright: An Interview with Thornton Wilder"[89] discusses the dramatic qualities in Wilder's early novels as stages in his development as a dramatist. The last major essay of the decade is Dayton Kohler's "Thornton Wilder,"[90] in which he discusses the themes and methods in each of the books, finding that Wilder "has traced the pattern of those traditional forces which he regards as the guiding influences of human activity: spiritual faith and the conduct of man's daily life."

The 1940s saw the publication of several important essays on Wilder. In addition to the earlier essays of McNamara and Brown that placed Wilder in a religious context, a similar approach is taken by Martin Gardner in his 1940 essay "Thornton Wilder and the Problem of Providence."[91] Joseph Campbell and Henry Morton Robinson's 1942 essay, "The Skin of Whose Teeth? The Strange Case of Mr. Wilder's New Play and *Finnegans Wake*," was a virulent attack on Wilder, accusing him of plagiarism.[92] The following year, Edmund Wilson in "The Antrobuses and the Earwickers"[93] defends Wilder against the Campbell-Robinson attack. A. R. Fulton's "Expressionism—Twenty Years After"[94] discusses the history and techniques of the expressionist style and relates it to *The Skin of Our Teeth*. Henry Adler's "Thornton Wilder's Theatre"[95] investigates Wilder's theatricality and the demands made on the imagination of the audience, showing how the plays are freed from chronological sequence, to achieve a "scope and poetry that celebrates the miracle of life."

The 1950s represented a most productive time for Wilder criticism. Joseph J. Firebaugh's "The Humanism of Thornton Wilder"[96] examines themes of Wilder's work through *The Ides of March* and finds him to be "a humanist who knows the underlying seriousness of comic events, a satirist who loves the human race." In Granville Hicks's essay "Our Novelists' Shifting Reputations"[97] an assessment is made to evaluate Wilder's critical standing. Hicks suggests that Wilder has never repeated himself and has never fit into a critical category. Paul Friedman's "The Bridge: A Study in Symbolism"[98] denies that Wilder's novel is an optimistic work; the fact that the bridge breaks suggests not the miracle of love but its failure, and this becomes apparent in the novel's final scene. Friedman finds that the novel offers profoundly tragic implications. Winfield Townley Scott's "*Our Town* and the Golden Veil"[99] argues that the play presents a "double point of view, an intermeshing of past and present. . . . [S]imultaneously we are made aware of what is momentary and what is eternal. . . . Wilder's art has reminded us that beauty is recognizable because of change and life is meaningful because of death." Donald Marston's "The Theatre of Thornton Wilder"[100] finds that Wilder does not commit the sins of his contemporaries: "to understand the moment in terms of the moment and to embrace the solution of the day." Francis Fergusson's "The Search for New Standards in the Theatre"[101] analyzes Wilder's theories of the group mind (developed in his essay "Some Thoughts on Playwriting") and finds that Wilder "wishes to make a show that will hold the undefined crowd, the greater number, and at the same time make it represent his own ideas, theories, or deepest intuitions," and in both *Our Town* and *The Skin of Our Teeth* "he has triumphantly accomplished this fact."

Arthur H. Ballet's "In Our Living and in Our Dying"[102] is an elaboration of his reasons for nominating *Our Town* as "the Great American Tragedy." John Gassner's discussions of Wilder's theatrical style in *Form and Idea in the Modern Theatre*[103] are important in placing Wilder's contributions to modern drama. In Henry Morton Robinson's "The Curious Case of Thornton Wilder,"[104] the author resumes the earlier Campbell-Robinson controversy, restating his claim that Wilder plagiarized *Finnegans Wake* for *The Skin of Our Teeth*, and makes similar charges concerning *The Matchmaker* and its source, Nestroy's *Einen Jux will er sich machen*. Archibald MacLeish discusses Wilder in terms of "The Isolation of the American Artist."[105] Gerald Weales's essay "Unfashionable Optimist"[106] argues that it is Wilder's "distinction . . . that banality emerges as . . . what it is . . . one kind of truth." H. Wayne Morgan's essay "The Early Thornton Wilder"[107] offers a discussion of Wilder's early novels and finds that his solution to the problems of his time was "renunciation of materialism, study of the past, and an intellectual Christianity. . . . [He] sought to control the tides of change that were breaking down the heritage on which he leaned. . . . He believed in rules in an age that hated rules." George D. Stephens's "*Our Town*—Great American Tragedy?"[108] serves as a rebuttal to Arthur H. Ballet's essay and denies that *Our Town* is a tragedy, believing the play to be a "symbolic picture of . . . romantic nostalgia."

In the 1960s a significant number of essays devoted to Wilder's work continued to be published. To open the decade, Wilder sustained a major attack in Dwight MacDonald's essay "Masscult and Midcult II."[109] A response was made by Granville Hicks in Wilder's defense: "The Highbrow and the Midcult."[110] David P. Edgell's "Thornton Wilder Revisited"[111] offers a discussion of the qualities that "must ensure Wilder a high place in the literary history of his times." Horst Frenz provides an overview of "The Reception of Thornton Wilder's Plays in Germany."[112] In "The World of Thornton Wilder,"[113] George Greene traces a move in Wilder's work toward a "freer representation" and finds a common characteristic in all of Wilder's characters: "Consciously or not, they are all committed to that temper of mind . . . which holds the human task to be subduing nature to the requirements of the soul." In "The Comedy of Thornton Wilder,"[114] Travis Bogard discusses Wilder's comedic view of life. Hermine I. Popper's "The Universe of Thornton Wilder"[115] asserts that "since the Depression, the center of literary preoccupation has shifted from economic to psychological determinism," and by maintaining that "individual decision is essentially a matter of moral judgment rather than psychological necessity, Wilder still stands apart from the throng." Popper finds Wilder's work animated by a special tension of opposing principles: "This struggle between the Puritan and the humanist principles—quite literally, a life-and-death struggle—is at the heart of Wilder's work." In his introduction to the 1963 edition of *The Long Christmas Dinner* collection of one-act plays,[116] John Gassner discusses the history of theatricalism and shows that Wilder is

at once a radical and traditionalist in employing a form of stylization that proclaims the theatrical nature of the drama instead of sustaining the so called illusion of reality required by the convention of modern realism. The artificial nature of the theatre was the established convention of classical, Oriental, Renaissance, Elizabethan, Neo-classic and Romantic theatre; realistic convention which became firmly established only in the second half of the nineteenth century, is a very late development. In returning to "theatricalism" or "theatre for theatre's sake," (rather than "theatre for the sake of illusion"), Wilder associated himself with tradition in dramatic art. But returning to tradition in the twentieth century was an innovation and Wilder's manner of returning to it was personal and unique, and it amounted to a minor revolution in the American theatre.

In 1967 an entire issue of *Four Quarters* was devoted to Wilder and included the following three essays: Richard H. Goldstone's "The Wilder 'Image,' " arguing that unlike many of his contemporaries, Wilder never merged a private life with a public personality and therefore does not "project an image"; Donald Haberman's "The Americanization of Thornton Wilder," holding that Wilder's ability to place *Heaven's My Destination* in an American setting reflects a new assurance and knowledge that may be seen in his work; and Hans Sahl's "Wilder and the Germans," examining the significance to postwar Germans of Wilder's plays.[117] In "A Green Corner of the Universe: *Our Town*,"[118] Thomas E. Porter writes about *Our Town* in terms of "rite and archtype." He includes a discussion of the role of the Stage Manager and responds to Francis Fergusson's essay "Three Allegorists: Brecht, Wilder, and Eliot" (included in this volume).

Compared with the number of essays in the previous years, the period from the 1970s to the present saw the lessening of a scholarly interest in Wilder's work. With his death in 1975 and the posthumous publications of "*American Characteristics*" *and Other Essays* and his *Journals*, only a few critical essays were published. In *God on Broadway*[119] Jerome Ellison writes that Wilder's conception of the deity is revealed in *Our Town* through the character of the Stage Manager. Ellison believes the character evokes "the transcendental God of Emerson" and sees parallels between "the third act limbo between time and eternity" and Jung's "hypothesis of the collective unconscious." In Douglas Charles Wixon's essay "The Dramatic Techniques of Thornton Wilder and Bertolt Brecht: A Study in Comparison,"[120] he finds that Brecht's plays tend to be political and ethical; Wilder's, philosophical and social. Their methods, nevertheless, are strikingly similar. Two new essays examined *The Eighth Day* in a religious context, in much the same way McNamara, Brown, and Gardner analyzed Wilder's earlier work in the 1930s and 1940s: Dalma H. Brunauer's "Creative Faith in Wilder's *The Eighth Day*" and Edward E. Ericson, Jr.'s "The Figure in the Tapestry: The Religious Vision of Thornton Wilder's *The Eighth Day*."[121] Prema Nandukumar's essay "Thornton Wilder: *The Eighth Day*"[122] offers a discussion of Wilder's use of heredity and environment in that novel as forces affecting the spiritual evolution of mankind. Nandukumar finds the novel a "masterpiece" that "will surely rank as one of the most beautifully sculptured and thought-provoking novels of our time" and sees in the character of John Ashley "the exemplum of the Karma Yogi of the *Gita*." Gideon Shunami believes Wilder and Dürrenmatt to be dramatic links between the epic theater of Brecht and the theater of the absurd of Ionesco, presenting this idea in his essay "Between the Epic and the Absurd: Brecht, Wilder, Dürrenmatt, and Ionesco (A Comparison of Two Major Genres in Modern Drama)."[123] My essay "When Farce Isn't Funny: The Original Production of *The Merchant of Yonkers*"[124] examines the reasons for the failure of the production and finds that the direction by Max Reinhardt (which missed the farcical spirit of the play), poor casting (the romantic actress Jane Cowl as the meddlesome Dolly Levi, who was unable to play farce), and an inadequate production by Herman Shumlin were chiefly responsible for the fiasco. Victor White's essay "*The Bridge of San Luis Rey* Revisited"[125] argues that the novel is a masterpiece and finds it astounding that the compassion is "the mood of gentle skepticism which runs through the book and anticipates by almost forty years the dominant mood of our time, when all certainties seem to have deserted us." My essay "Thornton Wilder: Broadway Production History"[126] discusses the writing as well as the first productions of and critical responses to *Our Town*, *The Merchant of Yonkers*, *The Skin of Our Teeth*, and *The Matchmaker*. In addition, the translations, adaptations, and productions of *Lucrèce* and *A Doll's House* are studied. With the fiftieth-anniversary production of *Our Town*, Lanford Wilson's essay "*Our Town* and Our Towns"[127] discusses influences and similarities between his own writing and Wilder's work. In the same issue of the *New York Times*, Mel Gussow's essay "Stage View: A Theatrical Vision Endures"[128] suggests that *Our Town* continues to live in the work of some of the best contemporary American playwrights, including Sam Shepard, David Mamet, and Lanford Wilson, in "finding the extraordinary within the most ordinary situations." Gussow also examines the "Beckett-like aspect in the author's intention. In *Our Town*, as in *Waiting For Godot*, one is born astride the grave."

This volume offers the first collection of critical essays devoted to the work of Thornton Wilder and represents more than 60 years of criticism. Some essays focus on Wilder's ideas; others investigate literary styles or the techniques he employed in his writing; and still others study Wilder in relation to such diverse writers as Cervantes and Proust. The essays have been arranged by genre—novels, dramas, and essays and journals—and placed in chronological order. Four essays appear for the first time in this volume: three are new, and one is a revision of a previously published essay that incorporates Wilder manuscript material recently made available for study at Yale University Library.

My essay "*The Alcestiad*: The Play and Opera" traces Wilder's preoccupation with the Greek myth and his attempts to dramatize it. For more than 25 years, the legend of Alcestis absorbed Wilder; her story embodies most of the themes and ideas with which he was concerned throughout his career. Wilder first recounted the legend in his novels, next wrote *The Alcestiad* as a play, and finally, in collaboration with composer Louise Talma, wrote the opera of *The Alcestiad*. This essay focuses on several European productions of *The Alcestiad* and the critical response to them.

David Castronovo has rewritten his previously published essay to incorporate the study of formerly unavailable one-act plays and an uncompleted work, *Wrath*, from *The Seven Deadly Sins* cycle.[129] *Wrath* reflects the darker vision Wilder was developing in *The Seven Deadly Sins* and suggests the direction in which his work was headed with the remaining plays in the cycle. With the study of completed and uncompleted drafts, Wilder's thematic design becomes clear. Since Wilder destroyed other cycle plays, he may have inadvertently spared *Wrath* or believed he would do additional work on it.

Paul Lifton's "Symbolist Dimensions of Thornton Wilder's Dramaturgy" is a study of the resemblances between Wilder's theater and that of the late nineteenth century French symbolists. The essay relates the symbolist movement to its rejection of Plato's belief that knowledge may be gained through reason and to its embracing of the Neoplatonic credo that knowledge may be gained by nonrational means, such as through intuition or mystical inspiration. Examples of the work of Mallarmé, Maeterlinck, and others inform the essay, and their aesthetic is explored, revealing significant correspondence in the plays of Thornton Wilder. Wilder's essays and *Journal* entries are studied for his beliefs that correspond to the aesthetics of the symbolists, and these are compared with his practices in his dramatic writing.

Finally, " 'Preparing the Way For Them': Wilder and the Next Generations," by Donald Haberman, examines the work of Wilder's artistic heirs in the drama from the 1940s to the present, by surveying German-language, English, and American playwrights. The essay discusses the impact of *The Skin of Our Teeth* in postwar Europe and some of the ways Wilder's writing for the stage has had a continuing life through the work of contemporary writers. While the essay focuses on the importance of Wilder to the work of Max Frisch and Friedrich Dürrenmatt, a brief sampling of plays by Caryll Churchill, Tennessee Williams, Edward Albee, David Rabe, A. R. Gurney, Ed Bullins, David Henry Hwang, and Lanford Wilson, among others, shows the way Wilder has shaped the attitudes of professionals and audiences, as well as his impact on new generations of playwrights.

By making this collection of essays available, it is hoped that the juxtaposition of critical perspectives will inspirit new dialogue between readers and critics. Perhaps now, 20 years after Thornton Wilder's death, renewed debate, new ways of engaging his work and renewed appreciation of it will emerge and rescue him from the purgatory of critical indifference.

Notes

1. Wilder's critical and scholarly writing includes his study of Goethe, Joyce, Stein, and Lope de Vega. Among his papers at Yale University Library are several hundred pages of Wilder's notes, principally on the prolific Lope. A consuming interest of Wilder's was the dating of the more than 400 extant plays of the Spanish dramatist.

2. At an early age Wilder developed his love for both literature and the theater. But Wilder was often in conflict in choosing the novel or drama as forms in which he wished to write. Examining his career in light of this tension, one may see that Wilder has wavered between both genres. His first efforts, *The Angel That Troubled the Waters* and *The Trumpet Shall Sound*, were both in dramatic form. His first three novels, *The Cabala*, *The Bridge of San Luis Rey*, and *The Woman of Andros*, were written between 1926 and 1930, during which time Wilder was searching for a theatrical style to embody his allegorical plays. The last of the novels is based on Terence's play *Andria*, and in using dramatic material Wilder may have tried to first write the novel as a play. *The Long Christmas Dinner* collection of one-act plays is Wilder's first successful attempt at using theatricalism for his stage work. His novel *Heaven's My Destination*, begun before *The Long Christmas Dinner*, was published after the play collection and is, in part, Wilder's answer to Michael Gold's challenge to set a novel in an American setting. In any event, following the novel's publication Wilder decided to abandon the novel and devote himself to playwriting, explaining, "All my work, all of the earlier writing has been one long apprenticeship for the theatre." ("Wilder Finds Novel an Outworn Vehicle," the *New York Times*, 15 November 1935, 19). This seemed to be true, and in the next several years Wilder produced his major full-length plays: *Our Town*, *The Merchant of Yonkers* (which was to be rewritten as *The Matchmaker*), and *The Skin of Our Teeth*. Following World War II, Wilder was unable to write a satisfactory play based on the myth of Alcestis and returned to the novel with *The Ides of March* and incorporated the myth into that work. Having been able to narrate the legend, Wilder was then able to dramatize it as *The Alcestiad*. When Wilder was unable to complete his final work in the drama, the two cycles of plays, *The Seven Deadly Sins* and *The Seven Ages of Man*, he returned to the novel to complete his last two works, *The Eighth Day* and *Theophilus North*.

3. Leon Edel, quoted on the front cover of the paperback edition of *The Alcestiad* (New York: Harper & Row, 1977).

4. Edmund Wilson, "Thornton Wilder," *New Republic*, 8 August 1928, 303–5.

5. Malcolm Cowley, "Two Americans of a Brilliant Generation," *New York Times Book Review*, 9 November 1975, 6–7.

6. Tyrone Guthrie, "The World of Thornton Wilder," *New York Times Magazine*, 27 November 1955, 26–27, 64–68.

7. U.S. Information Service, *Thornton Wilder: A Bibliography* (Bonn, Germany: U.S. Government, 1958).

8. J. M. Edelstein, *A Bibliographical Checklist of the Writings of Thornton Wilder* (New Haven, Conn: Yale University Library, 1959); and Heinz Kosok, "Thornton Wilder: A Bibliography of Criticism," *Twentieth Century Literature* 9 (July 1963): 93–100.

9. Jackson R. Bryer, "Thornton Wilder and the Reviewers," *Papers of the Bibliographical Society of America* 58 (First Quarter 1964): 35–49.

10. Michael Vincent Williams, "Thornton Wilder's Anglo-American and German Critics: A Bibliography" (Ph.D. diss., University of South Carolina, 1979).

11. Richard H. Goldstone and Gary Anderson, *Thornton Wilder: An Annotated Bibliography of Works by and about Thornton Wilder* (New York: AMS Press, 1982).

12. Claudette Walsh, *Thornton Wilder: A Reference Guide, 1926–1990* (New York: G. K. Hall, 1993).

13. Richard H. Goldstone, *Thornton Wilder: An Intimate Portrait* (New York: Saturday Review Press/E. P. Dutton, 1975).

14. Linda Simon, *Thornton Wilder: His World* (Garden City, N.Y.: Doubleday, 1979).

15. Gilbert A. Harrison, *The Enthusiast: A Life of Thornton Wilder* (New York: Ticknor & Fields, 1983).

16. Rex Burbank, *Thornton Wilder* (New York: Twayne, 1961).

17. Helmut Papajewski, *Thornton Wilder*, trans. John Conway (New York: Frederick Ungar, 1968).

18. Hermann Stresau, *Thornton Wilder*, trans. Frieda Schutz (New York: Frederick Ungar, 1971).

19. Bernard Grebanier, *Thornton Wilder* (Minneapolis: University of Minnesota Press, 1964).

20. Malcolm Goldstein, *The Art of Thornton Wilder* (Lincoln: University of Nebraska Press, 1965).

21. Donald Haberman, *The Plays of Thornton Wilder: A Critical Study* (Middletown, Conn.: Wesleyan University Press, 1967).

22. M. C. Kuner, *Thornton Wilder: The Bright and the Dark* (New York: Thomas Y. Crowell, 1972).

23. Mary Ellen Williams, *A Vast Landscape: Time in the Novels of Thornton Wilder* (Pocatello: Idaho State University Press, 1979).

24. Amos Wilder, *Thornton Wilder and His Public* (Philadelphia: Fortress Press, 1980).

25. David Castronovo, *Thornton Wilder* (New York: Frederick Ungar, 1986).

26. Donald Haberman, "Our Town": *An American Play* (Boston: Twayne, 1989).

27. Jackson R. Bryer, ed., *Conversations with Thornton Wilder* (Jackson: University Press of Mississippi, 1992).

28. Theodore Purdy, Jr., "Mr. Wilder's *Cabala*," *Saturday Review of Literature*, 8 May 1926, 771.

29. "First Novel of a New American Stylist," *New York Times Book Review*, 9 May 1926, 9.

30. "Laboratory Theatre Adds New Wilder Play to Repertory," *New York Herald Tribune*, 11 December 1926, 12.

31. "New American Play Is Quite Fantastic," *New York Times*, 11 December 1926, 15.

32. Laurence Stallings, "Book of the Month: *The Bridge of San Luis Rey*," *McCall's* (May 1928), 34, 124.

33. C., M. (assumed to be Malcolm Cowley), *"The Bridge of San Luis Rey,"* *New Republic*, 28 December 1927, 173–4.

34. Clifton Fadiman, "The Quality of Grace," *Nation* 125 (14 December 1927): 687.

35. Isabel Patterson, "To Justify the Ways of God to Man," *New York Herald Tribune Books*, 20 November 1927, 3.

36. T. S. Matthews, "The Publisher That Bothered Mr. Wilder," *New Republic*, 28 November 1928, 49.

37. Henry Hazlitt, "Mr. Wilder Turns to Terence," *Nation* 130 (26 February 1930): 246.

38. Edmund Wilson, "Dahlberg, Dos Passos, and Wilder," *New Republic*, 26 March 1930, 156–8.

39. Henry Seidel Canby, "Praise All Living," *Saturday Review of Literature*, 1 March 1930, 771–2.

40. Carl Van Doren, "Wilder's Third and Best," *New York Herald Tribune Books*, 23 February 1930, 1–2.

41. "Thornton Wilder's New Tale Has Classic Beauty," *New York Times Book Review*, 23 February 1930, 4.

42. Walter Prichard Eaton, "Recent Plays," *New York Herald Tribune Books*, 13 December 1931, 19.

43. Percy Hutchinson, "Mr. Wilder's Plays," *New York Times Book Review*, 13 December 1931, 21.

44. Sidney Olson, "Noted Authors' Latest Books Cause Reviewer Misgivings," *Washington Post*, 6 January 1935, 36.

45. Edmund Wilson, "Mr. Wilder in the Middle West," *New Republic*, 16 January 1935, 282–83.

46. Henry Seidel Canby, "A Baptist Don Quixote," *Saturday Review of Literature*, 5 January 1935, 405, 411.

47. R. P. Blackmur, "A Psychogenic Goodness," *Nation* 140 (30 January 1935): 135–36.

48. George Jean Nathan, "Theatre," *Scribner's Magazine* 103 (May 1938): 65–66.

49. Mary McCarthy, "Class Angels and Classless Curves," *Partisan Review* 4 (April 1938): 55–56.

50. Brooks Atkinson, "The Play: Frank Craven in Thornton Wilder's *Our Town*, Which Is the Anatomy of a Community," *New York Times*, 5 February 1938, 18.

51. John Mason Brown, "Two on the Aisle: *Our Town* a Beautiful and Remarkable Play," *New York Post*, 14 March 1938, 18.

52. John Mason Brown, "Two on the Aisle: Jane Cowl Seen in *Merchant of Yonkers*," *New York Post*, 29 December 1938, 8.

53. Brooks Atkinson, "The Play: Thornton Wilder Adapts an Old Farce into a Jest Entitled *Merchant of Yonkers*," *New York Times*, 29 December 1938, 14.

54. John Anderson, *"Merchant of Yonkers* Opens in Our Town," *New York Journal American*, 29 December 1938, 10.

55. Richard Watts, Jr., "The Theatres: Mr. Wilder's Frolic," *New York Herald Tribune*, 29 December 1938, 12.

56. Howard Barnes, "A Major Event of This or Any Season," *New York Herald Tribune*, 22 November 1942, sec. 6, 1, 3.

57. "Wilder Whimsey," *Newsweek*, 30 November 1942, 86–87.

58. Rosamond Gilder, "Broadway in Review: Old Indestructible," *Theatre Arts* 27 (January 1943): 9–11.

59. Wilella Waldorf, "Two on the Aisle: Mr. Thornton Wilder's Slapstick Trickery in *The Skin of Our Teeth*," *New York Post*, 21 November 1942, 8.

60. Richard Watts, Jr., "Ambitious Man," *New Republic*, 1 March 1948, 22–23.

61. Orville Prescott, "Books of The Times," *New York Times*, 18 February 1948, 25.

62. Paul Jordan-Smith, "Books and Authors: Julius Caesar Lives Again in Pages of Graphic Novel," *Los Angeles Times*, 22 February 1948, sec. 3, 4.

63. Amy Loveman, "Literary Highlights of 1948," *Saturday Review of Literature*, 4 December 1948, 60–61.

64. "Setting for Tragedy," (London) *Times Literary Supplement*, 31 July 1948, 425.

65. Robert Coleman, "Robert Coleman's Theatre: *The Matchmaker* a Hilarious Comedy," *New York Daily Mirror*, 7 December 1955, 38.

66. William Hawkins, "*Matchmaker* Is Delightful," *New York World-Telegram and Sun*, 6 December 1955, 22.

67. Of the six plays that were produced, *Infancy*, *Childhood*, and *Someone from Assisi* (Lust) are available in acting editions from Samuel French, Inc., New York City. *Childhood* was also published in the *Atlantic Monthly* 206 (November 1960): 78–84. *The Drunken Sisters* (Gluttony) is published with *The Alcestiad* (New York: Harper & Row, 1977) and also in *Atlantic Monthly* 170 (November 1957, 92–95). *Bernice* (Pride) has been published in periodicals only in Germany. *The Wreck on the Five-Twenty-Five* (Sloth) has been published in the *Yale Review* 82, no. 4 (October 1994, 22–41).

68. The title of Wilder's play is *The Wreck on the Five-Twenty-Five*, as reflected in his *Journals* and in a typescript of the work. References in critical literature have shown the title as *The Wreck of the Five-Twenty-Five*, and *The Wreck of the 5:25*.

69. Reviews are quoted in a memorandum from the American Embassy in Bonn to the U.S. Department of State, evaluating the plays performed at the Berlin Festival (Memo no. 1121, Office of Cultural Presentations, New York City).

70. Richard Watts, Jr., "Two on the Aisle: Three Plays by Thornton Wilder," *New York Post*, 12 January 1962, 54.

71. Walter Kerr, "First Night report: *Plays for Bleecker Street*," *New York Herald Tribune*, 12 January 1962, 12.

72. Howard Taubman, "Older and Bolder: Wilder Still Daring and Inventive, Writes Cycles for Arena Stage," *New York Times*, 21 January 1962, sec. 2, p. 1.

73. Eliot Fremont-Smith, "Books of The Times: Mr. Wilder's Grand Tapestry of Creation," *New York Times*, 27 March 1967, 31.

74. Melvin Maddocks, "Thornton Wilder Master Designer," *Christian Science Monitor*, 30 March 1967, 11.

75. Malcolm Cowley, "A Unique Case," *Washington Post Book Week*, 2 April 1967, 1–2.

76. Benjamin DeMott, "Old-Fashioned Innovator," *New York Times Book Review*, 2 April 1967, 1, 51–53.

77. Stanley Kaufmann, "Thornton Wilder," *New Republic*, 8 April 1967, 26, 45–46.

78. Peter S. Prescott, "Sorcerer's Wand," *Newsweek*, 22 October 1973, 127–28.

79. "Angelism in New England," (London) *Times Literary Supplement*, 12 July 1974, 741.

80. Geoffrey Wagner, "Newport Redivivus," *National Review* 25 (7 December 1973): 138.

81. In addition to the two collections discussed here, *The Alcestiad* was published in an English translation (New York: Harper & Row, 1977) from the text used for the German publication (1960). The two posthumous collections are based on Wilder's papers and journals, which are housed at Yale University Library. In the last few years before his death, Wilder

destroyed hundreds of pages of uncompleted work, early drafts and notes for work he would never be able to undertake. Wilder often quipped that the writer's best friend is the wastebasket. "There are no first drafts in my life," he would say. Wilder put his beliefs into practice, according to his literary executor, Donald C. Gallup. In his memoir *Pigeons on the Granite* (New Haven, Conn.: Beinecke Rare Book and Manuscript Library, Yale University, 1988, 187), Gallup recalls that Wilder would make periodic announcements that "another fifty pages" had been destroyed. For *"American Characteristics" and Other Essays*, many of Wilder's lectures were in note form and unable to be included. Gallup did include three of the lectures Wilder gave while in residence at Harvard University as the Charles Eliot Norton Professor, as well as several speeches and essays written for various publications. This work, along with the journals Wilder kept, represents the distillation of Wilder's thinking on many of the great books, diverse writers, and the philosophical and aesthetic concerns that have engaged intellectuals and artists for thousands of years. In editing *The Journals* Gallup consulted Wilder's family and discovered that his sister, Isabel, and brother, Amos, were surprised that Wilder "had been so hard on himself." After initial reluctance to permit publication of so intimate and personal a record, his siblings agreed that a judicious selection of items to be included in *The Journals* would add to Wilder's stature, especially in the academic community. Wilder began to record his thoughts and the events making up his life experiences at nine years of age. Though the earliest writings were lost, entries dating from 1912, 1916–17, and 1922–23 are extant. Gallup chose to include selections only for 1939–41 and 1948–61. Unfortunately, only one-third of Wilder's *Journals* are included in Gallup's volume. Among the excluded items were "passages of introspection and self-analysis, including dreams," as well as reactions to letters Wilder received from Albert Schweitzer and many others. What we are given in this "judicious selection" is the cerebral—the mind of Wilder at work. We are rarely permitted to see personal glimpses or the emotional side of Wilder, aspects of his personality that would help illuminate him as both man and artist. The work of future scholars will undoubtedly include efforts to make all the journals available so that more complete judgments on the life and work of Thornton Wilder can be made.

82. Riley Hughes, "Books," *Columbia* 60 (March 1980): 30–35.

83. Victor White, "American Literary Life through Wilder's Eyes," *Dallas Morning News*, 28 October 1979, G7.

84. Earl Rovit, "Biography," *Library Journal* 110 (August 1985): 88–91.

85. Gilbert A. Harrison, "Thornton Wilder's Literary Life," *Washington Post Book World*, 20 October 1985, 4.

86. Edmund Wilson, "Dahlberg, Dos Passos, and Wilder," *New Republic*, 26 March 1930, 156–8; "The Economic Interpretation of Wilder," *New Republic*, 26 November 1930, 31–32; "The Literary Class War: I," *New Republic*, 4 May 1932, 319–23; and "Mr. Wilder in the Middle West," *New Republic*, 16 January 1936, 282–83.

87. Michael Gold, "Wilder: Prophet of the Genteel Christ," *New Republic*, 22 October 1930, 266–68; Robert McNamara, "Phases of American Religion in Thornton Wilder and Willa Cather," *Catholic World*, 135 (September 1932): 641–649; and E. K. Brown, "A Christian Humanist: Thornton Wilder," *University of Toronto Quarterly* 4 (April 1935): 356–70.

88. Vernon Loggins, "Cleaving to the Dream," in *I Hear America: Literature in the United States Since 1900* (New York: Thomas Y. Crowell, 1937), 71–112.

89. Ross Parmenter, "Novelist into Playwright: An Interview With Thornton Wilder," *Saturday Review of Literature*, 11 June 1938, 10–11.

90. Dayton Kohler, "Thornton Wilder," *English Journal* 28 (January 1939): 1–11.

91. Martin Gardner, "Thornton Wilder and the Problem of Providence," *University of Kansas City Review* 7 (December 1940): 83–91.

92. Joseph Campbell and Henry Morton Robinson, "The Skin of Whose Teeth? The

Strange Case of Mr. Wilder's New Play and *Finnegans Wake*," *Saturday Review of Literature*, 19 December 1942, 3–4.

93. Edmund Wilson, "The Antrobuses and the Earwickers," *Nation*, 30 January 1943, 167–68.

94. A. R. Fulton, "Expressionism—Twenty Years After," *Sewanee Review* 52 (Summer 1944): 398–412.

95. Henry Adler, "Thornton Wilder's Theatre," *Horizon* 12 (August 1945): 89–99.

96. Joseph J. Firebaugh, "The Humanism of Thornton Wilder," *Pacific Spectator* 4 (Autumn 1950): 426–38.

97. Granville Hicks, "Our Novelists' Shifting Reputations," *English Journal* 40 (January 1951): 1–7.

98. Paul Friedman, M.D., "The Bridge: A Study in Symbolism," *Psychoanalytic Quarterly* 21 (1952): 49–80.

99. Winfield Townley Scott, "*Our Town* and the Golden Veil," *Virginia Quarterly Review* 29 (Winter 1953): 103–17.

100. Donald Marston, "The Theatre of Thornton Wilder," *Chrysalis: A Pocket Review of the Arts* 7, nos. 1–2 (1954): 3–13.

101. Francis Fergusson, "The Search for New Standards in the Theatre," *Kenyon Review* 17 (Autumn 1955): 581–96.

102. Arthur H. Ballet, "In Our Living and in Our Dying," *English Journal* 45 (May 1956): 243–49.

103. John Gassner, *Form and Idea in the Modern Theatre* (New York: Dryden Press, 1956): 14, 142–43, 155, 172, 176, 256.

104. Henry Morton Robinson, "The Curious Case of Thornton Wilder," *Esquire*, March 1957, 70–71, 121–26.

105. Archibald MacLeish, "The Isolation of the American Artist," *Atlantic Monthly* 201 (January 1958): 55–59.

106. Gerald Weales, "Unfashionable Optimist," *Commonweal* 67 (7 February 1958): 486–88.

107. H. Wayne Morgan, "The Early Thornton Wilder," *Southwest Review* 43 (Summer 1958): 245–53.

108. George D. Stephens, "*Our Town*—Great American Tragedy?" *Modern Drama* 1 (February 1959): 258–64.

109. Dwight MacDonald, "Masscult and Midcult II," *Partisan Review* 27 (Fall 1960): 589–631.

110. Granville Hicks, "Literary Horizons: The Highbrow and the Midcult," *Saturday Review*, 13 August 1960, 16.

111. David P. Edgell, "Thornton Wilder Revisited," *Cairo Studies in English* 2 (1960): 47–59.

112. Horst Frenz, "The Reception of Thornton Wilder's Plays in Germany," *Modern Drama* 3 (September 1960): 123–37.

113. George Greene, "The World of Thornton Wilder," *Thought* 37 (Winter 1962): 563–84.

114. Travis Bogard, "The Comedy of Thornton Wilder," *Three Plays by Thornton Wilder* (New York: Harper & Row, 1962), 405–26.

115. Hermine I. Popper, "The Universe of Thornton Wilder," *Harper's*, June 1965, 72–81.

116. John Gassner, "The Two Worlds of Thornton Wilder," introduction to *The Long Christmas Dinner* by Thornton Wilder (New York: Harper & Row, 1963), vii–xx.

117. *Four Quarters* 16 (May 1967): Richard H. Goldstone, "The Wilder 'Image,' "

1–7; Donald Haberman, "The Americanization of Thornton Wilder," 18–27; and Hans Sahl, "Wilder and the Germans," 8–9.

118. Thomas E. Porter, "A Green Corner of the Universe: *Our Town,*" in *Myth and Modern American Drama* (Detroit: Wayne State University Press, 1969): 200–224.

119. Jerome Ellison, "Wilder: *Our Town,*" in *God on Broadway* (Richmond, Va.: John Knox Press, 1971), 25–31.

120. Douglas Charles Wixson, "The Dramatic Techniques of Thornton Wilder and Bertolt Brecht: A Study in Comparison," *Modern Drama* 15 (September 1972): 112–24.

121. Dalma H. Brunauer, "Creative Faith in Wilder's *The Eighth Day,*" *Renascence* 25 (Autumn 1972): 45–56; and Edward E. Ericson, Jr., "The Figure in the Tapestry: The Religious Vision of Thornton Wilder's *The Eighth Day,*" *Christianity and Literature* 22 (Spring 1973): 32–48.

122. Prema Nandukumar, "Thornton Wilder: *The Eighth Day,*" in *Indian Studies in America Fiction*, M. K. Naik, S. K. Desa and S. Mokashi-Punekar (Delhi: Karnatak University [Dharwar] and Macmillan India, 1974): 163–84.

123. Gideon Shunami, "Between the Epic and the Absurd: Brecht, Wilder, Dürrenmatt and Ionesco (A Comparison of Two Major Genres in Modern Drama)," *Genre* 8 (March 1975): 42–59.

124. Martin Blank, "When Farce Isn't Funny: The Original Production of *The Merchant of Yonkers,*" *Players Magazine*, April-May 1975, 90–93.

125. Victor White, "*The Bridge of San Luis Rey* Revisited," *Texas Quarterly* 19 (Autumn 1976): 76–79.

126. Martin Blank, "Thornton Wilder: Broadway Production History," *Theatre History Studies* 5 (1985), 57–71.

127. Lanford Wilson, "*Our Town* and Our Towns," *New York Times*, 20 December 1987, sec. 2, pp. 1, 36.

128. Mel Gussow, "Stage View: A Theatrical Vision Endures," *New York Times*, 20 December 1987, sec. 2, p. 36.

129. The manuscript of *Wrath* is at the Yale University Library. Castronovo's comments on Wilder's intellectual and literary pursuits, which are incorporated into this revised essay, are taken from Wilder's *Journals*. The Seven Deadly Sins cycle, along with The Seven Ages of Man cycle, was undertaken by Wilder in the 1950s and deals, as he said, with "our lives and errors." He planned that the two projected cycles, containing 14 one-act plays, would be produced over six years and be unified by their subject matter if not their style; and by using four or five actors in each play and projecting a comic point of view, Wilder hoped to further unify the cycles. In an interview (Arthur Gelb, "Thornton Wilder, 63, Sums up Life and Art in New Play Cycle," *New York Times*, 6 November 1961, 1, 74), Wilder elaborated on these ideas, saying, "Because we live in the twentieth century overrun by very real anxiety, we have to use the comic spirit. No statement of gravity can be adequate to the gravity of the age in which we live," The first of the cycle plays to be produced was *The Drunken Sisters* (Gluttony), in 1955 in Edinburgh, where it served as a satyr play for *A Life in the Sun* (*The Alcestiad*). This was followed by the production of *Bernice* (Pride), and *The Wreck on the Five-Twenty-Five* (Sloth) at the Berlin Festival in 1957. Finally, in 1962 *Infancy, Childhood*, and *Someone from Assisi* (Lust) were presented under the title *Plays for Bleecker Street* at the Circle in the Square Theater in New York. During 1962 several newspaper items appeared regarding Wilder's progress. In January Wilder reported in the *New York Herald Tribune* (Joseph Morganstern, "The Demons Sit on His Shoulder," January 7, sec. 4, pp. 1, 5) that he had completed nine of the fourteen cycle plays. On 14 October an announcement appeared in the *New York Times* that two more plays were completed: *A Ringing of Doorbells* (Envy) and *Youth*, with still another two in their final stages of work. In his memoir *Pigeons on the Granite* (New Haven, Conn.: Beinecke Rare Book and Manuscript Library, Yale University, 1988, 182), Donald C. Gallup recalls attending a reading of a

cycle play, *Cement Hands* (Avarice). In addition to discussing the completed plays, Wilder in his *Journals* discusses ideas for several cycle plays, including the never published or produced *Youth*. While we do not know how many of the projected fourteen cycle plays Wilder actually completed and retained (see note 81) before abandoning the project, six are extant and were permitted productions: four of *The Seven Deadly Sins* and two of *The Seven Ages of Man*.

NOVELS

◆

Thornton Wilder: The Influence of Proust

EDMUND WILSON

Now THAT MR. THORNTON WILDER has become both a best-seller and a Pulitzer prize-winner, he is in an unfortunate situation. On the one hand, the literary columnists have accepted him as a Reputation and gossip about him with respect but without intelligence; and, on the other, the literary snobs have been driven by his tremendous popularity, by the obsequious gossips themselves, into talking as if they took it for granted that there must be something meretricious about him. Mr. Wilder remains, however, a remarkably interesting writer, with a good deal to be said about him which no one, so far as I know, has said.

One of the things about Mr. Wilder that I do not think has yet been said is that he seems to be the first American novelist who has been influenced deeply by Proust. In devoting some attention to this subject, I do not at all mean to imply a lack of originality on Mr. Wilder's part: on the contrary, it is quite extraordinary that a novelist so young should display, from the first page of his very first book, so accomplished a mastery of a form and a point of view so much his own. The Proust influence seems simply the influence of a first-rate senior writer on a first-rate junior one. And what Mr. Wilder has learned from Proust is not merely Proust's complex impressionism: the side of Proust that Sacheverell Sitwell imitated in *All Summer in a Day* does not figure in Mr. Wilder at all. He has listened to Proust's very heart, and his own has been timed to its beat. It is not so much a formula of style that Thornton Wilder has taken, though there are echoes of Proust's style, too, but a formula of emotion, of the criticism of life. And in order to estimate his work, we should try to discover which part of it represents the poet Wilder himself, from whom quite un-Proustian things may eventually be expected, and which part is mere repetition of cadences caught from the asthmatic master.

One of Proust's favorite formulas, then—which we find in almost every situation of *A la Recherche du Temps Perdu*—is that of an abject and agonizing love on the part of a superior for an inferior person, or at least on the part of a gentle person for a person who behaves toward him with cruelty. Mr.

From *The New Republic*, 8 August 1928, 303–5. Reprinted by permission of *The New Republic*, © 1928, The New Republic Inc.

Wilder seems infatuated with this, and he leans on it a little too heavily. It figures less conspicuously in *The Cabala* than in *The Bridge of San Luis Rey*; but the episode of Alix in the former book, which seems to me also the episode that carries the least conviction, is simply a reversal of the Proustian relationship in which we are shown a charming and sensitive man breaking his heart for an unworthy woman: the part played for Swann by Odette, for Saint-Loup by Rachel and for Proust's hero by Albertine, is played for Alix by Blair. One finds, also, everywhere in *The Cabala* unmistakable Proustian turns of phrase; the author has even taken over a favorite expression of Proust's—a sort of proverbial phrase in French, which I have never seen before in English: he likes to talk about somebody or other "making the fair weather" of somebody else, as Swann made *"la pluie et le beau temps"* of the Duchesse de Guermantes. And one finds in *The Cabala*, also, one passage where the typical Proustian note of hypochondriacal melancholy is brought almost to the point of burlesque: a Helen Darrell, a famous beauty, enters the story suddenly like one of those unannounced characters in Proust's social scenes. We are not told precisely what is wrong with her, but, like so many of the characters in *A la Recherche*, she is ill and very soon to die; none of her dearest friends dares to kiss her: they feel that she is blighted and doomed. "She was like a statue in solitude. She presuffered her death." Yet the unfortunate Alix envies her: "He would have loved me," she breathes in the hero's ear, "if I had looked like that. . . . She is beautiful. She is beautiful," he hears her mutter. "The world is hers. She will never have to suffer as I must." The dying beauty asks, before she goes, to be taken to say good-by to a saintly old French poet, who is also about to die. "One wonders what they said to one another as she knelt beside his chair: as he said later, they loved one another because they were ill." I have cited this passage at length because it shows Thornton Wilder when he has slipped into writing pure Proust and when, as it seems to me, he is least successful. Proust's characters are always ill, and Proust thinks that a languishing illness is the most pathetic thing on earth—but he has in French the special advantage of words made for him: *malade* and *maladie*, which he is able to introduce with a mournful and ominous accent that prevents us from becoming impatient with his eternal incurable invalids. Now, the words *ill* and *sick* hardly lend themselves to any such mournful magic: when, in English, you hear that someone is ill, you at once ask what treatment he is taking.

In *The Bridge of San Luis Rey*, the Proustian spirit pervades the book. The Marquesa de Montemayor is made to distil marvellous literature from her love for her selfish daughter, just as Vinteuil in Proust is made to distil marvellous music from his insulted love for his. The Marquesa, furthermore, is evidently a transposition from Mme. de Sévigné, who plays herself such an important role in Proust. The bad feature here, however, is that Mr. Wilder has followed Proust in exaggerating the cruelty of the beloved to the lover. This is sometimes hard to swallow in Proust himself, but then there is in Proust a bitterness that seems derived from hard experience; whereas with Mr. Wilder we feel that this violence is merely an effective device. I cannot quite believe, for example, in the harrowing scene in which Esteban is dressing Manuel's wound while Manuel abuses him so harshly, and I cannot believe at all in the scene where La Périchole refuses, after twenty years, to allow Uncle Pio to address her by her first name. Isn't there, also, something rather forced about the pining of Captain Alvarados for his daughter? Isn't it one case of hopeless love too many? At one point, Mr. Wilder allows himself to be carried into rewriting the death of Bergotte (by a natural attraction, certainly: no doubt, like Strachey's death of Victoria, it is destined to be imitated many times): "We come from a world where we have known incredible standards of excellence, and we dimly remember beauties which we have not seized again, and we go back to that world." ("*Toutes ces obligations qui n'ont pas leur sanction dans la vie présente semblent appartenir à un monde différent, fondé sur la bonté, le scruple, le sacrifice, un monde entièrement différent de celui-ci, et dont nous sortons pour naître à cette terre, avant peut-être d'y retourner. . . .*")

This is not, I must repeat, that Proust has been anything other for Wilder than the inevitable elder master that every young writer must cling to before he can stand on his own feet. Since I have cited so many passages in which Mr. Wilder has filled in with Proust, I must quote at least one in a similar key which Proust would never have written and which, in Mr. Wilder's own work, has a quite distinct ring of artistic authenticity: "He regarded love as a sort of cruel malady through which the elect are required to pass in their late youth and from which they emerge, pale and wrung, but ready for the business of living. There were (he believed) a great repertory of errors mercifully impossible to human beings who had recovered from this illness. Unfortunately there remained to them a host of failings, but at least (from among many illustrations) they never mistook a protracted amiability for the whole conduct of life, they never again regarded any human being, from a prince to a servant, as a mechanical object."

The effect of Thornton Wilder is, in any case, not at all like the effect of Proust, or like the effect of anyone else one remembers. From what one hears about him, one may get the impression that he is one of those contemporary writers who seem still to date from the nineties—that he is simply another "stylist," another devotee of "beauty"—that one will find him merely a pretty or a precious writer; but Mr. Wilder, when one comes to read him, turns out to be something quite different from this. He possesses that quality of "delightfulness" of which George Saintsbury has said that Balzac did not possess it but that Gérard de Nerval did. But he has, also, a hardness, a sharpness, that sets him quite apart from our Cabells, our Dunsanys, our Van Vechtens and our George Moores. He has an edge that is peculiar to himself, an edge that is never incompatible with the attainment of a consummate felicity. This felicity, which has nothing of the pose, of the self-conscious effort to "write beautifully," of the professional beautiful writer, is felt through the whole of his work and as much in the conception of the characters and the development of the situations as in the structure of the sentences themselves. It is the felicity of a true poet—not merely the contrived "style" of a literary man with a yearning for old unhappy fancy far-off things—and it makes possible for Thornton Wilder a good many remarkable feats that we should not have expected to see brought off. Mr. Wilder, for example, I understand, has never been in Peru, and ordinarily there are few things more deadly than the dream-country of the twentieth-century novelist. Yet the author of *The Bridge of San Luis Rey* has been able to give us a Peru that is solid, incandescent, distinct. Here is the Marquesa's pilgrimage to Cluxambuqua: "a tranquil town, slow-moving and slow-smiling; a city of crystal air, cold as the springs that fed its many fountains; a city of bells, soft and musical and tuned to carry on with one another the happiest quarrels. If anything turned out for disappointment in the town of Cluxambuqua the grief was somehow assimilated by the overwhelming immanence of the Andes and by the weather of quiet joy that flowed in and about the side-streets. No sooner did the Marquesa see from a distance the white walls of this town perched on the knees of the highest peaks than her fingers ceased turning the beads and the busy prayers of her fright were cut short on her lips." Then the church, the hawks, the llama. . . . It is the city of a fairy-tale, of course; but it is almost of the same quality as *Kubla Khan*. It is not without its preciosity; but this preciosity of Thornton Wilder's is at least as sound as that of *Vathek*.

Mr. Wilder has also a form of his own, which is highly individual and which seems to me to promise more than he has hitherto been able to accomplish. In *The Cabala*, the several heroes of the several episodes seem at first to have nothing in common save the accident of all being observed by the American who is telling the story; then we learn that they are the ancient gods fallen on evil times, and we realize that there is also a significance in their relations with the young American. In *The Bridge of San Luis Rey*, the different characters appear to have in common merely the fact that they were killed by the fall of the bridge; then gradually we are made to understand that their deaths at that moment had meaning, and that there is a meaning in the relations of the people who fell to the people who were left alive. *The Bridge of San Luis Rey* is more ingenious than *The Cabala*, and more completely worked out; but I do not find it completely satisfying. God works in too obvious a way. It is hard to believe that the author believes in the God of his book. The real higher power at work here is the author's aesthetic ideal, which is struggling to incarnate itself.

One ought to say something more about *The Cabala*, which has received less attention than *The Bridge* but which seems to me, in some ways, more interesting. The circle of clever people in Rome turn out to be the gods grown old; Christianity and modern society have finally proved too much for them. The Puritanism of the young American gives Pan (or Priapus?) such a feeling of guilt that he is driven to suicide; and Aphrodite breaks her heart for an American Adonis who pays no attention to her. A brilliant peasant Cardinal, who has spent most of his life as a missionary to China, robs Artemis—if, as I suppose, Astrée-Luce is Artemis—of her pagan religious faith. These are the gods of Europe contending with the influences of alien races. In the end, the young American goes to call on the Cardinal, whom he finds with *Appearance and Reality*, Spengler, *The Golden Bough*, *Ulysses*, Proust and Freud on the table beside him. In the course of the conversation, the Cardinal pushes them all to the floor: "Yes, I could write a book," he says, "better than this ordure that your age has offered us. But a Montaigne, a Machiavelli . . . a . . . a . . . Swift, I will never be." The moment after, as the visitor is going, the Cardinal remarks that he would like for his birthday a small Chinese rug. The young American departs for the States: "Why was I not more reluctant at leaving Europe? How could I lie there repeating the *Aeneid* and longing for the shelf of Manhattan?" The shade of Virgil appears to him. "Know, importunate barbarian," says the poet, "that I spent my whole lifetime under a great delusion—that Rome and the house of Augustus were eternal. Nothing is eternal save Heaven. Romes existed before Rome and when Rome will be a waste there will be Romes after her. Seek out some city that is young. The secret is to make a city, not to rest in it." . . . "The shimmering ghost faded before the stars, and the engines beneath me pounded eagerly towards the new world and the last and greatest of all cities."

Mr. Wilder himself, however, next turns up in Peru. I have already praised this fairy-tale country. I am told that it owes part of its vividness to its grasp of the Spanish character. Thornton Wilder's feeling for national temperaments—French, Italian and American—had already appeared in *The Cabala* as one of his most striking gifts. But I wish, for our sakes, and perhaps for his own, that he would now follow Virgil's advice and return for a time to New York. I wish that he would study the diverse elements that go to make the United States, and give us *their* national portraits. Mr. Wilder already knows Europe, and he also knows something of the Orient; and now we need him at home. I believe that this player on plaintive stops has more than one tune in his flute.

The Man Who Abolished Time

MALCOLM COWLEY

Thornton Wilder is the most neglected, in one sense, of our major living writers. The sense is purely critical, since his work has not suffered from popular neglect, except during a few of the early Depression years. Before that time his second book, "The Bridge of San Luis Rey," had been the most successful novel published in the 1920s by any of the new serious writers. In 1956 it was his plays that were popular; one of them was having a triumph on Broadway while a newer one was being produced at the Edinburgh Festival and an older one was being revived by amateur groups more often than any other play of the century.

There is possibly not a night in any year when "Our Town" is not being played somewhere in the Western world, often in a dozen towns at once, with the audience in each feeling that it was written especially for them. This very literary author has been accepted as a folk author, almost like Robert Frost, and he has received all sorts of semiofficial honors here and abroad. In Germany and Austria he is often praised as the leading American writer of his time; at home he has been given three Pulitzer Prizes and the Gold Medal of the National Institute, awarded once in five years for distinguished work in fiction. Yet for twenty years there have been no serious critical studies of his work.

I do not fully understand the reasons for his neglect. It is not a conspiracy of silence or a sign of hidden rancor; critics don't often hide their rancor. If there were real hostility there would be attacks and counterattacks, and these would lead to some understanding of Wilder's position in American letters. Instead there has been a sort of oversight for which one can easily find reasons, but not sufficient reasons. It can be partly explained by the enormous popular success of "The Bridge." In the 1920s most critics believed that a novel could be either a best-seller or a work of art, but couldn't be both. After "The Bridge" had led the best-seller lists for a year, its author was tacitly abandoned to the people, along with their other breads and circuses. But that was a long time ago, before he had done his major work.

Today the silence of the critics can be partly explained by the fact that Wilder has no specialty; he is a novelist, a dramatist, and an essayist,

From *Saturday Review*, 6 October 1956, 13–14, 50–52. Reprinted by permission of the publisher.

distinguished in all these fields. Each of his new books sets out from a different assumption and follows a different path; compare the elaborate setting of "The Ides of March," described in a series of invented documents, with the mere hint of a setting in "The Bridge," where the story is told against a flat backdrop labeled Peru; then compare them both with "Heaven's My Destination," which starts in a smoking car. The critics haven't known how to label him. Yet for all the diversity of his works, each dealing with another place and time—from the Ice Age to the Atomic Age and from the Andes to the Isles of Greece, passing through Omaha and Grover's Corners, New Hampshire—they have been animated from the beginning by the same spirit, one that is almost unique in our own time and country. Perhaps, by contrasting Wilder with other writers of his generation, we can find at least an approximate statement of what the spirit is.

Most of the other novelists born at the turn of the century had a geographical starting point, a sort of rock to which their early books were attached like a colony of mussels. One thinks of Hemingway's Michigan woods, of Faulkner's county in Mississippi, of Wolfe's North Carolina mountains, and of Summit Avenue in St. Paul, the unnamed scene of so many stories by Scott Fitzgerald. With this generation a strong sense of place re-entered American writing for almost the first time since Hawthorne and Thoreau. But the place that most of them cherished was the country of their childhood, where they had felt at home. In their far wanderings they were always thinking back on it or saying goodbye to it, and often they complained, like Wolfe in the title of his last book, that "You Can't Go Home Again."

(Wilder too is a great traveler, but he never had this sense of being exiled or expatriated, perhaps because there is no one place that he regarded as home. That may have been a result of the boyhood years he spent in China: they did not teach him the wisdom of the East, but they took him away from his birthplace in Madison, Wisconsin. He was no longer a Midwesterner, and he did not become a Californian in spite of his schooldays there. Today he is a little more of a New Englander, but chiefly he is an American whose home is wherever he opens one of his bound ledgers, uncaps a fountain pen, and begins writing about people anywhere.)

The others had a home place, but no longer had a family. That doesn't mean they had quarreled with their parents; the days of tears and final separations had ended for writers with the First World War. In the 1920s the young men simply went their way, but it was so different from the parents' way, there was such a gulf between generations, that sons couldn't talk sincerely with their fathers and be understood. They had rejected the standards by which the fathers lived.

(There was no such rejection in Wilder's early career. He never belonged to a conspiracy of youth, leagued in a moral rebellion against middle age. He had worshiped in his father's church and had started by following the profession of teaching that his father picked out for him. In a way he represented continuity and tradition, so far as they existed in American society.)

The others were new or at least tried to be new; they made experimental forays in all directions. Each of them wanted to write what might have been the first novel since the beginning of time, from a fresh vision of life, in a new language. Some of the minor writers, now forgotten, would have liked to abolish all literature before Joyce or Baudelaire or whoever might be their idol of the month. I have heard a toast drunk to Caliph Omar for burning the library at Alexandria.

(Wilder is devoted to books, the older the better, and he says that his writing life has been "a series of infatuations for admired writers." He likes to acknowledge that most of his plots are borrowed and to specify their sources, as in a note that precedes "The Woman of Andros": "The first part of this novel is based upon the 'Andria,' a comedy of Terence, who in turn based his work upon two Greek plays, now lost to us, by Menander." But he transforms the borrowed material, with a richness of invention that would be rare in any age, and becomes original through trying not to be.)

Each of the others had an ideal of art that was allied to symbolism, or to naturalism, or to impressionism, or was a mixture of all three. In any case the ideal was an outgrowth of the romantic movement, and some of the writers tried to make their lives romantic too, most often Byronic or Baudelairean.

(Wilder holds to the classical ideal of measure and decorum. Most of his infatuations have been for classical authors, including Sophocles, Catullus, Virgil, Mme. de Sévigné, and La Bruyère, as well as the severely classical Noh drama of Japan, though he has also taken lessons from Proust and Joyce. I suspect that his tastes in writing are more Roman than Greek, and more English Augustan than Roman. Yale in his undergraduate days was a center of eighteenth-century studies, and there has always been something of that century in his habit of mind; possibly he is the one contemporary author who would subscribe to most of the axioms that Pope advanced in his "Essay on Criticism":

> Those RULES of old discover'd, not devis'd,
> Are Nature still, but Nature methodiz'd.
> . . . .
> Regard not then if Wit be old or new,
> But blame the false, and value still the true.)

There is a still more fundamental difference between his work and that of his contemporaries. The others write novels about a social group—sometimes a small group, as in "Tender Is the Night," sometimes a very large one, as in "U.S.A."—or they write about an individual in revolt against the group, as in "A Farewell to Arms." The central relationship with which they deal is between the many and the one. Very often—to borrow a pair of terms from David Riesman—their theme is the defeat of an inner-directed hero by an other-directed society. They feel that the society and its standards must be carefully portrayed, and these writers are all, to some extent, novelists of manners. Wilder, on the other hand, is a novelist of morals.

Manners and morals are terms that overlap, sometimes confusingly, but here I am trying to use the two words in senses that are easier to distinguish. Manners would be the standards of conduct that prevail in a group, large or small, and hence they would change from group to group and year to year. Morals would be defined as the standards that determine the relations of individuals with other individuals, one with one—a child with each of its parents, a husband with his wife, a rich man with a poor man (not *the* rich with *the* poor)—and also the relations of any man with himself, his destiny, and his God. They are answers found by individuals to the old problems of faith, hope, love or charity, art, duty, submission to one's fate . . . and hence they are relatively universal: they can be illustrated from the lives of any individuals, in any place, at any time since the beginning of time.

The characters in Wilder's novels and plays are looking for such answers; his work is not often concerned with the behavior of groups. An outstanding exception might be his play "Our Town," in which the Stage Manager speaks with the voice of the community. But the community hasn't much to say about itself and won't admit to having local color; it might be any town, a fact that helps to explain the success of the play in towns all over this country, and other countries. The events it sets forth are coming of age, falling in love, getting married, and dying; in other words, they are not truly events, but rather examples of a universal pattern in human lives; and they are not greatly affected by the special manners of this one community.

Wilder's first novel was "The Cabala," which also starts by dealing with a group; but very soon the young narrator shifts his attention to its separate members, explaining that he is "the biographer of the individuals and not the historian of the group." The statement applies to the author himself, and in a more positive form: Wilder is not a historian. He had studied archeology at the American Academy in Rome and had learned to look backward and forward through a long vista of years; that sort of vision is a special quality of all his work. But what he sees at the end of a vista is what the archeologist often sees; that is, fragments of a finished pattern of life, in many ways similar to our own. It is not what the historian tries to see: a living community in a process of continual and irreversible change.

The other novelists of his generation were all of them historians. Their basic perception was of the changes in their own time, from peace to war, from stability to instability, from a fixed code of behavior to the feeling that "it's all right if you can get away with it." For them the First World War was a true event, in the sense that nothing was the same afterward. All of them were "haunted fatally by the sense of time," as Wolfe said of the autobiographical hero in his second novel, which was called "Of Time and the River." Hemingway's first book was "In Our Time," and he left it to be understood as ". . . in no other time."

Faulkner saw his time in the South as one of violent and progressive decay. Dos Passos tried to put thirty years of American life into one big novel. He invented a device called the Newsreel: it consisted of quotations from Chamber of Commerce speeches, newspaper headlines, crime stories, and the lyrics of popular songs, and it was intended to convey the local color of each particular year. Fitzgerald put some of the same material into the body of his stories; he wrote as if with one eye on the calendar. "The Great Gatsby" belongs definitely to the year 1923, when the Fitzgeralds were living in Great Neck, and "Tender Is the Night" could have ended only in 1930; no other year on the Riviera had the same atmosphere of things going to pieces. Both books are historical novels about his own time, which portrayed in them with such a long perspective that the books are permanent.

Wilder would never attempt to draw such a picture of his time. He is our great unsocial and antihistorical novelist, the artist of the anachronism. In all his work I can think of only one event that marks an absolute change; it is the birth of Christ, announced on the first and last pages of "The Woman of Andros." Chrysis and Pamphilus, in that novel, are premature Christians, and the author implies that they would have led happier lives if they had been born in the Christian era. He never mentions that other Christian event, the Fall: perhaps it plays no part in his theology. Everything else in his plays and novels—even the collapse of a famous bridge—is merely an example or illustration of man's destiny.

Nothing is unique, he seems to be saying; even the Ice Age will return, as will the Deluge, as will Armageddon. After each disaster man will start over again—helped by his books, if he has saved them—and will struggle upward until he is halted by another, or perhaps by the same disaster repeated in a different form. "Romes existed before Rome," the shade of Virgil says at the end of "The Cabala," "and when Rome will be a waste there will be Romes after her." Wilder does not think of history as an irreversible process or a river in flood; he thinks of it as a series of recurrent patterns, almost like checkerboards set side by side.

At this point I think we are beginning to see a design that unites his work. Wilder has written a dozen books, each strikingly different from all the others in place and time, in mood, and even more in method, yet all the books embody or suggest the same feeling of universal experience and eternal return. *Everything that happened might happen anywhere, and will happen again.* That principle explains why he is able to adopt different perspectives in different books, as if he were looking sometimes through one end of a telescope and sometimes through the other. In "The Ides of March" a distant situation is magnified, and Rome in 45 B.C. is described as if it were New York 2,000 years later. In "Our Town" he reverses the telescope and shows us Grover's Corners as if it had been preserved for 2,000 years under a lava bed and then unearthed like Herculaneum.

He has many other fashions of distorting time. There is a one-act play in which he presents a Christmas dinner that lasts for ninety years, with members of the family appearing from a bright door and going out through a dark door, to indicate birth and death. "The Skin of Our Teeth" tells the story of mankind in three acts and four characters: Adam, Eve, Lilith, and Cain. In the first act a glacial shield grinds down on Excelsior, New Jersey. In the second act, laid in Atlantic City just before the Deluge, an ark full of animals two by two is launched from the Million Dollar Pier. In the third act the great philosophers are portrayed as hours of the night. One of the characters explains, "Just like the hours and stars go by over our heads at night, in the same way the ideas and thoughts of the great men are in the air around us all the time and they're working on us, even when we don't know it." Spinoza is nine o'clock, Plato is ten, Aristotle is eleven, and Moses is midnight. Three thousand years of human thought are reduced to four hours, which pass in less than two minutes on the stage.

This foreshortening of time, which almost becomes an abolition of time, is an opportunity for the novelist as well as the dramatist. He is permitted to transfer any character from one historical period or pattern to another, so long as the character reappears on a corresponding square of the checkerboard. Thus, in "The Bridge," Mme. de Sévigné has a second life in Peru as the Marquesa de Montemayor. In "The Cabala" there is Keats, temporarily resurrected with his genius, his family, and his fatal illness; he dies in 1920, among a group of strange characters who might have been evoked from the Memoirs of the Duc de Saint-Simon, or who again might be classical gods and goddesses in modern dress.

Figures can be moved backward in time as well as forward. Edward Sheldon, the blinded and horribly crippled dramatist who lived for thirty years in retirement, dispensing wisdom to his friends, appears in "The Ides of March" as Lucius Mamilius Turrinus; and one suspects that Cicero, in the same novel, is a preincarnation of Alexander Woollcott. As for the hero of the novel, he is not a historical character, but a model or paradigm of the man of decision, as he might exist in any age. Wilder has called him Julius Caesar, just as Paul Valéry called his man of intellect Leonardo da Vinci, and just as Emerson gave the title of "Plato" to his essay on man as philosopher.

The mention of Emerson reminds us that he was another writer who denied the importance of groups or institutions and refused to think of history as a process. He discussed Plato and Shakespeare not against the background of their times, but as great contemporaries whom he might meet at the next dinner of the Saturday Club. . . . In the brilliant series of lectures that he gave at Harvard in 1950–1951 Wilder started with Emerson and the other classical American writers, notably Melville and Whitman. What he tried to deduce from their works was the character of the representative American, but what he actually presented, I suspect, was something of his own character. Here are three of his statements:

> From the point of view of the European an American is nomad in relation to place, disattached in relation to time, lonely in relation to society, and insubmissive to circumstances, destiny, or God.

> Americans could count and enjoyed counting. They lived under a sense of boundlessness. . . . To this day, in American thinking, a crowd of 10,000 is not a homogeneous mass of that number, but is one and one and one . . . up to 10,000.

> Since the American can find no confirmation of identity from the environment in which he lives, since he lives exposed to the awareness of vast distances and innumerable existences, since he derives from a belief in the future the courage that animates him, is he not bent on isolating and "fixing" a value on every existing thing in its relation to a totality, to the All, to the Everywhere, to the Always?

These are perceptive statements, but I would question whether they apply to most Americans today, or to many American novelists since the First World War. Their primary application is to Emerson and the big and little Emersonians—including Whitman, the biggest of all. In our day they apply to Wilder himself more than to any other living writer. If on one side he descends from Pope and Addison, or at least has something of their attitude toward the art of letters, on the other side he is an heir of the Transcendentalists. His work has more than a little of the moral distinction they tried to achieve, and like their work it deals with the relation of one to one, or of anyone to the All, the Everywhere, and the Always. Like theirs, it looks toward the future with confidence, though not with the bland confidence that some of the Emersonians displayed. "Every human being who has existed can be felt by us as existing now," Wilder said in another of his Harvard lectures, as if to explain and justify his foreshortening of history. "All time is present for a single time. . . . Many problems which seem insoluble will be solved when the world realizes that we are all bound together as the population of the only inhabited star."

Thornton Wilder: The Notation of the Heart

EDMUND FULLER

Wilder is unique among modern American novelists for possessing in the highest degree certain qualities currently undervalued and hence desperately needed among us. No one of his countrymen rests his work upon such an understructure of broad scholarship, cultivation and passion for the beauty and integrity of the English language. This equipment, rare in our time, gives tone to his work, especially the novels, and yet brings with it no taint of pedantry. To find work equally rich in allusion and grounded in humane learning, we must turn to English-born Aldous Huxley, although Wilder employs these attributes even more gracefully and unobtrusively than he. In a period when literary honors are bestowed often upon the craftless, the semiliterate and uncultivated, and in which the Yahoo has become hero, we need to recall that we have Wilder working among us. He helps to redeem the time.

He is notable for his versatility. Although he is not the only man writing both the novel and the play, no one else has written both at such a level of excellence, in such a marked diversity of modes, or in such form-renewing and form-extending ways as mark his work in the two media.

Wilder is a conspicuous exception to the common generalization that American writers tend to be youthful, writing of and from youth and immaturity, failing to mature in art as they age in years. He juxtaposes his always mature vision of life and character to our predominantly adolescent literature, while his range is greater than that of those established men who are most nearly his peers. There is an immense spread between the sophistication of *The Cabala* and the homely simplicity of *Our Town*, and Wilder is comfortably at home in both.

He is neither compulsive in his choice of material and method nor conditioned by some warped piping from a private clinical world. His view of life and behavior is broadly encompassing and humanely compassionate in the only true compassion, which is blended of sympathetic perception and clearly defined values.

He has the highest development and conscious control of style—having

From *Books with Men behind Them* (New York: Random House, 1962), 36–62. Reprinted by permission of the author.

no close rival among Americans in this respect—yet he spelled out the limits of style in *The Bridge*, in a passage about the Conde's relish for the famous letters of the Marquesa de Monte-mayor (which are like those of Mme. de Sévigné): ". . . he thought that when he had enjoyed the style he had extracted all their richness and intention, missing (as most readers do) the whole purport of literature, which is the notation of the heart. Style is but the faintly contemptible vessel in which the bitter liquid is recommended to the world. The Marquesa would even have been astonished to learn that her letters were very good, for such authors live always in the noble weather of their own minds and those productions which seem remarkable to us are little better than a day's routine to them." It is in this "whole purport of literature . . . the notation of the heart" that Wilder's genius is felt, and the flexible grace and individuality that attend his work in both his chosen media proceed from that "noble weather" of his own mind.

The novels are dazzlingly epigrammatic—a word that often carries with it a suggestion of glibness that does not fit this work. The epigram is a stylistic device, a perfectly shaped single thought, calculated to arrest attention and then, at its best, to start thought moving in a fresh direction. Such ability to shape and state things is sometimes given to shallow minds who waste it on minor witticism. In Wilder this gift is coupled with penetrating perception and wisdom. It helps him to communicate the depth and sharpness in which he sees character, motivation and impulse, and the significance that he discerns in things. . . .

Wilder is a gentle, not a savage, observer of folly. He blends folly with faith in the extravagant, picaresque, evangelical adventures of George Brush, the hero of *Heaven's My Destination* (1935). This fourth novel is startlingly different, in manner, method and material, from the other novels. Its tone is that of his plays, and I have wondered if, at some stage in its gestation, it may have hovered between the two forms. It is high parody, in somewhat the vein, and with the same deceptive simplicity, as *Candide* or *Joseph Andrews*. To descend somewhat in levels of comparison, there is even a touch of the Sinclair Lewis of *The Man Who Knew Coolidge*.

George, who is a textbook salesman and evangelist extraordinary, is the innocent fool, or the foolish innocent, in the kindliest sense of both the noun and the adjective. He is striving to be the fool in Christ, sowing the inevitable amazement, consternation and wrath that must ensue when Christ's fool runs at large among the worldly wise. This, in dark tones, was the concept underlying Dostoyevsky's *The Idiot*.

Wilder's George is also "the perfectly logical man," fulfilling conviction in action, practicing his preaching. To understand him it is necessary to observe the quotation from *The Woman of Andros* that Wilder uses as a text in the front matter of *Heaven's My Destination*: "Of all the forms of genius, goodness has the longest awkward age."

For all the sophistication that underlies the creation of George Brush—

indeed that was essential to it—Wilder loves this innocent and will not consent that we should do otherwise. His is the awkward age of a true goodness. Simple, it is; stupid, it is not. Nor is it easy. George suffers his own bitter crises of faith, and his occasional cry of "I don't want to live" is a genuine anguish. Among the most subtle and interesting devices of the book is the unseen figure called Father Pasziewski, seemingly comic in his context, but who becomes, through the simple bequest of a silver spoon, the instrument to free George from his darkest night of the soul. In this border terrain of folly and faith, Wilder sounds a cautionary note to the George Brushes of the world through Judge Carberry:

"Go slow; go slow. . . . The human race is pretty stupid. . . . Doesn't do any good to insult'm. Go gradual." . . .

It is in *The Ides of March* (1948) that we get his most ambitious image of the ancient world, in the most intricately constructed and ambitious of all the novels. Its spaciousness of concept creates a sense of a much larger work, physically, than it is in fact. Nowhere is his self-avowed "passion for compression" more successfully operable.

Here he takes his familiar liberties with time sequence and literal, factual matters, but he gives us a sense of a living Rome and a living Caesar. Through the difficult and adroitly practiced device of imaginary letters and documents, he evokes the most complex Caesar that I know in any work of art. This Julius's closest relative is Shaw's—that is, both are created in indifference to historical actuality as idealizations of a point of view (a device of the classical historians as well, as witness Herodotus' famous dialogue between Solon and Croesus). These Caesars have in common a detached, deliberative calm, and the relationship of each of them to Cleopatra is dominated primarily by a "passion for teaching." Yet Shaw's Caesar is a one-dimensional cartoon, withal brilliant, while Wilder's is complexly human with the special dimensions of genius.

Caesar's reflections on Roman society cut sharply into our own[:] ". . . the ostentation of vulgarity has become a political factor with which I must deal. The plebeian world is ameliorable in itself, but what can I do with a plebeian aristocracy? . . . it's now smart to talk pure *pleb.*"

The book is rich in its meditations upon liberty and rule, freedom and responsibility, interest and disinterest in public actions. The dual study of Caesar and Catullus (wholly as fanciful as Solon and Croesus) puts before us the statesman vis-à-vis the poet. Catullus is, in a sense, one face of this Caesar, who says, ". . . one of the things in this world that I most envy is the endowment from which springs great poetry. To the great poets I ascribe the power to gaze fixedly at the whole of life and bring into harmony that which is within and that which is without them." Is not this the transcendent aim of the great statesman? "I think there is only one solitude greater than that of the military commander and of the head of state and that is the poet's—for who can advise him in that unbroken succession of choices which is a poem? It is in this sense that responsibility is liberty; the more decisions that you are forced to make alone, the more you are aware of your freedom to choose. I hold that we cannot be said to be aware of our minds save under responsibility. . . ." *The Ides of March* is a text so rich that it requires exploration rather than reading.

Wilder's love of the ancient world, however, is not a flight from the modern one. He has been wise about that from the first. The returning American narrator of *The Cabala* is advised by Virgil, as he leaves Rome: "The secret is to make a city, not to rest in it."

Perhaps, finally, with Wilder, after love comes beauty as the second great theme. He said, in the Foreword to *The Angel That Troubled the Waters*, speaking of religion as a subject in art, ". . . in these matters beyond logic, beauty is the only persuasion." He has made it the instrument of his own persuasion in all matters. This may be what has shaped his style. The stamp of taste and the sure sense of the precise and subtle gradations of meaning that come with mastery of language and that are the essence of beauty in the written word are firmly in his possession.

And with beauty comes praise. Praise of life is constant with him. He knows the sometime kindness of death. He has the vision of something beyond death. He can remark the pain of living, as he gives words to the shade of Virgil: "Are you still alive? Alive? How can you endure it? All your thoughts are guesses, all your body is shaken with breath, all your senses are infirm and your mind ever full of the fumes of some passion or another. Oh, what misery to be a man. Hurry and die!"

Yet, like a descant over all his melodies is the note of praise.

One of the dead, a woman, in the poignant dual vision of the famous graveyard scene in *Our Town*, is reminded of childbirth, and remarks, almost with a laugh.

> I'd forgotten all about that. My, wasn't life awful
> (*With a sigh*)
> —and wonderful?

Simon Stimson, in the same scene, echoes Virgil's words above: "That's what it was to be alive. To move about in a cloud of ignorance . . . to spend and waste time as though you had a million years . . . to be always at the mercy of one self-centered passion or another." Mrs. Gibbs rebuffs him: "Simon Stimson, that ain't the whole truth and you know it." Emily herself, retreating from the pain of her return on her twelfth birthday, ends her cry of farewell to all people, places and things of life, with: "Oh, earth, you're too wonderful for anybody to realize you."

In *The Cabala*, the narrator visits the bedside of the dying poet (Keats transposed). He wounds the suffering man unintentionally by a casual slur upon Chapman's Homer, and so "discovered that he was hungry for hearing things praised. . . . The poet wanted before he left the strange world to hear some portion of it praised."

Again, in *The Ides of March*, Caesar at the bedside of another dying poet, Catullus, observes: "I am no stranger to deathbeds. To those in pain one talks about themselves, to those of clear mind one praises the world that they are quitting. There is no dignity in leaving a despicable world and the dying are often fearful life was not worth the efforts it had cost them. I am never short of subjects to praise."

Thornton Wilder, wise observer and celebrant of life, speaks in the dying courtesan, Chrysis, of Andros, as she is making "the most exhausting of all our adventures . . . that journey down the long corridors of the mind to the last halls where belief is enthroned." As she goes this course, she reflects: "I have known the worst that the world can do to me, and . . . nevertheless I praise the world and all living."

So, likewise, does Wilder, in the total body of this humane notation of the heart that is his work. In this shrewd, sometimes caustic observation of genus Homo and his history, we find one of the most searching, balanced and mature visions of ourselves as Man that any American writer offers us.

Wilder and Cervantes: In the Spirit of the Tapestry

Louis C. Pérez

Spanish literature, and more specifically Golden-Age literature, has held considerable interest for Thornton Wilder during his literary career. His novel *The Bridge of San Luis Rey* (1927), which appeared subsequent to his studies in Romance languages at Princeton, reveals this interest[1] as do the articles he published about the Spanish playwright Lope de Vega.[2] Some of Wilder's works seem to reflect if not the direct influence of, at least a very marked affinity with the works of Lope, Calderón, and Cervantes. The techniques used in *The Skin of our Teeth* and *The Matchmaker* suggest a certain familiarity with the works of these Spanish authors. The characters step out of the plays from time to time to comment, a technique used by Calderón in *El gran teatro del mundo*, and to a lesser extent by Lope in *Lo fingido verdadero*.[3] Also in *The Skin of our Teeth*, the broad treatment of man's record here on earth, beginning with Noah's flood, recalls the somewhat humorous observation Lope makes in his *Arte nuevo*

> . . . la cólera
> de un español sentado no se templa
> si no le representan en dos horas
> hasta el Final Juïcio desde el Génesis.[4]

Reminiscent too of Lope's *comedias* are the numerous characters in Wilder's plays.[5] Almost any one of the Spanish poet's well-known plays would bear this out. Both Lope and Wilder disregard historical truth when it interferes with their poetic creations: Wilder in *The Ides of March* and Lope in a large number of his theatrical pieces. Both Lope and Wilder show a preference for a minimum of stage scenery. However, in this last respect, we do know that Wilder had Shakespeare and Molière in mind.

Further, *The Skin of our Teeth* recalls one of Calderón's famous *autos*, *El gran teatro del mundo*, in which God plays the part of the author-director and

From *Symposium* 25 (Fall 1971): 249–59. Reprinted by permission of the Helen Dwight Reid Educational Foundation. Published by Heldref Publications, 4000 Albemarle St., N.W., Washington, D.C. 20016. Copyright © 1971.

distributes roles to the actors who will play their parts here on earth, since "all the world's a stage." The seven deadly sins are themes of this and other one-act sacramental plays of Calderón. Wilder has written seven one-act plays utilizing the seven deadly sins. But the affinity to which I refer is to be seen not only in one or two details of the American author's works, but in a combination of many. Beside the ones already mentioned we might add Wilder's practice of addressing himself to the people—all the people—a practice which places him closer to the Spaniard of the seventeenth century than to the Frenchman of that period. And like Lope, Wilder also seeks the participation of his audience.[6] Another likely comparison is that, while in Wilder's plays the mother has a sacred and central role, in the *comedias de capa y espada*, the mother, precisely because she is too sacred a person to be involved in plots of love intrigue, does not appear.

To my knowledge, Thornton Wilder has made no formal written contribution to an understanding of *Don Quixote*, though it is obvious that he knows the novel and the gentleman of la Mancha—in *Heaven's My Destination*, for example, Brush reveals noticeable quixotic traits.[7] Also in his latest novel, *The Eighth Day*, one of his main characters, Beata Ashley, reads to her children from *Don Quixote*. Beata "found not humor but truth in the adventures of the knight for whom the world was filled with evil necromancers and with those bitter injustices which a man must put right."[8] There is some justification for suspecting that the author is suggesting, in this novel, the influence great books have on an individual's life: Don Quixote's idealism and heroic struggle could be inspirational to the entire family—to Beata, to the daughters, and to the son who achieves success in Chicago. In our reading of *The Eighth Day* we are often reminded of *Don Quixote*. There are many important thematic and artistic similarities between these two novels, particularly in regard to the function of the tapestry. Both authors suggest the important role that the tapestry plays in their work, both disregard the technical differences between a true tapestry and other comparable arts (i.e., rug, embroidery, etc.).[9] Both refer to the reverse side of the woven item for important revelation and relation to literature, and both unveil their literary device late in their respective works. Cervantes speaks of the tapestry just after the middle of the first part of *Don Quixote* and then again toward the end of the same part. Wilder relates *The Eighth Day* to the tapestry in its last pages.

The tapestry has long been present in literature, beginning with Homer, who tells us that Helen wove into a great web the struggles that Trojans and Achaians endured for her sake. And in regard to historical representation, it is noteworthy that one of the important records we have of the Norman invasion of England is preserved on tapestry or, perhaps more accurately, in an embroidery often referred to as the *Bayeux Tapestry*. It was logical for Cervantes to relate the novel to the tapestry. In his time tapestries were highly esteemed, perhaps even more than paintings,[10] since they had a twofold purpose: a practical one and a decorative and entertainment one as well. They were used as substitutes for windows or often as room dividers; and in the theatre (which brings us closer to the realm of art) they were used to set off a corner as a dressing room for the actors. We find references to their decorative and entertainment value often in the literature of sixteenth-and seventeenth-century Spain.[11] In *Don Quixote* itself we have an inkling of the frequency with which tapestries were displayed. In the second part, our hero, now famous, stops at an inn where he is "given lodging in a lower room, the walls of which were covered with some odd bits of painted serge of the kind found in villages in place of leather hangings" (*DQ*, II, LXXI, 972). While he is waiting to be served, his attention is drawn to these *painted tapestries*, one of which depicted the rape of Helen by Paris and the other the story of Dido and Aeneas. Cervantes takes the opportunity to comment on the artistic merits of these tapestries: "On one of these was depicted, by a very crude hand, the abduction of Helen, when the bold guest bore her off from Menelaus, and on the other was represented the story of Dido and Aeneas, with the queen standing on a high tower and signaling with half a sheet to the fugitive, who was now at sea on a frigate or brigantine. Helen did not appear very reluctant about going, for she was laughing slyly and roguishly, but the beauteous Dido was shedding tears the size of walnuts" (*DQ*, II, LXXI, 972). Later that day, Alvaro Tarfe, friend of the pseudo Don Quixote[12] arrives at the inn, and the author points out that he too is accommodated in a room "similarly adorned with painted serge" (*DQ*, II, LXXII, 974).

References to tapestries or painted cloths with histories and epics abound in Cervantes' works.[13] He is interested in the tapestry not only for its decorative and background value, but most importantly for its esthetic implications, just as Wilder is. Cervantes points to the relationship that exists between his narrative technique and that of the tapestry, and comments on how the thread of the main theme intertwines with the threads of the interpolated tales, which add to the enjoyment of the whole:

> [we] are able to enjoy not only the charm of his [Don Quixote's] veracious history, but also the tales and episodes interpolated in it, which in a manner are no less pleasing, artful, and true than the history itself.
> Pursuing, then its *hackled*, *twisting*, *winding thread* of plot, the work in question goes on to relate. [. . .] (*DQ*, I, XXXVIII, 233)[14]

And toward the end of the first part of the novel, Cervantes is even more explicit. One of the characters, the Canon, reveals the author's ideas on the novel when, after an extensive commentary on narrative technique, he suggests what ought to be done in the writing of a novel and ends by saying:

> All of which being done in an easy-flowing style, with a skilled inventiveness that draws insofar as possible upon the truth of things, the result would surely

be *a web woven of beautiful and variegated threads*, one which when completed would exhibit such *a perfected beauty of forms* as to attain a most worth-while goal of all writing, which as I have said is at once to instruct and to entertain. These books [of chivalry], indeed, by their very nature, provided the author with an unlimited field in which to try his hand at the epic, lyric, tragic, and comic genres and depict in turn all the moods that are represented by these most sweet and pleasing branches of poetry and oratory; for the epic may be written in prose as well as verse. (*DQ*, I, XLVII, 427–28)

Don Quixote may very well be a prose-epic, as Cervantes suggests, but there is no denying that the form is influenced by the tapestry. Translators and critics who have been unaware of this have all too often incorrectly concluded that some of the episodes of *Don Quixote*, such as the "Story of the One Who Was Too Curious for His Own Good," were extraneous. Henry Edwards Watts, in his translation (*Don Quixote de la Mancha*, New York, D. Appleton and Company, 1899) completely eliminated this episode. He obviously deemed it superfluous or unnecessary to the whole work. It is not my purpose here to explain how this extraordinary episode is indispensable to the whole novel. Suffice it to say that in the *Curioso impertinente* Cervantes has summarized or woven the main threads of the previous episodes of the novel and put them in one panel which falls in the baroque center of the first part of the novel. The author realized only too well that the thematic and artistic technique of the tapestry due to its pictorial effectiveness and comprehensiveness could be transferred to the novel. Hunter alludes to this sisterhood of the arts when he observes that "Tapestries are one of the most effective forms of literary expression the world has ever known. Through them the stories of Vergil's *Aeneid* and Ovid's *Metamorphoses* were made vivid to the Romans."[15] Does not *The Eighth Day*, too, have many elements of the epic? Could Ashley not be construed as the wandering hero, enveloped in an aura of legend with assistance from the supernatural and confronted with an enemy? Does not Wilder's book have a didactic or religious purpose, and like some epics embody the ideals of a nation? The parallels between the epic and *The Eighth Day* are many, even to the details such as a shipwreck and the founding of a city.

What strikes the reader as truly significant, regarding the tapestry technique, is that both Cervantes and Wilder viewed not only the front of the tapestry but also its reverse side, a fact which cannot be explained as simply mere whim on the part of both authors. In Cervantes' case, although it at first appears (in the following quote) that he is commenting solely on the inaccuracy of translations, a closer look reveals that it is the second part of the statement that is pertinent to our study—all the threads of the novel must blend smoothly with one another for the purpose of unity: "But, for all of that, it appears to me that translating from one language into another, unless it be from one of those two queenly tongues, Greek and Latin, is like gazing at a Flemish tapestry with the wrong side out: even though the figures are visible, they are full of threads that obscure the view and are not bright and smooth as when seen from the other side" (*DQ*, I, LXII, 923). Wilder's purpose, though he alludes to the smoothness of the configuration on the front of the tapestry, is to emphasize that, if we are part of the tapestry, and therefore too close to it, we cannot see the design:

> The Deacon was gazing intently at the home-made rug at his feet and Roger's eyes followed his. It had been woven long ago, but a complex maze-like design in brown and black could still be distinguished.
> "Mr. Ashley, kindly lift the rug and turn it over."
> Roger did so. No figure could be traced on the reverse. It presented a mass of knots and of frayed and dangling threads. With a gesture of the hand the Deacon directed Roger to replace it.
> "You are a newspaperman in Chicago. Your sister is a singer there. Your mother conducts a boardinghouse in Coaltown. Your father is in some distant country. Those are the threads and knots of human life. You cannot see the design." (p. 428–29)

Wilder and Cervantes are weaving rhetorical tapestries. For Cervantes, Don Quixote, together with a number of important themes rhythmically intertwined, is a character-thread contributing to the unity of his cloth. Wilder's approach is slightly different. While there is unity in the repeated and varied themes—*the builders*—there is no one character actively present from beginning to end, though Ashley's thread is seen throughout, and referred to from time to time in the different episodes or panels which go into the weaving of *The Eighth Day*.

Wilder begins his tapestry-weaving, strangely enough, in the middle. The technique of *in medias res* and the tapestry pictorial technique are at once combined. Wilder then works out from there. Fremont-Smith sees it this way: "It is the particular knot on the back of the tapestry Mr. Wilder has chosen to start with. Its threads span out in all directions, and through time, back to the eighteen-eighties, forward in detail in 1905 and then in glimpses to the present."[16] In fact Wilder seems to present us with a series of panels, as if in a medieval triptych,[17] all related to the central panel. The panels may be viewed separately. Just as the parts of his novel could stand alone and be understood as individual frames, for the division of his novel is not conventional; it does not divide into chapters. We have implied that the panels could stand out from one another. This is so if we stand relatively close to the work of art, but studying them at a distance, we are struck by the thematic unity of the panels or the sections of the novel.

A tapestry in Cervantes' time, logically enough, was a woven painting.[18] He treated it as such. Wilder seems to follow the same line of thinking. The idea of the woven threads running rhythmically throughout the tapestry may be adapted to the novel through themes or scenes. The pictorial aspect may be used for other effects. If this conjecture is defensible, it is quite likely that Wilder, like Cervantes and other writers of the Spanish Golden Age, has been persuaded by what Horace stipulates in his *Ars Poetica*—*ut pictura poesis*—that poetry is like painting, and that some paintings are to be viewed from up close and others from a distance. The Spaniard of the sixteenth and seventeenth centuries took Horace's observations quite literally; we have many indications of their acceptance or adherence to this precept in their work.[19] Some tried to reproduce a painting which could be seen from up close, others from a distance and yet others both, producing at different distances, different effects.

Is it not also possible that Wilder, consciously or otherwise, shares the esthetic aims of the last group? Is Wilder trying at one and the same time to give us pictures to be seen relatively close up for one kind of effect and from a distance to give us a more universal picture? Very likely. At all events, this double intention was Cervantes' aim. The portrait of Don Quixote, for example, is to be seen from up close. Cervantes is quite definite about this: "and as he sat there, with no stirrups and his legs hanging down, he looked like nothing so much as a figure in some Roman triumph painted or woven upon a Flemish tapestry" (*DQ*, II, XLI, 772). However, it was not Cervantes' ultimate intent to depict his novel only in isolated portraits and scenes, but to display the entire tapestry, thus underscoring—as Wilder does—that all scenes, all persons, all humanity, are related in some way; and this becomes evident by tracing different threads. We are made aware of the relationship between all persons and episodes in life, if we place ourselves at a point which permits us a universal view of things.

The Castilian author is a complex artist, but the knowledge or revelation that his art is that of the tapestry invites us to appreciate his narrative technique, to discover the rhythmic threads of the themes, characters, and episodes which he has introduced with a great deal of variation. He labors meticulously, even on the small threads (i.e., the ballad and the proverb). The ballad, in this regard, is a most fortuitous example in *Don Quixote*: an allusion, a direct reference, lines half-hidden in prose, then an imitation of the ballad, and finally, as in the case of Durandarte, the ballad itself is dramatized and retold in prose by the old man Don Quixote meets in the cave of Montesinos.

The main philosophic thread in *The Eighth Day* and *Don Quixote* is the same: the secret of a happy and full life is in creating. In Wilder's novel the key word is *builders*: in *Don Quixote* it is *righting* wrongs. In both instances, the secret is in the doing, in the carrying out of a program. To do nothing is to die spiritually. This is what the hero of Chrysis' fable in *The Woman of Andros* realizes when he is permitted to be the participant and the onlooker in life: "the living too are dead and that we can only be said to be alive in those moments when our hearts are conscious of our treasure."[20]

Ashley in Wilder's tapestry is but a figure in the whole design whose thread ends somewhere out at sea, just as Alonso Quijano, alias Don Quixote, is in reality only a figure. The entire tapestry is the important thing—the tapestry which reveals how we are all intertwined,[21] affecting one another's lives—influencing one another's fate. I would suspect that coincidence is the poet's way of insisting on our interrelation and inter-dependence on one another. These coincidences are not inartistically contrived.[22] *We have to act in life*, have a program and through our actions bring meaning and movement to other lives, and these in turn to others, *ad infinitum*.

No one who has read *Don Quixote* doubts that the noble *hidalgo* is a kind of messiah, just as Ashley surely is. Eliot Fremont-Smith seems to agree: "Ashley works. Quietly, inventively, humorously, this very ordinary man who is also a Messiah of a kind, moves humanity slightly forward."[23]

It is Don Quixote who saves the duke and duchess from the monotony of their meaningless existence. His presence is so meaningful, so spiritually necessary to them that they scheme to bring him back into their midst a second time so that they may save themselves from nothingness by becoming a part of his adventure in life. And just as in Cervantes' novel the good qualities of the hero produce a favorable effect on Sancho and other characters, so it happens in *The Eighth Day*. Among the things that Constance wants most in the world is "to know hundreds and thousands of people everywhere. [. . .] I keep a list of the people I know. I know one hundred and four people. That doesn't include all the boarders. I have another list for them— the ones that I only say 'good morning' to when I'm waiting on table and cleaning their rooms. I think about people—don't you?—and the more you know the better you think" (pp. 432–33). It is love for humanity that Constance proclaims. Just like her father before her in the case of the Indians, and just like Don Quixote, whom we so often see hurrying or spurring his nag along to catch up with a traveler in order to know him, to ensnare him in his thread. If the spirit of both books were not one of love for humanity and our inextricability from life, the form—the tapestry—would lose part of its artistic meaning. For it is the duty of the artist to reflect in his art his view of life, and the tapestry through its rhythmic threads is well suited for this: "I am interested in those things that repeat and repeat in the lives of millions."[24] For "history is one tapestry" (p. 435). The history of humankind is such, in spite of the fact that "no eye can venture to compass more than a hand's breadth" (p. 435).

Ashley's greatness and his serene life is in knowing that "there is no happiness equal to that of being aware that one has a part in a design" (p. 413). Likewise Don Quixote, whose faith in himself and whose convictions that the future would speak in glowing and glorious terms of his adventure and admirable concern for others, is a well-woven thread in Cervantes' novel.

It is a well-known fact that Cervantes wrote *Don Quixote* partly in reaction to the picaresque novel and the spirit it reflected of his era—a cynical and negative comment on life. Cervantes sought to underscore that little is gained by mere destructive criticism, unless a constructive program is also proposed. *Don Quixote* was an attempt to beat down the negativism and despair of his time, mirrored in the picaresque, and to propound the creative aspect, the true essence of life. Are Wilder's novels unconsciously an answer to the school of atheistic existentialism? We do know that "the atheistic implications of Sartre's philosophy were repugnant to Wilder."[25] *The Eighth Day* ends with the following enigmatic statement, although every reader knows where its author stands: "There is much talk of design in the arras. Some are certain they see it. Some see what they have been told to see. Some are strengthened by seeing a pattern wherein the oppressed and exploited of the earth are gradually emerging from their bondage. Some find strength in the conviction that there is nothing to see. Some" (p. 435). David J. Gorden interprets this ending as meaning that "the book ends with an incomplete sentence to suggest that we cannot see the whole design."[26]

Both Wilder and Cervantes chose the strongest form possible for rendering their philosophies—the tapestry conveys well their message—the irrevocable fact that we are all involved in mankind and all our acts are not only recorded in the great tapestry of history but influence directly or indirectly the lives of others. Yet "The human race cannot be saved by one man or one group of men, but only with the sum total of individual effort."[27] In this regard Sabina's words in *The Skin of our Teeth* go to the crux of the matter: "Pass up your chairs, everybody [to keep the fires burning and man from freezing]. Save the human race"—here on earth. For it is unquestionably certain, that both humanists, Wilder and Cervantes, are deeply concerned with mankind's existence here on earth. And "the notion that we are not necessary to anyone, that attachments *weave* and *unweave* at the mercy of separation, satiety and experience"[28] should be dispelled and our stay here on earth be one of exultation and love. The hero in *The Woman of Andros* saw this only too well. When he was released from the terrible dream of "watching life and living it . . . [he] fell upon the ground and kissed the soil of the world that is too dear to be realized."[29] But most important, it is in the spirit of the tapestry that we should live life.

Notes

1. "His recent study in Romance languages at Princeton makes itself apparent in *The Bridge*, through allusions to Spanish literature of the Golden Age," comments Malcolm Goldstein in *The Art of Thornton Wilder* (Lincoln: University of Nebraska Press, 1965), pp. 50–51.
2. "Lope, Pinedo, Some Child-Actors, and a Lion," *Romance Philogy*, 7 (1953), 19–25. "New Aids toward Dating the Early Plays of Lope de Vega," *Varia Variorum. Festgabe für Karl Reinhardt* (Münster/Köln: Böhlau-Verlag, 1952), 194–200.
3. Robert J. Nelson informs us that the form of a play within a play is "not English— no more than it is Spanish or French or Italian. Nor is the device peculiar to one historical

moment, [. . .]. The play within a play is a dramatic technique [. . .]" *Play within a Play* (New Haven: Yale University Press, 1958), p. ix. However, the fact remains that Wilder's stage manager stepping in and out of the action and directing the other players is very close to the role of the author-director of Calderón's *El gran teatro del mundo*: too close to be summarily dismissed. And like Cervantes, Wilder also experiments with this idea in the novel. In *The Woman of Andros* (New York: Albert & Charles Boni, 1930), the hero is accorded permission to return to life from the dead but with the condition "that it must be with a mind divided into two persons,—the participant and the onlooker: the participant who does the deed and says the words of so many years before, and the onlooker who foresees the end" (p. 35).

4. Quoted from Federico Sánchez Escribano y Alberto Porqueras Mayo, *Preceptiva dramática española del renacimiento y el barroco* (Madrid, 1965), p. 131.

5. Goldstein, *Art of Thornton Wilder*, p. 102.

6. "The sympathetic participation of the audience was most engaged when their collaborative imagination was called upon to supply a large part of the background." Donald Marston, "The Theatre of Thornton Wilder," *Chrysalis*, 7, 1–2 (1954), p. 6.

7. Brush says "I didn't do anything. I just told a bank president that banks were immoral places and they arrested me." *Heaven's My Destination* (New York: Harper & Brothers, 1935), p. 26. In another episode Brush magnanimously gives a hold-up man his liberty and some money (pp. 207–10). Then he explains to Mrs. Efrim "don't be mad at me. I had to act that way to live up to my ideals" (p. 211). Compare this with the episode of the galley slaves: "Of how Don Quixote freed many unfortunate ones who, much against their will, were being taken where they did not wish to go." Miguel de Cervantes, *The Ingenious Gentleman Don Quixote de la Mancha*, trans. Samuel Putnam (New York: The Viking Press, 1949), I, 22, 167–77. All references are to this edition. Like Don Quixote, Brush is considered crazy, "crazy in a sort of nice way" (p. 278). In *The Woman of Andros*, Chrysis, it seems, is a female Don Quixote.

8. Thornton Wilder, *The Eighth Day* (New York, Evanston, and London: Harper & Row, 1967), p. 67. All references are to this edition.

9. "Se referirán con la palabra equivoca, a paños bordados, o a paños tejidos con 'muestras' de figuras o animales repetidos uniformemente (pues el 'tecnicismo' del arte industrial nunca quedo establecido de modo inequivoco)." Felipe de Guevara, *Comentarios de la pintura* (Madrid: edición de Antonio Ponz, 1788), p. xi. Guevara, who lived during Charles V's reign, wrote around 1535.

10. "After the middle of the fourteenth century, tapestries became the form of art most prized by kings and nobles, as is shown by the inventories of the period." George Leland-Hunter, *Tapestries of Clarence H. Mackay* (New York, 1925), p. 17.

11. See Guevara, *Comentarios de la pintura*, pp. xi–xii.

12. The reader is reminded that in 1614 Avellaneda published what he termed the second part of *Don Quixote*. A gentleman by the name of Tarfe appears in it. Cervantes used this same character in the second part of his *Don Quixote* (1615) to discredit Avellaneda's book.

13. We find many examples in practically all of Cervantes' works. Beside *Don Quixote* we have examples in *Persiles y Sigismunda*, in his shorter novels, and in some of his plays.

14. The italics in this quote and in the following ones are added.

15. George Leland Hunter, *Tapestries, Their Origin, History and Renaissance* (New York, 1912), p. 295.

16. *The New York Times*, March 27, 1967, p. 31.

17. We might, however, add that Wilder's triptych consists of seven panels if we include the Prologue, which is actually the center panel.

18. "Diéronle los antiguos mejor y mas proprio nombre del que agora tiene porque la llamaron Pintura texida." Felipe de Guevara, *Comentarios*, p. 54.

19.   See Marcelino Menéndez y Pelayo, *Historia de las ideas estéticas en España* (Santander, 1947), II, 149–53; Francisco Cascales, *Tablas Poéticas* (Madrid: Sancha, 1779); Darnell H. Roaten, F. Sánchez y Escribano, *Wölflin's Principles in Spanish Drama*, 1500–1700 (New York, 1952).

20.   *The Woman of Andros*, p. 36.

21.   In this regard Edith Oliver, in a review of *The Eighth Day*, observed that: "Almost every racial strain is at least touched on," *The New Yorker*, May 27, 1967, p. 147.

22.   Denis Donoghue comments that: "In books of this kind [*The Eighth Day*] the satisfactions of belief are considerable, when they come; as in the account of John Ashley's escape, his riding westward to the Mississippi, his selling the horse to Mrs. Hodge. Or later, the report of Lansing's relation with his wife. Here the author's purposes, however complicated, *coincide* with his mere story, or with what he makes of his story." *The New York Review of Books*, August, 1967, p. 12.

23.   *The New York Times*, March 27, 1967, p. 31. "He is, I believe," says Edith Oliver, "meant to be a kind of saint—the author's idea of a saint—'A man of faith' but of no recognizable religion, with his ' inner quiet, at homeness in existence.' " *The New Yorker*, May 27, 1967, p. 146.

24.   I disagree with Kauffmann who sees rhythmic repetition as unnecessary: "Still worse is the book's treatment of its theme, which is the *Our Town* theme of universality: the similarities of men and women of all times and places, the links between us all, the fact that no horizon is the end of any human landscape. Instead of dramatizing this theme or allowing it to permeate his novel, Wilder states it regularly so that we cannot miss it." *The New Republic*, April 8, 1967 p. 26.

25.   See Goldstein, *Art of Thornton Wilder*, p. 21. Chrysis, in *The Woman of Andros*, fights against this feeling of aloneness: "I am alone. Why have I never seen that before? I am alone" (p. 40); "I have lived alone and I shall die alone" (p. 46). But she concludes "The fault is in me. It's my lack of perseverance in affection" (p. 46).

26.   *The Yale Review*, "New Books in Review," Oct. 1967, p. 108.

27.   Donald Marston, "The Theatre of Thornton Wilder," p. 10.

28.   *The Woman of Andros*, p. 40.

29.   Goldstein, in *Art of Thornton Wilder*, p. 61, similarly finds that "far from recommending a narcotic contemplation of the after life, Wilder speaks out for the vigorous pursuit of purely human relationships."

Theophilus North

GRANVILLE HICKS

Of the eight eminent writers of the twenties and thirties about whom Malcolm Cowley writes in "A Second Flowering," only one is still alive, Thornton Wilder. Wilder survives not merely as a man but also as a writer. In 1962, when he was 65, he retired to the Arizona desert to meditate upon a novel, which became "The Eighth Day" (1967) and won a National Book Award. Now, in his 77th year, he has another book, "Theophilus North," which might conceivably equal the popularity of his second book and first best seller, now half a century old, "The Bridge of San Luis Rey."

From the beginning each of Wilder's books has been a new departure. "The Eighth Day," a combination of mystery story and family chronicle, differed from anything he had previously written in tone, narrative method and setting. "Theophilus North" takes off in an even more surprising direction. Although it is fair enough, as such things go, for the publisher to call it a novel, a term more and more loosely used, it is a novel made up of closely related short stories. So far as I can remember, Wilder has published no short stories in the past, though many short plays, and so once more we find him at work in a medium that is new to him. The stories, moreover, as stories, are adroit, amusing and altogether successful in an old-fashioned way.

The principal unifying factor is Theophilus North, who is both narrator and hero. Like T. Wilder, T. North was born in Wisconsin in 1897, the son of an influential newspaper editor, and received part of his education in China, his father being Consul General in Hong Kong and Shanghai. He spent a year during World War I in the Coast Artillery and returned to Yale to get his A.B. in 1920. He—the pronoun still refers to either T. Wilder or T. North—taught for some years at a private school in New Jersey and took his M.A. at Princeton. But outward characteristics of this order often seem to play a small part in Wilder's work, and it may be that the resemblances here are part of some game with which Wilder is amusing himself. At any rate it is clear that the novel, or whatever you choose to call it, is not autobiographical in any important way. Whether in some subtler sense North stands for Wilder is a harder question to dispose of.

From *New York Times Book Review*, 21 October 1973, 1. Copyright © 1973 by The New York Times Company. Reprinted by permission.

Wilder's plan for a collection of closely related stories requires an approximate unity of time and place, and it is further necessary that North, in order to perform his dual role, must be able to observe and participate in a variety of actions on several social levels. Wilder solves the problems with an ingenuity that is concealed by his offhand manner. Having settled by chance in Newport, Rhode Island, in the summer of 1926, after giving up his job in the New Jersey prep school, North supports himself by teaching tennis to boys and girls and by reading in any of several languages to people who need his services. Soon he knows the city well, and comes to believe that in Newport, as in Schliemann's Troy, there are nine cities. He sees most frequently the inhabitants of the sixth city, the very rich, and those of the seventh, their servants, and strongly prefers the latter to the former. In general, though he makes something of the nine cities, sociohistorical generalizations are not Theophilus's primary interests, nor are they Wilder's.

There are a dozen incidents in which Theophilus proves helpful to inhabitants of Newport. His specialty is saving marriages and smoothing the course of true love, but he also practices his own brand of exorcism on a haunted house, thwarts the avaricious heirs of a gifted old man, saves a young man from being the victim of a talent for what North calls "calligraphic mimicry," helps a legless boy live up to his potentialities and eases the passing of the venerable Tante Liselotte. Although at the outset Theophilus announces his desire to keep to himself and not be involved in the life of Newport, he turns out to be a habitual Good Samaritan, or perhaps one might compare him to an uncommonly conscientious and imaginative Boy Scout.

Sometimes Theophilus does his good deed by means of a trick that might have been employed by O. Henry, but the trick always turns out to have deeper implications than O. Henry would have given it. In "Diana Bell," for instance, Theophilus prevents Diana from eloping by giving her and her lover opportunity to bore one another. Wilder tells the story with humor and gusto, but Theophilus is concerned with more than the snobbish wishes of Diana's parents, and he has something to say about incompatibility. In the same way a little common sense is enough to dispose of the neurotic symptoms of the aging but by no means moribund Dr. Bosworth; a large part of his trouble, however, is what Theophilus calls "the death watch," the vigilance of heirs to speed a rich relative on his path to the grave, and that is harder to deal with. In a couple of stories literature plays an important part in North's therapy, and in others he is—or at any rate appears to his neighbors to be—a faith healer. (Like Hawthorne, Wilder makes ambiguous use of the supernatural.)

Wilder's tone remains consistently lively, is often comic, and the book is extraordinarily entertaining. There are those, I have no doubt, who will call it corny, and sometimes it comes recklessly close to sentimentality—as "Our Town" does, or, for that matter, "The Skin of Our Teeth" and "The

Matchmaker." (Theophilus sometimes makes me think of Dolly Levi.) Occasionally, I admit, I felt that a story might have been written for some woman's magazine, perhaps one that flourished about 1826. But in spite of an excess of sweetness now and then and some obvious manipulation for the sake of happy endings, the stories hold the reader in a firm grip.

It might be enough to say that the book is fun to read and let the matter rest there, but Wilder's works as a rule have multiple meanings, and I have a persistent sense that these stories are saying something, though not in a loud voice. According to Cowley, Wilder describes himself as "fundamentally a happy person." Cowley continues: "He likes to find the goodness or greatness in people and books. He is optimistic by instinct, in the fashion of an older America." At the same time there is in his makeup a tough streak of pessimism. "The Bridge of San Luis Rey" was widely believed to carry a message of consolation and hope, which is probably why it sold so well, but in the end of Brother Juniper's examination of the lives of the victims of the bridge's fall he can conclude only that there was "perhaps an intention."

In "The Eighth Day," when Dr. Gillies is asked to speak to the inhabitants of Coaltown on Dec. 31, 1899, the eve of a new century, he describes to them in flamboyant terms the wonderful age that is coming. But Wilder breaks in to inform the reader: "Dr. Gillies was lying for all he was worth. He had no doubt that the coming century would be too direful to contemplate—that is to say, like all the other centuries." He lies because of the young men in the audience: "It is the duty of old men to lie to the young. Let these encounter their own disillusions. We strengthen our souls, when young, on hope; the strength we acquire enables us later to endure despair as a Roman should."

If Wilder is an optimist, his opportunism operates only in the short run, for his view of man's fate is by no means cheerful. But he does see that there are happy passages along life's way, and he seems to believe that we should make the most of them, not merely in the sense of seizing the day but also as experiences to be taken into account in our judgment of the human condition.

What Theophilus North learns in Newport is that most people could be happier than they are, and experimentation teaches him that sometimes he can improve their lot. His first name proclaims that he is a lover of God, but we see him as one who loves his fellow man which—as Leigh Hunt observed—may be the same thing. As for the second name, it may be a reminder of the cold wind of skepticism. It is like Wilder that he should celebrate 50 years of distinguished writing by producing a book that is gayer in spirit than anything he had previously written, that generously displays his varied talents and that asks more questions than it answers.

It might be argued that Theophilus is what some critics would call a Jesus-figure. He heals the sick after his own fashion, and his deeds attract a large following. Members of the establishment denounce him for stirring up the people. But I don't want to push this as far as it might be pushed. It is more useful to suggest that Theophilus in various complicated ways fulfilled his early ambition to be a saint. He lists saintliness first among the nine ambitions that he held at one time or another in his youth. Eventually he abandoned this ambition as beyond him, but all his ambitions influenced his life. "The past and the future are always *present* within us."

PLAYS

◆

Three Allegorists: Brecht, Wilder, and Eliot

FRANCIS FERGUSSON

I

A number of contemporary playwrights, of whom Brecht, Wilder and Eliot are among the most accomplished, are now writing some form of allegory. They reject the tradition of modern realism, perhaps because little remains to be done with direct reflections of contemporary life: the pathos of the lost individual or the decaying suburb has been done to death since Chekhov. They do not seek some form of theater-poetry based on folk forms or myths or rituals, or on symbolism on the analogy of the *symboliste* poets, as so many theater artists did in the twenties. They seek to use the theater in the service of their consciously worked-out moral or philosophical ideas. They do not, however, write thesis plays à la Brieux, in which some scheme of social reform is openly debated and "proved" on the stage; nor do they write Shavian intellectual farces, in which the point is in the game of ideas itself. Their aim is not discussion in any sense, but teaching: they use the stage, the characters, and the story to demonstrate an idea which they take to be the undiscussible truth. The truths which Brecht, Wilder and Eliot propound are very different; but they all write allegory according to the literal definition in the Oxford Dictionary: "speaking otherwise than one seems to speak."

One must be very detached from the contemporary theater and its audiences in order to write allegory of this kind. Brecht, Wilder and Eliot do not expect their audiences to share their intimate perceptions, whether "realistic" or "poetic." Such detachment is the natural result of the failure of the art theaters of the twenties. After World War I much of the creative energy of the theater went into small theater groups which tried to build special audiences like those of ballet, chamber music or lyric poetry. Playwrights who worked for such groups tried to cultivate their art first and their audiences second; they were encouraged to embody their visions in the theater medium as directly as possible. In that context the thought-out indirectness of allegory seemed cumbersome and artificial. But the contemporary allegorists despair of the effort to recruit an audience of connoisseurs. They accept the commercial theater (especially Wilder and Eliot) as the only

From *Sewanee Review* 64 (1956): 544–73. Permission by the editor, SEWANEE REVIEW.

theater we can have; and the problem they set themselves is to use that non-conducting medium—necessarily *indirectly*—for their didactic purposes.

All three of these allegorists are extremely conscious of what they are doing. One can study their philosophies not only in their plays but in their theoretical writings, and all of them have written technical studies of playwriting which reveal the knowing methods they use in making their plays. But in other respects they are dissimilar and unrelated. Each of them has followed a lonely road to his achievement, and speaks through the stage as though he were alone with his undiscussible truth. For that reason it is something of a tour de force to consider them together, as though they were voices in a dialogue; as though they were devoting their thought and their art to some common enterprise in the modern theater.

Nevertheless they all seek with some success to address the mysterious modern crowd; their plays may run at the same time in the same city. And all of them are obliged to come to terms with the theater itself, stage, actors, and audience; and the art of handling those elements, though seldom studied in its full scope, is not unknown. Brecht, Wilder and Eliot seek to work out *new* theatrical forms, and Brecht owes much of his peculiar force to his direct defiance of the tradition. But one may patiently put them back into relation to the tradition by enquiring what they do with the inescapable elements of plot, characterization, language, and the conventions of make-believe. In this way one can, I think, find a basis for comparing them and for estimating the meaning of the present trend toward allegory. . . .

II

The philosophy which Thornton Wilder presents in his plays, especially the two most famous, *Our Town* and *The Skin of Our Teeth*, is at the opposite pole from Brecht's. Brecht is exclusively concerned (like Barth in his "Theology of Crisis") with his obsessive vision of the emergency of our time. His Marxism is in essence partisan, and his theater lives by conflict. Wilder on the other hand tries to take his stance above all parties; he preaches the timeless validity of certain great old traditional ideas, and his theater is almost devoid of conflict, wooing its audience gently. Wilder's philosophy—that of a most cultivated man—is more sophisticated than Brecht's and more subtly presented. But on the evidence of the plays I think one can call it a sort of religious Platonism: deistic, but not more Christian than Unitarianism or Ethical Culture.

Brecht has paid his respects with characteristic vigor to those writers who even in our time reiterate the eternal verities: "It is true," he writes in *Fünf Schwierigkeiten*, "that Germany is falling into barbarism, and that rain falls downward. Many poets write truths of this kind. They are like painters who decorate the walls of a sinking ship with still lifes." If he read Wilder's still lifes he would characterize them in just such scornful terms. And as one turns from Brecht to Wilder one must be struck with the sudden quiet, and wonder what relevance these plays have to the actual texture of our lives. Yet Wilder's plays succeed at least as well as Brecht's in holding a modern crowd for two hours in the theater, and Wilder's art is at least as knowing, forewarned and forearmed, as Brecht's.

A very early play of Wilder's, perhaps his first, was produced by the American Laboratory Theatre in 1926, and has, I think, never been printed. It is a heavy allegory about a householder (God) who goes away on a journey, leaving his servants in charge. When he returns he finds that they have been faithful or unfaithful in various ways, and rewards them accordingly. This play is appropriately entitled *The Trumpet Shall Sound*, and it reveals Wilder's philosophy and his allegorical art at a crude, early stage. The distance between it and *Our Town* measures his extraordinary growth as technician. We have some of the experiments and finger exercises he did in the next eight years: his short plays, his adaptation of *A Doll's House*, his translation of Obey's *Viol de Lucrèce*, and his valuable technical essay, "Notes on Playwriting." On the evidence of the plays it appears that Joyce, Gertrude Stein, Obey, and in general the literary and theatrical great of "Paris in the twenties" have been his masters. But his art has been very little studied: we marvel at his results, but have not investigated his stage magic. This essay can therefore be no more than a preliminary exploration.

Our Town is Wilder's masterpiece to date. His nostalgic evocation of Grover's Corners, New Hampshire, at the turn of the century, is fed, more than any of his other works, with the sources of poetry: old, digested memories and associations. The atmosphere of the little town convinces before all thought, as poetry does. But at the same time a New England village before World War I is a natural illustration of the faint religious humanism which Wilder wants to present allegorically. The Stage Manager–Lecturer directs our attention to the protagonist (the town) and the narrative sequence from the cradle to the grave. By the end of Act I it is evening, and we have heard *Blest Be the Tie That Binds* sung offstage by the Ladies' Choir and then whistled by Mr. Webb. George and Rebecca Gibbs, as children, are leaning out an upstairs window enjoying the moonlight:

REBECCA: I never told you about that letter that Jane Crofut got from her minister when she was sick. . . . He wrote Jane a letter and on the envelope the address was like this: It said: Jane Crofut; The Crofut Farm; Grover's Corners; Sutton County; New Hampshire; United States of America.

GEORGE: What's funny about that?

REBECCA: But listen; it's not finished: The United States of America; Continent of North America; Western Hemisphere; The Earth; The Solar

System; The Universe: The Mind of God—that's what it said on the
envelope.

This passage was perhaps inspired by the very similar address which young
Stephen Daedalus writes in his geography book; but it works beautifully at
this point in the play, and the moral—that we live, whether we realize it
or not, in the Mind of God—emerges naturally from the context of old-
fashioned village childhood. In Act II Wilder uses the terrors and sentimental
tears of a long-past marriage to suggest the same idea more gently; and in
Act III he uses Emily's funeral and her ghostly return to earth on her
fourteenth birthday for the same purpose: to present Grover's Corners *sub
specie aeternitatis*. In the whole play the homesick vision and the Platonic-
religious teaching work harmoniously together.

Wilder's "Notes on Playwriting" show that, like Brecht, his art of
allegory is completely knowing. Like Brecht again, he stresses the conventional, make-believe quality of the stage—in opposition to the realists'
"illusion"—for the purposes of allegory. All theater "lives by convention,"
he writes, and "a convention is an agreed-upon falsehood, a permitted lie."
. . . "The convention has two functions: (1) It provokes the collaborative
activity of the spectator's imagination; and (2) It raises the action from the
specific to the general. . . . The stage continually strains to tell this generalized truth and it is the element of pretense that reinforces it." That is an
excellent description of the way the theatrical conventions of *Our Town* work.
The bare stage and the Stage Manager who directly addresses the audience
or tells the actors what to do enlist the audience in make-believe: induce it
to imagine the little town waking up, years ago, in the dark of early morning.
At the same time the frank theatricality of these conventions warns us not
to take the characters too seriously as people: they are presented only by
make-believe, as half-playful illustrations of a "generalized truth." It is this
"generalized truth"—that we exist in the Mind of God—which we are to
watch for, and when we get it we shall have the whole point and message
of the play.

Wilder maintains, in his "Notes," that all drama is essentially allegory,
"A succession of events illustrating a general idea," as he puts it. "The
myth, the parable, the fable are the fountainheads of all fiction," he writes,
"and in them is seen most clearly the didactic, moralizing employment of
a story. Modern taste shrinks from emphasizing the central idea behind the
fiction, but it exists there nevertheless, supplying the unity to fantasizing,
and offering a justification to what otherwise we would repudiate as mere
arbitrary contrivance, pretentious lying, or individualistic emotional association-spinning." This radically Platonic view of poetry—that its only justification is that it may be a means of teaching moral truth—might be disputed
at some length. But I suppose it must be the belief of all three of our
contemporary allegorists; Brecht would certainly agree in principle, for his

plays are very obviously constructed as "a succession of events illustrating a general idea." But it is worth noting that Brecht's "truth" is the opposite of Wilder's—which suggests that moralizing is no more immune than poetry to the human weakness for arbitrary contrivance, pretentious lying, and individualistic emotional association-spinning.

In the art of both Brecht and Wilder plotmaking is basic, for the plot, while presenting the story, must be at the same time a demonstration of the idea. Wilder relies on plotting even more than Brecht; by its means, he explains, the playwright controls stage, actors, director and designer for his purposes. "He learns to organize the play in such a way that its strength lies not in appearances beyond his control, but in the succession of events and in the unfolding of an idea, in narration." He accomplishes precisely this feat by means of the plot—the succession of events—in *Our Town*. It is primarily the narrative sequence from morning to night, from the cradle to the grave, through the marriage to the funeral, which carries the play; and it is this sequence also which continually leads to the *idea*. Brecht arranges his plots in such a way as to present onstage only struggles; he avoids all pathos on the ground that it would demoralize the audience which he is grooming for the Revolution. But Wilder, in the interest of his opposite philosophy, bases the three acts of his play precisely upon the pathos of the great commonplaces of human life, birth, marriage and death; and he shows no conflict at all.

The plot with its unfolding idea is so effective, in *Our Town*, that it almost makes the play go without reference to the individual lives of its people. But not quite: the stage is after all not the lecture platform; one must put something concrete upon it. "Because a play presupposes a crowd," Wilder writes, "the dramatist realizes that the group mind imposes upon him the necessity of treating material understandable by the greater number." It is apparently in accordance with this principle that he has selected the concrete materials of *Our Town*: the characters, which are clichés of small-town life rather than individuals; the language they speak, which (in spite of its authentic New England flavor) is distressingly close to that of plays written for high schools and Sunday schools, or to the soap operas of radio, or to vapid "family magazines." If one looks at a few passages from the play apart from the movement of the plot—George and Emily absorbing their cherry phosphates, or George having his tearful talks with his father-in-law to be—the effect is embarrassingly stale and pathetic. It is evident that Wilder himself is not much interested in George or Emily. He hardly imagines them as people, he rather invites the audience to accept them by plainly labeling them; as sentimental stereotypes of village folksiness. They are therefore understandable by the greater number, and they serve to present the story and illustrate the moral. But they betray, I think, the worst weakness of Wilder's type of allegory. The distance between the life onstage, which the audience accepts because it is so familiar in this sense, and the idea which the author has in mind is too great. The "greater number" blubbers at the platitudes of character and situation, while the author, manipulating his effects with kindly care, enjoys the improbable detachment of the Mind of God.

André Obey's *Noah* is akin to *Our Town* in several respects; I even think it possible that it may have given Wilder some of the clues for his play. *Our Town* is based on the "world" of small-town Protestantism at the turn of the century, and *Noah* upon the "world" of French peasant religion. Both plays therefore owe some of their appeal to nostalgia, and when *Noah* is played one can hardly "get" it without an effort of sympathy which may be called sentimental. But once we make-believe that vanished world, we get a vision of human life which is full of the weight of experience. The imagined characters are intensely alive; we see at every moment how Noah is groping and struggling. It is his experience which leads us to the idea—or rather the vision—which the play presents. At the end we are made to feel what Noah's faith has cost him, and therein lies the strength and the authority of the play. But the dreamy situation of *Our Town* does not cost anyone anything, and that, I think, is why the idea may strike us as sentimental and pretentious. The idea is clear; in a sense it is appropriately illustrated in the atmosphere and the customs of Grover's Corners. But it is not incarnate in the characters and the language which make up the actual texture of the play.

In spite of this weakness *Our Town* is a "natural" for Wilder and his philosophy: the basic inspiration is propitious, the remembered village and the idea to be taught do harmonize. But in *The Skin of Our Teeth* Wilder set himself an even more difficult problem: that of presenting his religious Platonism in an urban context, and at a time—the beginning of World War II—of general crisis. In that play both the theatrical virtuosity and the weakness, or limitation, of Wilder's kind of allegory are very clear.

Wilder is reported to have received the inspiration for *Skin* at a performance of *Hellza'poppin*, an extravaganza in the corniest style of old-fashioned vaudeville. But Campbell and Robinson, who attended the opening of *Skin* just after they had completed their *Skeleton Key to Finnegans Wake*, demonstrated in two well-documented articles in *The Saturday Review* that the play is a simplified dramatization of Joyce's mysterious work. There is probably no one but Wilder with enough imagination and enough understanding both of Joyce and of vaudeville to combine the two. But now that the work is done we can see what a brilliant notion it was to translate Joyce's dreamlike and ironic meditation on the eternal recurrences of human history into the ancient jokes, irrational horseplay and shameless sentimentality of burlesque. Burlesque provides Wilder with his "material understandable to the greater number," an urban folksiness corresponding to the village folksiness of *Our Town*; and *Finnegans Wake* suggests a plot-scheme and an abstract cast of characters to give narrative and rational form to the whole.

The plot of *Skin* is closely analogous to that of *Our Town*. The protagonist is Humanity, which corresponds to Grover's Corners. The three major crises on which the three acts are based, the Ice Age, the Flood, and War, correspond to Our Town's Birth, Marriage and Death. Just as Birth, Marriage and Death must be suffered by all villagers, and recur in every generation, so the crises in *Skin* are felt as common, similar, and recurrent ordeals, which must be suffered in every generation. *Skin*, like *Our Town*, is essentially a pathos, with little conflict—and that little unconvincing. The moral of the tale is the same: we have our being within the eternal verities, or the Mind of God. Thus at the end of Act I, when the Antrobus household in Excelsior, New Jersey, is getting ready to survive the Ice Age, Antrobus insists on saving Moses, Homer and the nine Muses (who are bums on the streets of New York) "to keep up our spirits." Moses and Homer each quote a bit from their works, in Hebrew and Greek respectively; and then all join in singing *Tenting Tonight*. At the end of Act II the Flood provides a more sinister hint of the truth behind our heedless lives (like the marriage in *Our Town*); and at the end of Act III bits from Spinoza, Plato, Aristotle and Genesis are quoted by members of the backstage staff. The quotations proclaim the intellectual love of God, and are supposed to be thought of as hours of the night, from nine to midnight, passing over our heads like the stars: an effect very much like the one in *Our Town*, when George and Rebecca are seen in the moonlight, with stars beyond, and beyond that the Mind of God.

All of this works very well in the theater, when "the greater number" is there to guffaw at the scenery when it leans precariously, the wise cracks aimed at the peanut gallery, and the racial jokes in the cozy style of *Abie's Irish Rose*; or to grow still and dewy-eyed when the old familiar tunes are heard. But if one happens to be feeling a little morose—smothered perhaps by so thick an atmosphere of sheer warm-heartedness—or if one tries the experiment of reading the play in cold blood, the marriage of Plato and Groucho Marx may fail to appeal. It is too evident that the "material," the actual texture, of the play, is a pastiche. The language is a collection of clichés, the characters unfused collections of familiar labels. Antrobus, for instance, consists of old jokes about the suburban householder, the middle-aged philanderer, and the Shriner on a binge, but he is also labeled the inventor of all human culture. The combination has no imaginative or intellectual unity at all. It is amusing and good-natured to set Moses, Homer and the nine Muses to singing *Tenting Tonight*, but what does Wilder's "greater number" get out of this reassuring effect? The austerity of the Ten Commandments, or tearful associations with last summer's bonfire at Camp Tamiment?

A reading of *Our Town* and *The Skin of Our Teeth* suggests that Wilder's extraordinary freedom and virtuosity in the theater is gained through eluding rather than solving the problem which most playwrights feel as basic: that of embodying form and meaning in character and language. If he had addressed himself to that problem in *Skin*, Antrobus, as the father-pilot of the race, would have had to sound a little more like Spinoza and a little less like George F. Babbitt. But Wilder has seen how it is possible to leave the "greater number" in peace with the material understandable to it, and Plato in peace in the supratemporal realm of the Mind of God. He is thus able to be "for" Plato (as politicians of every persuasion are for Peace, Freedom and Prosperity), and at the same time devote his great gifts to entertaining the crowd or "group mind."

This type of allegory is perfectly in accord with the Platonic kind of philosophy which it is designed to teach. The great Ideas are timeless, above the history of the race and the history of actual individuals. Any bit of individual or racial history will do, therefore, to "illustrate" them; but history and individual lives lack all real being: they are only shadows on the cave wall. It may be part of Wilder's consciously intended meaning that the material understandable to the greater number—comic-supplement jokes, popular tunes—*is* junky and illusory. That would be one explanation of the bodiless and powerless effect of his theater, as compared, for instance, with Brecht's. Brecht's vision is narrow and myopic, but a sense of the reality (at however brutal a level) of individual experience is truly in it. Brecht's philosophy is, of course, a philosophy of history, and leads him naturally to sharpest embodiments in the temporal struggle. But Wilder's philosophy lacks the historic dimension, and its intellectual freedom is therefore in danger of irrelevancy, pretentiousness and sentimentality.

Wilder's art, as I pointed out above, has not yet been critically digested or expounded. Wilder occupies a unique position, between the Great Books and Parisian sophistication one way, and the entertainment industry the other way, and in our culture this region, though central, is a dark and almost uninhabited no man's land. Partly for that reason, his accomplishments must seem rather puzzling and paradoxical. The attempt which I have been making, to take him seriously as allegorizing moralist, may be much too solemn. His plays belong in the theater; they have their proper life only there, like the tricks of a stage magician. When the man pulls the rabbit out of the hat, the glamour of the occasion suffices: it is inappropriate to enquire whether he has really materialized a new creature, or only hauled out, by the ears, the same old mild vegetarian pet. . . .

III

It is the peculiarity of the kind of allegory represented by Brecht, Wilder and Eliot that the author *assumes* the truth and the acceptability of the moral to be taught. It is this which distinguishes contemporary allegory from the old-fashioned thesis-play, in which the thesis is directly discussed and supposedly proved to the satisfaction of all parties to the dispute. Thus Brecht assumes his Marxian doctrine as something his audience can get through apothegmatic references, signals instantly clear to those who know. And in analogous ways Wilder and Eliot assume their Platonic or religious philosophies, reminding their audiences of the ancient truths rather than arguing, or trying to induce a fresh perception. All three allegorists, in other words, write "as if" their audiences were with them: this attitude is the basis of their didactic strategies.

But in order to teach that way in the theater, each playwright must put on the stage some aspect of human life, some mode of action, which his audience will recognize, and which at the same time harmonizes with the idea to be taught. All of them would presumably accept Wilder's dictum, that the basis of the playwright's art is in "the unfolding of an idea"; yet each one, in the necessary effort to bring life to the stage, instinctively "imitates an action." In each case the *action* of the play is the connecting link between the audience and the author's ideas. And I believe that the action is a better index of the *actual* spiritual content of the plays than the ideas which the playwrights wish to teach.

Thus Wilder writes "as if" we were all good-hearted home folks together (his diagnosis of the assumption underlying our popular entertainment): "I don't think the theater is a place where people's feelings ought to be hurt," says Sabina in *The Skin of Our Teeth*. And in *Our Town* we read, in the "serious talk" that George and Emily have in their late teens:

EMILY: I always expect a man to be perfect and I think he should be.

GEORGE: Oh . . . I don't think it's possible to be perfect, Emily.

EMILY: Well, my father is, and as far as I can see your father is. There's no reason on earth why you shouldn't be too.

GEORGE: Well, Emily . . . I feel it's the other way round. That men aren't naturally good; but girls are. Like you and your mother and my mother.

George and Emily, like Sabina and the other characters in Wilder's two plays, are trying to "feel good," and it is that action which the audience sympathetically imitates, sharing its Sunday school righteousness and its smiling tears of delicious embarrassment. Wilder counts on the analogy between this bathetic attempt to feel good and the action recommended in the classic counsel: "Be ye therefore perfect even as your Father in heaven is perfect." Through this analogy he proposes to remind us of the Good, the True and the Beautiful in the Mind of God. But the analogy, if it exists, is extremely remote; and the idea, if one tries to apprehend it at any sort of adult level, is not incarnate in the action. It remains a bodiless allusion, hardly appropriate to the squirms and sniffles we indulge in while feeling good with George and Emily.

Brecht, approaching the modern crowd from an opposite angle, writes "as if" we were all condemned to the single-minded pursuit of material satisfaction, nimbly filching each other's shirts (and wives) in the myopic old game of pleasure and power. The idea he wishes to teach—by allusion—is the Marxian Utopian idealism; but what gives his plays their carrying power is again the least common denominator of action. It is the sardonic hilarity of the squabble that we share and enjoy.

Eliot is of course a far more serious and searching moralist than Wilder or Brecht. And the plan of *The Confidential Clerk* calls for a more balanced, varied and comprehensive composition of analogous actions leading to the perception of an order, rather than to a mere idea. The action, according to plan, would be "to discover what I really wish for." At the bottom of the scale would be Sir Claude, with his timid, snobbish diagnosis of his wishes; at the top, Colby, when he finally sees that his true wish would be obedience to God. But in order to establish contact with the audience he has in mind Eliot is obliged to write "as if" we were all brought up in good society, careful in matters of taste, keeping a stiff upper lip for politeness' sake; embarrassed by metaphysics. And on this basis, he, like Wilder, can realize only a very reduced version of the action his plot calls for. What we actually see and feel in that drawing room are plausible types endeavoring to formulate their dim wishes within the limits of social convention. And in the ensuing conversations there is little to choose between Colby and Sir Claude: the action, thus circumscribed, is so narrow that the difference between salvation and damnation is hardly perceptible. The hierarchy Eliot wishes to teach is present only as it is somewhat artificially alluded to in talk.

Wilder and Eliot both seek to teach certain ideas derived from the central religious-humanistic tradition, and in thinking over their results one is led to wonder—rather idly, perhaps—what it would take to reincarnate the ancient vision. Eliot speaks, in his essay on Baudelaire, of "the adjustment of the natural to the spiritual, of the bestial to the human, and the human to the supernatural." One can see how this formula might apply to *Lear*, for example: the natural, the spiritual, the bestial, the human and the supernatural are all present with the weight and authority of experience; all alive with the imagined lives of the characters and their relationships; all "adjusted" to one another in countless suggestive ways. But one cannot see how, even if a genius like Shakespeare were available, any such comprehensive picture of human nature and destiny could be squeezed into our show shops. Eliot and Wilder do not, of course, make the attempt. Their plays are designed in accordance with their diagnoses of the "group mind" of the contemporary theater. Therein is their originality, and also their technical interest and their significance as signs of the times. It is discouraging to find that they connect with their audiences only by way of nostalgia, flattering daydream, or "wish"—finding thereby no way to incarnate their meanings, teaching only by concepts and allusion.

Brecht's plays do not have this bodiless quality. His materialistic philosophy does not connote the problem of "incarnation": you might say that his characters are *all* "carne," and that the destructive half of his revolutionary creed—each thing meeting in mere oppugnancy—is brilliantly realized in his theater. But the other half, the Marxian Utopia, is at least as unrealized as Eliot's and Wilder's moral and religious ideas. If one regards Brecht as a Marxian idealist one may feel in his work as well as in that of Wilder and Eliot, the force of Yeats's nightmare:

> Things fall apart; the centre cannot hold;
> Mere anarchy is loosed upon the world,
> The blood-dimmed tide is loosed, and everywhere
> The ceremony of innocence is drowned;
> The best lack all conviction, while the worst
> Are full of passionate intensity.

The aims of those who seek to make an allegorical form for the modern theater, in order to teach the group mind indirectly, by way of some mode of action which they can recognize and accept, would seem to be natural and right. But it is hard to see how this effort can get much farther in our theater as it is. Brecht, Wilder and Eliot, with their varied talents and their extraordinary technical resourcefulness, have shown us what is possible in that line.

Thornton Wilder Says "Yes"

BARNARD HEWITT

None of Thornton Wilder's critics mentions *The Matchmaker*, perhaps because it is offered as an adaptation not as an original work, but more likely because it is labeled a "farce" and serious critics of the drama have almost always ignored farce as mere diversion for the unthinking. Moreover, farce has been pretty much out of favor in the theatre for nearly thirty years. However, there are signs that it may be returning to fashion: witness the success not only of *The Matchmaker* but of *Hotel Paradiso*. Moreover, Eric Bentley has rediscovered farce as a subject for analysis by the critic and theorist of drama. His essay "The Psychology of Farce," which introduces the volume of French farces recently published in the Mermaid Dramabook series, gives every appearance of being only a beginning. We may expect more on the subject from Bentley, and other critics may well follow his lead.

If *The Matchmaker* is subjected to analysis, it is likely to draw adverse criticism of the same kinds that have been leveled against *Our Town* and *The Skin of Our Teeth*. Since *The Matchmaker* is acknowledged to be an adaptation of an Austrian play by Johann Nestroy, which was based upon an English play by John Oxenford, perhaps no one will look for further borrowings. But if they do, they will find that the scene in Act I in which Dolly Levi describes to Horace Vandergelder Ernestine Simple's wonderful qualifications to be his wife, in which she flatters Horace and extracts money from him, is right out of Molière's *The Miser*. Before any critic cites this as further evidence that Thornton Wilder is lacking in original creative power, let us hope he will recall that Molière's *The Miser* drew very heavily upon Plautus' *Aulularia*.

What do we discover, if we examine *The Matchmaker* according to Eric Bentley's view of farce? Bentley finds the function of farce in Freud's *Civilization and Its Discontents* and describes that function as follows: ". . . when we buy civilization, as we do, at the price of frustration, the frustrated impulses become a potential source of trouble. The pressures are enormous and perpetual. We ought to welcome any relief from them, however slight or trivial,

From *Tulane Drama Review* 4 (Winter 1959): 110–20. Reprinted by permission of the heirs of Barnard Hewitt.

provided it is harmless. Dreams are the commonest relief but are usually unpleasant. The most pleasurable relief is to be found in the arts." One of these arts is farce. The farce, like the dream, pictures the disguised fulfillment of repressed wishes. Many repressed wishes are gross and all are in revolt against our culture. Since the family is at the center of our culture, gross wishes are mainly directed against the family. "Outrage to family piety and propriety," says Bentley, "is certainly at the heart of farce." Hence, the farcical ubiquity of the bed. The energy which is one of the earmarks of farce derives from the repression of primitive instinct. The violence, which is another of its earmarks, is aggression against established forms, against established values. The physical exertions of the characters in farce provide release and relief for conflicts which for the most part lie buried beneath the conscious life of civilized man. To quote Mr. Bentley once more: "Man, says farce, may or may not be one of the more intelligent animals; he is certainly an animal, and not one of the least violent; and one of the chief uses to which he puts his intelligence, such as it is, is to think aggression when he is not committing it."

From Bentley's point of view, farce is a moral and highly useful form of drama. It provides in enjoyable and harmless fantasy a substitute for aggressive thoughts and destructive actions—wife-beating, adultery, rape, incest, patricide—to which we are all impelled by the beast within us. Farce is an efficacious tranquilizer. An evening at *Hotel Paradiso* is as good as an hour on the psychiatrist's couch.

Thornton Wilder's *The Matchmaker* is full of energy, but the energy is not destructive. The wildly absurd action of the play is precipitated and complicated by the determination of its principal characters to lead freer, fuller lives than circumstances have imposed upon them. Cornelius Hackl one day rebels against the narrow limits of his life in Yonkers as Horace Vandergelder's chief clerk, and, with his youthful assistant, Barnaby Tucker, sets out for a day of adventure in New York, determined before he returns to have a good meal, get almost arrested, spend all his money, and kiss a girl. Ambrose Kemper is determined to marry Horace's niece Ermengarde in spite of her uncle's opposition. Irene Malloy, weary of the restrictions which widowhood, her millinery business, and standards of decorum placed upon her, kicks over the traces. She goes to dinner at the Harmonia Gardens with what she thinks are two gay blades. Dolly Levi is determined to marry Horace Vandergelder in order to put his money into circulation and thus make the world a pleasanter place for her and lots of other people.

Horace Vandergelder stands for the cautious, careful, safe existence— everything the others are rebelling against. Horace prides himself on his good sense. In comparison with him, nearly everyone is foolish. To be young is foolish. To fall in love is foolish. To marry is foolish. To be poor is foolish. In order to be rich one must work hard and spend money only for necessities. To be sensible, therefore, is to be old and rich like Horace Vandergelder.

And yet the revolt against Horace and the cautious, careful life he stands for is without malice, without vindictiveness. It is entirely light-hearted. The two clerks encourage some cans of tomatoes in Horace's store to explode, thus providing an excuse for their holiday, but the cans of tomatoes were spoiled to begin with. Otherwise Horace does not suffer from their revolt. Horace is not forced or tricked into allowing Ermengarde to marry Ambrose; he does so of his own free will. Dolly Levi succeeds in marrying Horace, but she does not deceive him. He knows she is going to help him spend his painfully accumulated money, but he wants to marry her anyhow.

This is not hard to believe, for we know that Horace, in spite of all his talk about what is sensible and what is foolish, in spite of his treatment of Ambrose and Cornelius and Ermengarde, is not really so different from the rest of them. In the first act, immediately after his stuffy sermon on folly and good sense, he declares that he is contemplating getting married again, not only in order to have his house run with order, comfort, and economy (a *sensible* reason) but also because he hankers after "a little risk and adventure after many years of caution and hard work," (a very *foolish* reason). Having taken one cautious step out of his safe, sensible, and lonely world into the adventurous, foolish, and convivial world, he inevitably takes another step, and another, until he is running with the majority of mankind. To use Dolly Levi's words, he has "joined the world," he has "rejoined the human race."

Thus, Horace only *seems* to be a symbol for the sensible, humdrum side of life, against which everyone else is rebelling. Underneath his crusty exterior he longs as much as anybody to shake off the shackles of security and good sense. Once the crusty exterior is cracked, it rapidly disintegrates.

Cornelius, Ambrose, Dolly Levi, and Irene Malloy do not represent repressed wishes in revolt against our culture. Their revolt is not aggression against the established forms, the established values of our civilization. They are not really rebelling against anything outside themselves. They are in conflict with the drive toward self-preservation, security, and peace, which exists in most human beings side by side with its opposite, the drive toward change, adventure, and excitement.

Aggression in *The Matchmaker* is not directed against the family. Indeed, the opposite is true. Aggression, if it can be called that in this play, is directed against ideas and attitudes which discourage marriage. The immediate result of the rebellions it presents is three marriages, all of which have every prospect of being happy marriages, thus strengthening the family and the culture of which it is the center.

In *The Matchmaker*, Wilder has used the form and method of farce to celebrate—in very simple, almost childlike terms—the radical, the pioneering, the exploring, the creative spirit in man. Even if one ignores the playwright's statement of his theme as he puts it into the mouths of some of his characters or overlooks these explanations in the hurly-burly of the action, this meaning, as Harold Clurman has noted "is in the doing of it, the sheer physical exhilaration of its theatrical pattern." *The Matchmaker* is gay; it is exhilarating. It is not a tranquilizer but a tonic. . . .

If Thornton Wilder is an optimist, his is no shallow optimism. He recognizes that pain, cruelty, failure, and death are a part of living but he feels strongly that they can never completely define life. Gerald Weales has observed that Wilder, like the heroine of his novel *The Woman of Andros*, seems to say, "I have known the worst that the world can do. . . . Nevertheless, I praise the world and all living." He says "yes" to life.

Thornton Wilder says "yes" to the theatre also. He recognizes and accepts the fact that theatre is a collaborative art, that director and actors necessarily intervene their bodies, minds, and imaginations between the playwright and his vision of his play. In his essay "Some Thoughts on Playwriting," he says he seeks "to organize the play in such a way that its strength lies not in appearances beyond his control, but in the succession of events and in the unfolding of an idea, in narration." The details of the physical realization of his play he is happy to leave to actors and director. He recognizes too that a play is addressed not to individuals but to a group, and he accepts the fact that the "group-mind imposes upon him the necessity of treating materials understandable by the larger number."

Above all, Thornton Wilder believes in the theatricality of the theatre. The theatre, he says, is a world not of illusion but of pretense, of make-believe. It lives by conventions, that is, by agreed upon falsehoods, by permitted lies. "When it tries to assert that the personages in the action 'really are,' really inhabit such and such rooms, really suffer from such and such emotions, it loses rather than gains credibility." Convention, he maintains, provokes the spectator to collaborate in the dramatic creation, and it raises the action from the specific to the general. The element of pretense reinforces the continual effort of the stage to present generalized truth.

Of course, the theatre of "illusion," as Wilder uses the term, is also a theatre of pretense. No one mistakes its personages for real people. And, like the theatre of "make-believe," it depends upon conventions—agreed upon falsehoods, permitted lies. But its conventions are different conventions. They tend to make the audience a spectator rather than a collaborator; they tend to make the drama particular rather than general.

The theatre of "illusion"—as opposed to the theatre of "make-believe"—is, in a way, theatre that denies itself. Not only the realistic theatre of Belasco and Stanislavsky but the symbolistic theatre of Gordon Craig and Adolphe Appia seeks to create by means of text, actors, scenery, and light a world separate from the audience—not the world of the theatre, but the world of Peter Grimm or Madame Ranevsky or Hamlet or Tristan and Isolde.

The proscenium arch is not only the symbol of that separation but the principal means whereby the illusion is created.

Thornton Wilder's plays in one way or another break down the barrier of the proscenium arch. They involve the spectator directly by frankly making him once more a participant in a theatrical experience. These plays have been and continue to be highly successful. They point the way the living theatre should go, for if it is to survive as anything but a luxury for the few, it must discard the conventions of "illusion" and revive the older conventions of "make-believe." It should leave the creation of "illusion" to the moving picture and to television, both of which are infinitely better equipped for it. The theatre should reaffirm itself as an art of "pretense" not of "illusion," of living actors not real people, and of an active not a passive audience.

Thornton Wilder is important in today's American theatre because he is a believer, a yea-sayer. He says "yes" to the life of the theatre, still struggling to escape the strangling embrace of realism and illusion. And through the theatre he says "yes" to human life. In what sometimes seems an unbroken chorus of aggression and rejection by contemporary American playwrights, his is one strong, affirmative voice.

Thornton Wilder and the Tragic Sense of Life

ROBERT W. CORRIGAN

Of all modern American dramatists, none is more difficult to pin down than Thornton Wilder. He is thought of, together with O'Neill, Miller, and Williams, as one of our "Big Four," and yet his reputation is based on only three full-length plays and was made on one. And whereas reams of criticism have been written on the other three playwrights, only an occasional article on Wilder is published. This is all the more surprising since no one seems to agree about his work. For some he is the great American satirist; for others he is a soft-hearted sentimentalist; and for still others he is our only "religious" dramatist. Furthermore, no American playwright is more respected by contemporary European dramatists than is Wilder; Brecht, Ionesco, Düerrenmatt, and Frisch have all acknowledged their debt to this "great and fanatical experimenter." Therefore, it is about time that we reevaluate his work.

From his earliest volumes of one-acts, *The Angel That Troubled the Waters* and *The Long Christmas Dinner*, to his last full-length play, *The Matchmaker*, Wilder has dealt boldly and affirmatively with the themes of Life, Love, and Earth. Each of his plays is a hymn in dramatic form affirming life. But the important question is: What is the nature of this affirmation? It is not, as some would have it, Christian. To begin with, Wilder has no belief—at least as expressed in his plays—in a religion that is revealed or historical. These are basic premises of Christianity. To be sure Wilder is deistic, but as almost all of his critics have pointed out, he is essentially a religious Platonist; and this position must ultimately reject the historic dimension as meaningful. Francis Fergusson ties these two ideas together when he writes: "The plays are perfectly in accord with the Platonic kind of philosophy which they are designed to teach. The great Ideas are timeless, above the history of the race and the history of actual individuals. Any bit of individual or racial history will do, therefore, to 'illustrate' them; but history and individual lives lack all real being; they are only shadows on the cave wall."

From *Educational Theatre Journal* 13 (October 1961): 167–73. Reprinted by permission of The Johns Hopkins University Press.

Mary McCarthy approaches this another way when she writes of *The Skin of Our Teeth*:

> In other words, if George misses the five-fifteen, Chaos is come again. This is the moral of the piece. Man, says Mr. Wilder, from time to time gets puffed up with pride and prosperity, he grows envious, covetous, lecherous, forgets his conjugal duties, goes whoring after women; portents of disaster appear, but he is too blind to see them; in the end, with the help of the little woman, who has never taken any stock in either pleasure or wisdom, he escapes by the skin of his teeth. *Sicut erat in principio*. . . .
>
> It is a curious view of life. It displays elements of Christian morality. Christ, however, was never so simple, but on the contrary allowed always for paradox (the woman taken in adultery, the story of Martha and Mary, "Consider the lilies of the field"). . . . No, it is not the Christian view, but a kind of bowdlerized version of it, such as might have been imparted to a class of taxpayer's children by a New England Sunday School teacher forty years ago.

Now, I happen to believe that both Fergusson and Miss McCarthy (even in their admiration for Wilder) overstate their arguments, because Wilder, except in his preface to *The Angel that Troubled the Waters*, has never thought of himself as a Christian or a religious playwright. He best states his position when he writes: *"Our Town* is not offered as a picture of life in a New Hampshire village; or speculation about the conditions of life after death. . . . It is an attempt to find a value above all price for the smallest events of daily life." Wilder is talking about *Our Town*, but what he says applies to all of his work. In short, Wilder is a humanist, an affirming humanist, a "yeasayer to life" as Barnard Hewitt calls him.

When we examine the nature of Wilder's humanistic affirmation, what do we discover? His plays celebrate human love, the worth and dignity of man, the values of the ordinary, and the eternity of human values. From the little boy in Wilder's first play who says: "I am not afraid of life. I will astonish it!" to Dolly Levi and her cohorts in adventure in *The Matchmaker*, Wilder has always been on the side of life and life is seen to be most directly affirmed through love. Love, then, is his most persistent theme and it has been for him an inexhaustible subject. Of its worth he is convinced, but it is interesting to note that Wilder has never been able to make any commitments as to the reasons for its worth. Wilder can deal with life and love directly and concretely; but when he moves to the edges of life, the focus becomes less sharp. Certainly, Wilder deals with death—he is not afraid of it, but death in his plays is terminal. When Mrs. Soames says in Act Three of *Our Town*: "My, wasn't life awful—and wonderful," Wilder is reminding us that beauty is recognizable because of change and life is meaningful because of death. But as both John Mason Brown and Winfield Townley Scott have pointed out, Wilder never deals adequately with Death's own meaning. And as for what's beyond death? The Stage Manager in *Our Town* tells us: "You know as well as I do that the dead don't stay interested in us living people for very long. Gradually, gradually, they let go of the earth. . . . They get weaned away from the earth—that's the way I put it—weaned away. Yes, they stay here while the earth-part of 'em burns away, burns out, and all that time they slowly get indifferent to what's going on in Grover's Corners. They're waitin'! They're waitin' for something that they feel is comin'. Something important and great. Aren't they waitin' for the eternal part in them to come out clear?" But what is this eternal part, this Platonic essence, which in our imperfect awareness of living is only a shadow on the wall of the cave? What is death's meaning? The Stage Manager has just told us: "everybody knows that *something* is eternal. And it ain't names, and it ain't earth, and it ain't even the stars. . . . [E]verybody knows in their bones that *something* is eternal, and that something has to do with human beings. All the greatest people ever lived have been telling us that for five thousand years and yet you'd be surprised how people are always losing hold of it. There's something way down deep that's eternal about every human being." So, we are right back where we started: Life is reality and eternity is the perfected essence of that reality to which we are too often blind and of which we can't stand too much.

It is this tendency, a tendency consistent with his Platonism, to reduce the dimension of eternity so that it can be encompassed by life itself, that has led me to believe, although he has written no tragedies, that Wilder has essentially a tragic rather than a Christian or even religious view of life. To be sure, Wilder has not created any Ahabs or Lears, but this is not because he lacks a tragic vision. He happens to believe, as did Maeterlinck, that there are times in each of our lives when we are conscious of moving into the boundary situations of the tragic realm, and that furthermore, life's tragedies can best be seen in the drama of the everyday, in life's smallest events. For this reason he does not dramatize great conflicts in order to capture the quintessence of tragedy. I think it is important to see the validity of this, although we must point out that while this approach is tragic it is not always dramatic. And this, I think, accounts for the fact that Wilder's plays are usually referred to as "hymns," "odes," "songs," and so on, and most critics feel that there isn't much conflict in their plots. It might be helpful to take a specific example to illustrate Wilder's position on this matter.

Over and over again in Wilder's work, the belief is stated directly and indirectly that "life is what you make of it." The fullest discussion of the idea is in his novel *The Ides of March*, where Caesar says: "Life has no meaning save that which we confer upon it." Later he says: "Am I sure that there is no mind behind our existence and no mystery anywhere in the universe? I think I am. . . . How terrifying and glorious the role of man if, indeed, without guidance and without consolation he must create from his own vitals the meaning for his existence and the rules whereby he lives." Many of us believe this idea when stated in its simpler form: "Life is what we make of it." But we are unaware that this is really an existential position and that Wilder is very close to Sartre's "Man is condemned to be free."

In fact, upon reflection, we discover that in starting from "Life is what we make of it," Wilder is really in the mainstream of the modern drama beginning with Ibsen and Strindberg. And this is a dangerous position and usually in the drama has led to despair. The image of man in this drama is an image of collapse. Certainly, Kierkegaard saw this in the already quoted passage from *Fear and Trembling*: "If there were no eternal consciousness in a man, if at the foundation of all there lay only a wildly seething power which writhing with obscure passions produced everything that is great and everything that is insignificant, if a bottomless void never satiated lay hidden beneath all—what then would life be but despair." Most modern dramatists have answered with "that's all!" But Wilder hasn't, even though he holds a position that should lead this way. I think he averts despair—and also tragedy, even though his view of life is essentially tragic—with a kind of Santayana-like belief in life. In fact, Wilder's Platonism can make sense only if it is seen as coming through Santayana. Wilder is, as probably most of us are, saved from despair and its paralyzing effects by what Santayana has called "animal faith." Many will admit that by the rules of logic life is little more than an irrational nightmare in which the only reality is that grotesque illusion which we happen to believe in at a given moment; but somehow our animal faith, which bids us believe in the external world, is much stronger than all the logical arguments which tend to make life seem absurd. As Joseph Wood Krutch put it: "Everybody acts as though he believed that the external world exists; nearly everybody acts as though he believed that his version of it is a dependable one; and the majority act as though they could also make valid value judgments about it." It is this belief, this animal faith, that permits Wilder to say "Life is what you make of it," and still come up in affirmation on this side of despair. All his plays might be described by that verse of Theodore Spencer's (and I think Wilder and Spencer have great affinities):

> Oh how to praise that No,
> When all longing would press
> After the lost Yes!
> Oh how redress
> That disaster of No?

But although Wilder can assert meaning to life, the meaning is almost in the assertion itself and this is not a very comfortable position to be in. One gets the feeling that Wilder has to keep saying it to make sure that it is true. The danger of this position is that it lacks the necessary polarity and tension for full meaning. This in itself keeps Wilder from being a religious dramatist. In all great religious drama—the works of Sophocles, Calderón, *Everyman*, and in more recent times the later plays of Hofmannsthal, Eliot, and even Fry—there is the backdrop of religious belief which gives meaning to and informs the hero's "life is what you make of it." There is the greater stage. The medieval theatre and the Spanish theatre of Calderón exhibit this, and this is what Hofmannsthal tried to achieve at the Salzburg festivals with his productions of *Everyman*, *The Great World Theatre*, and *The Tower*. In all of these plays the actors—man—are faced with a moral choice under the very eyes of God and his angels upstage. The scaffold of these multiple stage structures not only serves as a magic mirror for the visible world and its invisible order, but the invisible order is made visible. For in these plays the idea of man as a player on the world's stage becomes the very principle of the *mise-en-scène*. For God, the master, speaking from the top of the scaffold, actually orders the world to produce a play under his eyes, featuring man who is to act out his part on earth.

More important than the absence of a religious dimension to Wilder's work, however, are the many experiments he has made in theatrical technique to compensate for this lack of an ultimate perspective. It is a commonplace in talking about modern literature to comment on the loss of a community of values and the disappearance of public truths in our time. It is equally well known that writers tend to compensate for the lack of a community of belief with new techniques of expression. The problem for the dramatist is how to make a highly individual standard of values appear to the audience to be a natural objective standard. Most of the modern dramatists have attempted to meet this problem by focusing on the psychology of their characters. In so doing they leave begged the question of value by confining the world of the play to the limits of an individual character's mind and then assessing value solely in terms of the consciousness of that mind. Thus, an incident in *Hedda Gabler* may not be important by any communicable standard of human significance, but if the universe is confined to her mind and Ibsen makes us look deeply enough into it, we can at least see it as important in that tiny context. In this way psychology makes possible such a drastic limitation of context that a private world can be the subject of a tragedy. Furthermore, by new techniques of presentation that private world and its values can be made, at least for the duration of the performance, convincing.

Wilder has not been interested in psychology and has never used psychological techniques to solve the "modernists' " problems in the theatre. This accounts, I think, for his great influence on the Continental avant-garde dramatists who are rebelling against our psychologically oriented theatre. Wilder sought to achieve the sense of an ultimate perspective by immaterializing the sense of dramatic place on stage. The bare stage of *Our Town* with its chairs, tables, and ladders, together with the Stage Manager's bald exposition, are all that he uses to create the town. The same is true of *The Skin of Our Teeth*; you never really know where the Antrobuses live, nor when. This is his second dominant technique; by destroying the illusion of time, Wilder achieves the effect of any time, all time, each time. But this is risky business, for without the backdrop of an ultimate perspective to inform a play's action, it can very easily become sentimental or satirical, or even pretentious. Wilder at his best keeps this from happening, but his only weapons are wit and irony. And a production which does not succeed in capturing these qualities (as, alas, most college and school productions do not) is bound to turn out bathetic and sentimental; when technique is used as a compensation for the ultimate perspective, the resultant work of art always lies precariously under a Damoclean sword.

It is important that we see the dangers in Wilder's methods, but that a tragic sense of life informs his plays is best illustrated by his sense of destiny. In Wilder's novel *The Woman of Andros*, Chrysis tells her guests a fable of the dead hero who receives Zeus's permission to return to earth to relive the least eventful day of his life, on the condition that he see it both as onlooker and participant[:] "Suddenly the hero saw that the living too are dead and that we can only be said to be alive in those moments when our hearts are conscious of our treasure; for our hearts are not strong enough to love every moment." He quickly asks to be released from this experience, and it is the opinion of Chrysis that "All human beings—save a few mysterious exceptions who seemed to be in possession of some secret from the gods—merely endured the slow misery of existence, hiding as best they could their consternation that life had no wonderful surprises after all and that its most difficult burden was the incommunicability of love." Eight years later Wilder incorporated this into the last scene of *Our Town*. When Emily comes back on her twelfth birthday, she discovers that "we don't have time to look at one another. I didn't realize. So all that was going on and we never noticed. . . . Oh, earth you're too wonderful for anybody to realize you. Do any human beings ever realize life while they live it?—every, every minute?" The answer, of course, is no, and Emily must conclude with "That's all human beings are! Just blind people."

What Wilder is saying here is that human beings cannot stand to have a sense of destiny—the awareness that there is a continuity in all our acts, the awareness that every present moment comes from a past and is directed to a future. Only at moments, usually of emotional crisis, do we have this sense of destiny, this sense of awareness of the future. It is this sense of destiny that is the great human reality and the tragedy of life lies in our fragmentary and imperfect awareness of it. Wilder is aware, like Eliot, that "human kind cannot bear very much reality," but his plays fall short of tragedy because he takes the Platonic escape, he moves into a world that denies the reality and the nemesis of destiny. Nor does he have the solution of an Eliot. For in denying, finally, the reality of destiny he shuts out the possibility of ever providing the means to perfect our fragmentary and imperfect vision. He fails, to use Karl Jaspers' phrase, to go "Beyond Tragedy." That Wilder lacks this dimension is not to discredit him, however, for no other American dramatist more fully affirms that miracle of life which so much modern drama would deny.

Thornton Wilder's Small Gem

WALTER KERR

I am told that somewhere in the Talmud there is a passage justifying the intense affection most people lavish on their grandchildren. Why do we bestow such disproportionate love upon our children's children? Because, the wry passage explains, "they are the enemies of our enemies."

The image of the child as The Enemy has stirred several times recently on off-Broadway stages. It is what gives the flavor of only slightly sweetened alum to Thornton Wilder's "Childhood," the middle playlet in a trio of new one-acters expressly written for Circle in the Square. As mother Betty Miller wipes her hands of the batter she has been mixing and moves onto her suburban lawn to remind the children to kiss daddy when he comes home (it is apparently a ritual that daddy must be kissed on Friday nights, with the work week done), she is alarmed to find the youngsters concealing themselves, a bit shamefaced, behind the shrubbery. She knows at once what they have been up to. They have either been playing that the house is on fire or their other favorite game, "funeral."

As father Dana Elcar comes home, the children do not kiss him; they vanish, in a tumble, into the house, leaving him to practice his golf swing (which is what he really wants to do) and to wonder vaguely why he hasn't been formally welcomed. In due time, he learns why. The stage dissolves, courtesy of a canny electrician and Mr. Wilder's knack for coining phrases that elude time and slip through space, into what is for the children a daydream and for the parents a nightmare.

With measured dignity and lissome grace, dark Susan Towers leads towheaded Debbie Scott and a smaller, soberer Philip Visco to a prepared graveside. A fearful accident has succeeded in making them orphans (the boy wants to know if they will be paid for having achieved such remarkable status), but before they take off on a bus to savor their freedom they wish to do the Decent Thing. They will recite their parents' eulogies with candor and with honor, grudging nothing, blinking nothing. Mother was all right, though not as loving as she might have been: "she liked us best when we were sick." Father was a responsible provider, though a dull conversationalist.

From *New York Herald Tribune*, 28 January 1962; © 1962, New York Herald Tribune Inc. All rights reserved. Reprinted by permission.

Everything good is acknowledged; everything bad is judiciously forgiven, especially now that it is over. The little minds are cool, precise, impartial.

Mr. Wilder does not end his prying into a subconscious that might be shattering if it were ever openly faced with these chilling, though admirable, obsequies. He packs the happy mourners into a bus headed for Indian territory and for rising floodwaters; while the journey is occupying the matter-of-fact children and charming all the rest of us, we notice that Mr. Elcar is the bus driver and Miss Miller, in black, a forlorn passenger keeping to herself in the very last seat. A second insight has been drawn over the first, though both remain transparent as in a double exposure: having disposed of mother and father, the children are careful to restore them in less committed, more manageable forms. One can speak man-to-man to a driver; one can feel kindly toward a bereaved stranger. It might be nice to know these people if it were possible really to know them.

In the sustained simultaneity of dispassionate rejection and a guarded welcome-back, Mr. Wilder seems to pluck out of the air, like a magician's egg, the perverse and contradictory truth of the matter. Only an unnecessary trace of moralizing ("it's like family life, we're all stuck in this bus together") scars the perfection of an illusionist's performance, and that very little. Mr. Wilder is as likely to be understood, and commended, at Saturday matinees as he is on Friday nights. "Childhood" belongs in the American theater's small-gem collection along with "A Happy Journey to Trenton and Camden" and "Pullman Car Hiawatha."

Music to My Ears: Hindemith on Wilder

A unique blend of talents introduced a new composite of beauty in Paul Hindemith's setting of Thornton Wilder's *The Long Christmas Dinner* at its first performance in America at the Juilliard School under the composer's direction. A kind of microsketch for *Our Town*, this predecessor by seven years (1931) views the life cycle of the New England Bayards in terms of the annual Christmas dinner. It spans marriages and births, reunions and separations, from the building of the homestead to its abandonment ninety years later by the youngest generation. Periodically, there is the most poignant leavetaking of all, as death claims its relentless due.

Wilder's single act runs without interruption for three quarters of an hour, a sizable stretch of music for any composer. But, at this time of his productive life, Hindemith may be trusted to choose wisely what interests him, and work well to interest us in what interests him. From its beginning with the tune of "God Rest Ye Merry, Gentlemen" thoroughly Hindemithed (which is to say, reconstituted in woodwinds and low brass) to its reprise at the end, this is a fluid, beautifully sonorous musical setting. As the time approaches, one senses that Hindemith's feeling for structure will make that reprise inescapable, but it is a tribute to the art with which he has spanned the incidents and emotions in between that the inescapable is also the inevitable.

Wilder has made his own adaptation of the play for Hindemith, but it remains substantially an unversified text. There are few set pieces as such, but the interchange of thought develops, every so often, into a trio (an intricate canon of deceptively simple sound) or a sextet (in the manner of a chorale prelude) which varies the vocal texture and renews interest in the resumption of dialogue. An orchestra of about thirty is utilized, and it occasionally suggests, through skilful use of the low woodwinds, French horn, and muted strings, the sound of a small organ or harmonium. This is a touch of local color much in keeping with the surroundings.

As the generations come and go (they emerge from a white framed door at stage right and disappear at death through a black-shrouded portal at stage left), they acquaint us with the joys and woes to which family life is prone: the good marriage and the bad, the children that grow to maturity and those that are carried off young, the spinster and the youth who is a war victim. What might, in the hands of another, court cliché becomes, in

From *Saturday Review*, 30 March 1963. Reprinted by permission of *Saturday Review*.

Wilder's, the touch of nature that makes us all kin, and Hindemith has responded in kind. The values of the richly written score were clearly discernible. An artful and affecting work, it should have frequent performances both by professional and workshop groups.

The Alcestiad: The Play and Opera

MARTIN BLANK

When Thornton Wilder said that some plays take twenty-five years to write,[1] he was undoubtedly referring to *The Alcestiad*. The earliest traces of his preoccupation with the Greek legend can be seen in his 1930 novel *The Woman of Andros* when his character Chrysis says, ". . . [S]ome Alcestis will touch me and will show me the meaning of all these things." During the next several years, through the 1930s, he worked on the play intermittently; in a letter to Wilder dated 28 September 1938, Michael Myerberg makes reference to an *Alcestiad* on which the author had been working.[2] The following 20 January an announcement appeared in the *New York Times* that Wilder was writing a play based on the Alcestis myth, "presumably for next season."[3] Less than six months later, however, on 18 June 1939, a similar notice appeared, stating that Wilder had given up the idea for the play.[4]

Meanwhile, Wilder had been at work on *The Skin of Our Teeth*, had seen it produced, and had volunteered for service in World War II. As Wilder states, after his discharge "[I] took up a theme which I had already partially developed before the war. I had spent a year on it only to find that my basic ideas about the human situation had undergone a drastic change. I was not able to define the change until the writings of Kierkegaard were called to my attention by my theologian brother (Amos)."[5] In August 1945 Wilder wrote to his friend Elizabeth Artzybasheff that after "jerky starts and many discouragements the central intention becomes clear, solving many incidental problems of 'style' as well as episode (and) plotting," and he was well into the second act.[6] Two months later, in October, he thought the play would be finished by Christmas and hoped it would be a "detonation in the American theatre."[7] By March 1946, however, Wilder had *The Alcestiad* "laid aside (not being able to) cope with her views on the essence of life until I've settled my own."[8] Still under the influence of existentialism, Wilder undertook an adaptation of Jean-Paul Sartre's play *Les Morts Sans Sepulture*, called *The Victors* in Wilder's version, and began writing his novel *The Ides of March*. Wilder stated that the novel "can be said to be written under the sign of Kierkegaard" (Van Gelder, 122). He apparently was unable

This essay was written specifically for this volume and is published here for the first time by permission of the author.

to dismiss the Alcestis myth, or perhaps believed it would never come to be realized as a play, because what eventually became the first act of *The Alcestiad* can be seen in narrative summary at the close of book 1 of *The Ides of March*, as part of the "Alcestiad of Catullus." In the intervening years, however, Wilder was able to complete a dramatization of the myth, and in a letter of December 1954 he speaks about his inability to work on a German version of *The Matchmaker*, because he was involved with writing another play.[9] We may assume Wilder was referring to *The Alcestiad*.

Constructed like a Greek tetrology, *The Alcestiad* has three acts, each focusing on separate actions, and the play is in turn followed by a satyr play, *The Drunken Sisters*. The plot of *The Alcestiad* covers 30 years—from the marriage of Alcestis and Admetus to her death. The first act occurs on a day ten years prior to the action in Euripides's play and uses another legend involving King Admetus. In this myth Zeus commanded Apollo to descend to earth and to live for one year as a man among men. Apollo chose to live as a herdsman in the fields of King Admetus. Wilder uses this legend and has the young Alcestis refusing to marry Admetus because she wants to live devoting her life to God. She wants Apollo, whose true identity is unknown to her, to give her a sign that he exists and that life has meaning. When her naive hopes for certainties are shattered, she gives herself in love to Admetus. In the second act Wilder follows Euripides's plot. Alcestis sacrifices herself for Admetus, who is mortally ill, and agrees to die for him; she is then rescued from the underworld by Hercules, who battles with death to bring her back to life. In the third act Wilder makes use of still another legend, and this takes place twenty years after her death and resurrection. A plague has gripped the city; the barbaric King Agis has usurped the throne and put Admetus to death. Alcestis has been spared but reduced to servitude. Epimenes is the only child of hers to survive, and he has fled. When he and his friend Cheriander return to Thessaly to kill Agis, Alcestis dissuades them, since she has taken mercy on Agis, and she turns their efforts to ridding the city of its plague.

While the narrative is forward moving, each act is self-contained and serves as a variation on the play's themes, a technique Wilder used in *The Skin of Our Teeth*. In *The Alcestiad* a major theme presented is self-sacrifice as an expression of love, "with the levels worked out in ascending order to culminate in an epiphany and mystical union in Act III."[10] In writing about his play, Wilder has stated:

On one level my play recounts the life of a woman—of many women—from bewildered bride to sorely tested wife to bewildered old age. If I were now to change the scene of the play from Thessaly to medieval Iceland or to ancient India, the task would involve extensive alterations, but very few of them would be required in the role of Alcestis. On another level, it is a wildly romantic story of gods and man, of death and hell and resurrection, of great loves and great trials, of usurpation and revenge. On another level, however, it is a comedy about a very earnest matter. . . . Following some meditations of Søren Kierkegaard, I have written a comedy about the extreme difficulty of any dialogue between heaven and earth, about the misunderstandings that result from the incommensurability of things human and divine. Kierkegaard described God under the image of the "unhappy lover." If He revealed Himself to us in His glory, we would fall down in abasement, but abasement is not love. If he divested Himself of the divine attributes in order to come nearer to us, that would be an act of condescension, and love does not admit of condescension. This is a play about how Apollo searched for a language in which he could converse with Admetus and Alcestis and with their innumerable descendants; and about how Alcestis, through many a blunder, learned how to listen and interpret the things that Apollo was so urgently trying to say to her. Yet, I am aware of other levels, and perhaps deeper ones that will only become apparent to me later.[11]

The satyr play, a comic afterpiece, was written to follow *The Alcestiad*. In *The Drunken Sisters* Wilder expands on the theme of choice and free will by concentrating on Apollo's efforts to make the three Fates drunk and alter their decree, thus allowing Admetus to live. They will change their edict of death, but the Fates must have a substitute. They stipulate, however, that the person can't be an unknowing victim. Man must choose willingly. Although events seem unalterable, Wilder suggests that they are still determined by man.

The year before, in the summer of 1954, Wilder worked with Tyrone Guthrie at the Edinburgh Festival on the tryout of *The Matchmaker*, and Guthrie was to direct the new play as well. They were hoping for a similar response to *The Alcestiad*, with Edinburgh "a breaking in," allowing Wilder to bring the play to New York. It was to be staged there by Jed Harris, who held an option on it. For this production Tanya Moiseiwitsch, who designed *The Matchmaker*, was engaged in a similar capacity, and Tennent Productions, Ltd., coproducers of the British production of *The Matchmaker*, also served to cosponsor *The Alcestiad*, which became known as *A Life in the Sun* for this engagement. The title was accepted over Wilder's objections. (Wilder said he did not want theatergoers to get the impression that his play dealt with "people sprawling on the beach on the Riviera absorbing the sunlight"[12] The play was commissioned for a three-week engagement, and it was to be performed on the platform stage of the Church Assembly Hall at the festival. No stage curtain was to be used. The platform stage was ideal for the play, Wilder believed, with entrances and exits made through the audience, breaking down the barriers to immediacy and confrontation that the proscenium presented. Yet the play, unlike *The Matchmaker*, fell victim to "Guthrie's tendency to overdirect." Wilder objected to the unnecessarily large cast Guthrie used and to "such Guthrie touches as putty sores on the actor's arms."[13] Rehearsals did not go well. Irene Worth, who had appeared at the festival in 1949 in T. S. Eliot's version of the myth, *The Cocktail Party*, was engaged for the leading role. To costar with her as Admetus, Wilder had Montgomery Clift signed for the part. Clift, who had created the role of Henry in *The Skin of Our Teeth* and with whom Wilder wished to work again, withdrew from the company early in rehearsals[14] and was followed by Michael Goodliffe, who in turn resigned. The next actor to be hired was Robert Hardy, who opened in the play. These replacements were symptomatic of the distress in which the production found itself. During rehearsals Guthrie cut the text drastically,[15] presumably with Wilder's permission, in an attempt to enliven a script that was not translating well on to the stage.

The critical response was not good. Anthony Hartley of the *Spectator* felt "boredom and irritation when watching it." The tone of the play, Hartley commented, was robbed of all classicism by the introduction of pseudo-Shakespearean characters (a nurse and a comic porter), whose homespun humor was out of place: "It is to the credit of Tyrone Guthrie that he managed to extract some dramatic moments from the wreckage. Alcestis is played by Irene Worth with great dignity and pathos. . . . It is a pity that all this talent should have been wasted on a play that is pretentious to very little purpose."[16] Henry Hewes, reviewing the play for the *Saturday Review*, found the inordinate amount of action and homilies crammed into the last act confusing: "In choosing the ballad form, Mr. Wilder has refused excitement of suspense for the grand style, in which emotion is heightened by poetry. He has written a prose counterpoint to a strong and well established legend which makes the comments more interesting than the main action." Hewes found that Guthrie seemed to have worked in a somewhat different direction from Wilder's intention, because in his emphasis on the ensemble and in groupings one missed the poetry that Wilder was careful not to write. The actors, he believed, paid the penalty for Guthrie's open stage production in sacrificing what might have been a credible performance in a "conventional" production.[17] W. A. Darlington, reporting in Edinburgh for the *New York Times*, found the play profound but far from lucid, the play never rising as high as it aimed: "Those who try and follow him are swept off their feet and drowned. . . . One comes away from the play feeling that all the characters have been talking too much and saying too little that is significant. As a result, when significant things are said they are apt to be swept away by the flood and lost." The one enthusiast for the play, the *Daily Express*, called it "One of the most startlingly strong, movingly dramatic and poetic pieces the English speaking stage has created in years." Speaking for the majority, Darlington held that if the play fails "it is a failure in the grand manner. It will be remembered for many fine things, some quiet scenes of comedy and Irene Worth's moving sincerity as Alcestis."[18]

Based on the poor reception in Scotland, Wilder did not bring the play to New York in the autumn of 1955 as he had expected. Wilder was in

Europe early in 1956 and on returning home planned to work on the play, having a finished script for a Broadway presentation later that year (Calta). That November he still had not completed a script to his satisfaction to give to Jed Harris. He was taking time to work on the last act of the play, the act that was giving him trouble and never did satisfy him. At that time he could not predict when a completed script might be ready.[19] Meanwhile, Wilder permitted a translation of the play to be presented for the German Book Fair of 1957, during which he received the Peace Prize of the Booksellers. Wilder collaborated on the translation with Herbert E. Herlitschke, the translator of all of Wilder's previous work into German. The first performance in that language took place in Zurich in June 1957 and was looked on as a major dramatic event.[20] A capacity audience gave the play an enthusiastic reception, with the cast and Wilder taking thirty curtain calls. Wilder was delighted with the production of Leopold Lindtberg. Rolf Langnese composed original music for it, and the setting of Admetus's palace was designed by K. L. Otto. Maria Becker played Alcestis and Peter Juehr the role of Admetus. Unlike the Edinburgh production, in which *The Drunken Sisters* was inserted between acts 1 and 2, the Zurich production followed the play with the satyr play.[21]

Following its impressive Swiss production, the play first appeared in West Germany in Frankfurt that October and was hailed as "a ray of light from the new world."[22] One critic found much irony, tender melancholy, and unbroken vitality in the play.[23] Another found that the tone of the second act might have been better for the rest of the play, which seemed too didactic and less dramatic than Wilder's other work. This reviewer believed that at times the play offered meditation rather than conflicts, philosophizing rather than action. Despite these faults, the production was well received, with most of the praise for the acting going to Hans Dieter Zeidler in the seriocomic role of Hercules.[24] For the production Teo Otto's platform setting was projected out in front of the proscenium into the auditorium. Otto, who was working in a conventional theater, tried to bring the play as close to the audience as possible and used one of the exits as part of the scene—the Hell Mouth into Hades. The production was staged by Hendrich Koch, and the role of Alcestis was played by Gisela von Collande.[25] The next month, November 1957, the play was produced at Vienna's Burgtheater, where it received a warm reception and "loud cheers at the end." Wilder was deeply moved as he thanked the audience in German and took at least ten curtain calls.[26] In March 1958 *The Alcestiad* premiered in Hamburg, where the production was hailed as a thoughtful modern reinterpretation of one of the most moving mythological stories of classical times. *The Drunken Sisters*, presented after *The Alcestiad*, as in Frankfurt, was done grotesquely, with surrealistic masks, and the broad fun of the piece was considered an ingenious device to end the serious theme on a comic note (Frenz, 136). One critic raised the question of whether the addition of the satyr play does not prove that the German interpretation is more serious and the production less relaxed than Wilder intended it to be.[27]

In this production the director, G. R. Sellner, approached the play somewhat differently than his predecessors. Sellner believed that although the play is set in an ancient, mythological milieu, the historical setting is not a main issue. The historical is juxtaposed with the modern, and this can be seen clearly in the character of Teiresias, for example, who is continuously confused and mixes up people's names. If one approaches the play from the present day, the play therefore comes into focus. Sellner found in the English text a reference to Admetus's palace, comparing it with a "ranch," and the effect he tried to achieve in the setting was to emphasize the peasantry, the colloquial, the herdsmen who work Admetus's farm, and to help achieve this he costumed Hercules in blue overalls, so that when Admetus asks him where he is coming from and he replies, "From work, Admetus, from work," in the voice of an "automechanic," the reality of Hercules is established. So Sellner had Franz Mertz design the set with wooden doors and de-emphasize the grandeur of the palace. Therefore, Sellner noted, against this background and in the colloquial speech of the characters the story unfolds, and the object of the play becomes not the myth of antiquity but the immediacy of the entire story of Western man. Sellner believed that Wilder was concerned with setting a "new" story in motion, removing from the legend what had become dead in previous versions, including those of Goethe, Grillparzer, and Offenbach. Wilder, then, wanted to create new life with the legend, and Sellner, to achieve this goal in his production, tried to find theatrical equivalents for Wilder's drama. Sellner saw the play as "heart, faith, confidence of man in one another and confidence of the Godly in man." He went on to explain that Wilder sees Apollo as a messiah, closer to a Christian image of God than the pagan. Wilder's tone is one of naive wonder, which Western man and his saturation with history cannot experience. Wilder therefore abolishes 2,500 years, making a new union with the myth that does not exclude Christ, but rather includes him in the guise of Apollo. Kurt Lothar Tank found that in Sellner's strong production there is a convincing, new projection of the myth for our time: "Wilder's play—however strange this may sound—is filled with a stronger power of belief than is Euripides." The satyr play is not just an addendum to the production but is interwoven into the entire theme—the human attempt at interpretation of divine messages that come to men in mutilated or distorted form, so that the means to illuminate the meaning of life that appears to be insufficient may indeed communicate to us. Love itself is not the meaning, but only a symptom that life has significance. In the final scene between Apollo and Alcestis, Wilder's objective becomes clear: "And whom should I thank for so much serenity?" asks Alcestis, while walking toward the grave. Apollo responds, "Friends don't put this question to each other. Those who have loved each other don't put this question to each other."[28]

The idea of writing the libretto for an opera was not new; Wilder wanted to compose an opera when he was 14.[29] As an adult he first discussed the possibilities of collaboration with Paul Hindemith. Nothing was to come of this until 1960, however, when Hindemith began work on adapting Wilder's one-act play *The Long Christmas Dinner*.[30] But before he began his work with Hindemith, Wilder had met Louise Talma. Talma, who was born in France to American parents, was reared and educated in New York. She studied at the Juilliard School of Music and with Nadia Boulanger at Fontainbleu. She had composed two piano sonatas, a string quartet, and an oratorio, "The Divine Flame," but was perhaps best known for her "Toccata for Orchestra." When Talma and Wilder met at the MacDowell Colony in New Hampshire in 1952, he broached the subject of collaboration.[31] Talma agreed. Their plan was to write an original, full-length chamber opera on a contemporary American theme. Wilder had hoped to solve "the problem of opera with much use of spoken dialogue."[32] They started work on this project in January 1954 and devoted more than a year to it,[33] but after Talma became familiar with *The Alcestiad*, they abandoned their initial efforts and began work on Wilder's play. Talma had first heard Wilder read the play at a private party and "began to hear the music of the opera even while he was reading" ("Singing Greeks," 54). In a letter to Wilder, she explained her reaction to the play and berated him for his modesty regarding the work:

When you talked to me in your letters last winter, you said you "just" wrote it in darkness. It's irrational. It's more than that. You know certainly that you wrote this play under inspiration. You told me your piece was not unified and wanted me to comment on that. I was inclined to rebuke you for your question. However, I didn't because I was too amazed and can only ask you now: weren't you amazed by the play? Last night, when I came home, in one moment I realized that the man who wrote this must have had a unified purpose in mind. (While listening to music), I heard exactly the sound for the introduction of Apollo and the sound for the dialogue with Death and Apollo that I wanted. Bitter meeting with Alcestis and Apollo and I heard another sound I wanted for bitter, scornful Admetus. Each scene forms itself piece by piece. Even as I write this ideas come even more clear. How could someone better compose the meeting with Hercules and Death without music? You don't know how (to do it) yourself, but you certainly realize how music accomplishes this end, and finally, music with such clarity to go Alcestis one step more.[34]

Theirs was not the first opera based on the Alcestis legend: Handel, Gluck, and Lully had written versions as well. Talma, a professor of music at Hunter College, was unable to work full-time on this project as Wilder would have liked: "Wouldn't it be better if we could give up the whole year for this?" Wilder was deeply involved at this time with the Edinburgh production of the play and was unable to get the concentration he needed "to bring to fruition our first ideas."[35] After his unhappy experience with *A Life in the Sun*, Wilder was able to work in France and wrote to Talma, "I see that we will build a grand opera, not an old chamber opera like we first thought of, but something ambitious. The central point is correct . . . namely, the opera of a drama of opposites which appear behind the everyday world, but it will no longer be a chamber piece, but magnified into grand opera."[36] The composition of the music took three years and another two to score it. In his libretto Wilder had shortened the first two acts, but it is not until the third act that the cuts and rewriting are markedly different from the play.[37] One of the major changes was the exclusion of the satyr play and the addition of the chorus, which Wilder had to incorporate into the libretto. As in the play, each act of the opera was complete unto itself, but each act also was part of the full-length work, with an overall unity. Wilder set his libretto partly in free verse and partly in prose.[38] He began to write it with the idea that it would be set to music, keeping one principle in mind: pay attention to open vowel sounds. An example cited by Wilder is the song in *Measure for Measure* "Take, O Take Those Lips Away." He achieved the effect they both wished, and Talma did not have to ask him to make any changes in the dialogue. [39] One of Wilder's lines that she particularly liked for its singable quality is "Send me the sign I have waited for / Call me, Call me."[40] Talma did not write any overtures or preludes. Instead, the emphasis was placed on the text and its relationship to the music.

Harry Buckwitz, director of Frankfurt's municipal theaters, heard part of the opera in New York in 1960 and obtained the first rights to production.[41] He presented the opera 1 March 1962 under his stage direction and featured the mezzo-soprano Inge Borkh in the title role. During rehearsals Talma worked with the principals and chorus,[42] and the production marked the first time that a work by an American woman composer was produced by a major European opera house.[43] The "cubistically inspired" set, designed by Hein Heckroth, represented the ancient Thessalonian palace situated in primitive craggy mountains and was surmounted by a Calder-like mobile. Critic Ernst Thomas wrote that most modern operas based on plays had the ideas extracted and made subservient to the music. This was not a problem with *The Alcestiad*. The libretto, he found, was not much different from the play and was changed principally by incorporating scenic symbols and allowing time for the music to develop. Talma, however, did not find correct musical terms for her composition, with the music an accompaniment rather than an integral part of the piece. Thomas goes on to say the intent to write grand opera is not reflected in the music. There is an appreciation of the greatness of the assignment, but no idea of the musical demands of the scenes. She has learned from Stravinsky, Schoenberg, and Hindemith but does little more than link scenes together lightly. Thomas concludes that she achieves a gray tone without any spontaneous impulse or freedom of expression. The opera is one of opposites: the noble and debauched Hercules, the respect and parody of the ancients as seen in Teiresias, the boorishness and faithfulness of the four shepherds. But these opposites are not conveyed musically.[44] Heinz Joachim thought the work a deep and meaningful creation. The music, potentially full of feeling, serves as background, one step behind the text. It never reaches out for the musical essence of a thought. It is self-conscious and tactful but does not encounter the wonder and miracle of the resurrection and mortal fulfillment. The music, when it encounters the words, destroys the poetry.[45] Dr. George Bonter found a French tone to Talma's musical construction, an aspect characteristic of Boulanger's students. The music is clean-sounding and rhythmic, with a stark sense of the dramatic. Talma has variety, but without marked individuality. The libretto is excellent and does not overpower the music.[46] The Zurich press covered the premiere. One newspaper thought the work "beautiful and interesting."[47] Another said that Wilder is a great poet, and the opera's premiere in Frankfurt shows the poor state of opera in America. The premiere was a well-deserved, great success.[48] The critics noted that Talma's music was atonal, using the 12-tone scale. One thought the work was inspired by Bartók (Gybling). Another noted that her style was contrapuntal, using two or three voices mostly, with the lyrical dominating. She uses small choruses and dramatic episodes, profiting greatly from her chamber-music style in tone coloring, creating something new in opera. She is technically in command, and while there is no growing development, she has a firm grasp of the tragic conception.[49] The production itself was well received, with the stark, strong meaning of the libretto realized.[50]

Notes

1. *WYBC Microphone*, 13 April 1954, Thornton Wilder Collection, Yale University Library.

2. Donald Haberman, *The Plays of Thornton Wilder* (Middletown, Conn.: Wesleyan University Press, 1967), 39. At that time Myerberg, who was to produce *The Skin of Our Teeth*, was serving as Wilder's agent in his negotiations with Max Reinhardt on the production of *The Merchant of Yonkers*, which was to be presented in December of that year.

3. *New York Times*, 20 January 1939, New York Public Library Theatre Collection, Thornton Wilder File.

4. *Ibid.*, 18 June 1939.

5. Robert Van Gelder, "Interview with a Best Selling Author," *Cosmopolitan*, April 1948, 122; hereafter cited in text. Before resuming work again on *The Alcestiad*, Wilder offered to translate and adapt Luigi Pirandello's play *To Clothe the Naked* for producer Cheryl Crawford, who read it and rejected Wilder's offer (letter to Elizabeth Artzybasheff, 5 August 1945, Thornton Wilder Collection, Yale University Library).

6. Letter to Elizabeth Artzybasheff, postmarked 11 August 1945, Thornton Wilder Collection, Yale University Library.

7. Letter to Elizabeth Artzybasheff, 23 October 1945, Thornton Wilder Collection, Yale University Library.

8.   Letter to Elizabeth Artzybasheff, postmarked 31 March 1946, Thornton Wilder Collection, Yale University Library.

9.   *Brief an Rudolf Hirsch*, 152, letter dated 2 December 1954, Thornton Wilder Collection, Yale University Library.

10.   Rex Burbank, *Thornton Wilder* (New Haven: College and University Press, 1961), 124.

11.   Program of *A Life in the Sun*, produced at the Edinburgh Festival, 1955, 16, New York Public Library Theatre Collection.

12.   Louis Calta, "Wilder Planning to 'Rework' Play," *New York Times*, 1 March 1956, New York Public Library Theatre Collection, Thornton Wilder File; hereafter cited in text.

13.   Lee Beltzer, "The Plays of Eugene O'Neill, Thornton Wilder, Arthur Miller, and Tennessee Williams on the London Stage, 1945–1960," Ph.D. diss., University of Wisconsin, 1965, 904.

14.   Starting in 1948 Wilder was intermittently working on a play, *The Emporium*, and at its inception had Montgomery Clift in mind for a leading role (*New York Times*, 23 June 1954, New York Public Library Theatre Collection, Thornton Wilder File).

15.   Malcolm Goldstein, *The Art of Thornton Wilder* (Lincoln: University of Nebraska Press, 1965), 147.

16.   Anthony Hartley, "Contemporary Arts—Festival Blues," *Spectator*, 2 September 1955, 305.

17.   Henry Hewes, "Broadway Postscript," *Saturday Review*, 10 September 1955, 42–44.

18.   W. A. Darlington, "Wilder at Edinburgh," *New York Times*, 28 August 1955, New York Public Library Theatre Collection, Lester Sweyd Collection.

19.   *New York Times*, 16 November 1956, New York Public Library Theatre Collection, Thornton Wilder File.

20.   Horst Frenz, "Wilder in Germany," *Modern Drama* 3, no. 2 (September 1960): 135; hereafter cited in text. Wilder probably made some alterations in the text between its English language and German productions. Almost two years had elapsed (August 1955 to June 1957) between productions, and Wilder in the meantime was trying to get a satisfactory text for Jed Harris, an aim he never achieved. The critical reception on the Continent would indicate that the major repairs had been made since its world premiere in 1955. Wilder has always been popular in Germany, however, as Frenz's study makes clear. In 1929 Wilder characterized his work in a way that may help explain this popularity: "I think of my work as being French in form and manners (Saint-Simon and LaBruyere); German in feeling (Bach and Beethoven); and American in eagerness" (Erich Posselt, ed., *On Parade* [New York: Coward-McCann, 1929]): 168.

21.   *New York Times*, 29 June 1957, New York Public Library Theatre Collection, Thornton Wilder File.

22.   Rudolf Lange, *Hannoversche Allgemeine Zeitung*, 9 October 1957, quoted in Frenz.

23.   Karl Korn, *Frankfurter Allgemeine Zeitung*, 7 October 1957, quoted in Frenz.

24.   Willy H. Thiem, *Frankfurter Abendpost*, 7 October 1957, quoted in Frenz.

25.   Harry R. Beard, "Thornton Wilder's *Alcestiad* in Germany," *Christian Science Monitor*, 30 November 1957, New York Public Library Theatre Collection, Thornton Wilder File.

26.   "Vienna Hails Wilder's Play," *New York Times*, 6 November 1957, New York Public Library Theatre Collection, Thornton Wilder File.

27.   Willy Has, *Die Welt*, 8 March 1958, quoted in Frenz.

28.   Kurt Lothar Tank, "I Have Come to Set a Story in Motion: Thornton Wilder's *Alcestiad*, a New Encounter with the Ancient—Talk with Director G. R. Sellner," *Sonntagsblatt*, 23 March 1958, New York Public Library Theatre Collection, Thornton Wilder File.

29.   "The Singing Greeks," *Time*, 23 March 1962, 54; hereafter cited in text.

30. "American Christmas," *Time*, 29 December 1961, 25.
31. *New York Times*, 2 March 1962, New York Public Library Theatre Collection, Thornton Wilder File.
32. *New York Times*, 4 May 1955, New York Public Library Theatre Collection, Thornton Wilder File.
33. Ruth Berges, "The World's Music," (Evanston, Ill.) *Musical Courier*, May 1962, 34.
34. Letter from Louise Talma to Wilder, 3 May 1955, in *The Alcestiad* program, Grosses Haus, Frankfurt, 3 March 1962.
35. Letter to Louise Talma, 27 August 1955, in *The Alcestiad* program, Grosses Haus, Frankfurt, 3 March 1962.
36. Letter to Louise Talma, 12 September 1955, in *The Alcestiad* program, Grosses Haus, Frankfurt, 3 March 1962. Wilder was to write a chamber opera, with Paul Hindemith—*The Long Christmas Dinner*—in 1961.
37. "Thornton Wilder's *Alcestiad* as an Opera," *London Times*, 17 April 1962, 15.
38. *New York Times*, 2 March 1962, New York Public Library Theatre Collection, Thornton Wilder File.
39. Talma did, however, have to eliminate text from the German version of the libretto prepared for the Frankfurt production by Wilder's translator.
40. *Time*, 23 March 1962.
41. *New York Times*, 2 March 1962.
42. *Frankfurter Allgemeine Zeitung*, 26 February 1962.
43. *New York Times*, 2 March 1962.
44. Ernst Thomas, "*The Alcestiad*," *Frankfurter Allgemeine Zeitung*, 3 March 1962.
45. Heinz Joachim, "There Are No More Miracles," *Die Welt*, 3 March 1962.
46. Dr. George Bonter, "The Opera about the Purpose of Life," *Salzburger Nachrichten*, 3 March 1962.
47. W. G., "A Woman Opera Composer," *Die Tat*, 10 March 1962.
48. Walter Gybling, "Wilder's *Alcestiad* as Opera," Tges *Anzeifer*, 12 March 1962: hereafter cited in text.
49. G. A. Trumpff, "Wilder's *Alcestiad* Set to Music," *Dusselddorfer Nachrichten*, 8 March 1962.
50. H. H., "A Myth with Musical Accompaniment," *Neue Ruhr-Zeitung Essen*, 3 March 1962.

Strange Discipline: Wilder's One-Act Experiments

David Castronovo

Wilder's one-act plays are short journeys packaged in modern experimental forms, highly charged minutes in which he arranges his obsessions into new arresting patterns. During the 1920s and early 1930s—and again in the late 1950s—he turned to small structures in order to concentrate his meaning. No "idea was too grandiose . . . for me to try and invest it in this strange discipline." His themes are no different from those of the early novelistic period: the awesome and strange feelings generated by being alive in a world larger than ourselves, the isolation of existence, the possibility that love is redemptive and not destructive, the irony and ridiculousness of human plans and desires. But for all the continuity, there is a radical change in shape; the plays draw attention to their form, whereas the novels—for all Wilder's affinities to the modernist tradition—are generally quieter in their effects. The one-act plays—whether those in *The Angel That Troubled the Waters* (1928), or *The Long Christmas Dinner and Other Plays in One Act* (1931)—are crafted in ways that upset conventional theater expectations and that create new recognitions.

Dispensing with well-made plots, illusions of real events taking place on stage, conventions of the box stage with actors looking out at an audience, and people whose destinies proceed from previously established patterns of action, Wilder in effect breaks with the nineteenth-century theater of realism. While he is subtle rather than bold in his assault on the trappings of the well-made play, he is nevertheless a writer whose best short dramas are likely to become classics of American stage innovation. Often he selects unpromisingly ordinary or familiar material: the rituals of Christmas dinner, bedtime on a train, a car ride across a state. He likes to dramatize what playwrights generally leave out or sum up in a line. His subject matter and settings are given intensity and power because he seems, as Edmund Wilson has said of Sherwood Anderson, to have discovered permanent truths all by himself—and for the first time. This freshness of approach—at first a mystery

From *Thornton Wilder* by David Castronovo. Copyright © 1986 by The Ungar Publishing Company. Reprinted by permission of the publisher.

to a theatergoer who wonders why his attention is captured by characters who say good-bye to each other on a street in Newark—is actually the result of technical experiments and subtle dislocations.

Wilder's one-act works typically do not experiment with dialogue and diction. Their assault on the conventional goes to the very heart of drama: the strategy is to attack the vital organs of a well-constructed play—plot, motivated characters, resolutions. He transplants components of his own— stage managers who interrupt the plot flow, props that draw attention to themselves, inanimate objects that speak, visual jokes, spectacular, impossible stage effects, undramatic repetitions. As readers or audience, we sometimes feel that the playwright is the strangest phenomenon in American-theater history: a man whose works are combinations of eighth-grade assembly plays and dramas by Strindberg or Pirandello. At once naive and capable of the most complex symbolic art, Wilder takes his place beside the other twentieth-century artists who abandon slick craftsmanship and replace it with new and seemingly cruder techniques. Such experiments, of course, are always forays into the unknown and possibly the unsuccessful.

The Angel That Troubled the Waters is the first phase of the one-act experimentation: the plays gathered in this volume are largely closet dramas "stimulated by literature," as Gilbert Harrison has noted in *The Enthusiast: A Life of Thornton Wilder*. They are Wilder's first attempts to reject naturalistic theater, and are often engaging intellectually, if not entirely satisfying as drama. Dissolving stage logic and verisimilitude, they succeed in becoming theater pieces of the mind—strange explorations of people who labor under various kinds of stresses and obsessions. They have points of tension rather than paraphrasable plots. Sometimes preposterous and often diffuse, they are always disengaged from the traceable causalities of well-made plays. To ask if most of them would "play" is about as sensible as asking if a biblical parable would make a good movie: they are small dramas that resonate with moral implications and that play best on the stage of one's own imagination. They also dislocate the whole set of nineteenth-century-theater expectations by emphasizing extravagant or childlike, naive special effects.

Beginning with *Nascuntur Poetae*—a play about artistic initiation— Wilder embodies his themes in wild and seemingly undramatic forms. In five pages of text, the playwright makes us enter "some incomprehensible painting of Piero di Cosimo; a work of pale blues and greens." A boy in the painting has been told, by a woman in a chlamys, of the chosen—artists who now "sit apart, choosing their successors." He is to be one of their number—and the play's only conflict is his fears about the impending mission. Such a situation sounds like the effort of a prep-school student who is cultured and sensitive; yet the real charm and significance of the play are not to be found in conflict or characterization, but in a few lines and an overall confidence in its vision. The child, like Pio and the Marquesa, is to assume the role of artist-sufferer and pursuer of a love more sustaining than ordinary love. "For you there shall be ever beyond the present a lost meaning and a more meaningful love." The boy, anticipating the Marquesa, is "not yet brave," not ready for his spiritual destiny. Wilder is fond of Dantesque imagery—"shadow of the wood," "the profound shade"; he also has set up one of his enduring themes—the isolated and anxious progress of a special soul. Protestant in its emphasis on the boy's election, clumsily Catholic in its medievalism, the play is another Wilder combination of resources.

Another apprentice work that Wilder chose to publish in 1928 is *Childe Roland to the Dark Tower Came*. Once again, there are continuities with major themes and patterns—as well as very obvious dislocations from realistic technique. The disengagements are most pronounced in the medieval setting: "The sun has set over the great marsh, leaving a yellow-brown Flemish light upon the scene." Childe Roland—the strange questor mentioned in *King Lear*, and given life by Robert Browning in his poem of agony and doubt—seeks refuge in Wilder's playlet. Wounded and seeking the peace of death after his harrowing campaign, Roland is another Wilder creation who has reached the limits of his own endurance. In the midst of Roland's pleas for admittance to the dark tower, Wilder injects a scene note that is completely out of keeping with the play's tedious, stagey dialogue: "The marsh is a little put out by all this strong feeling." Ironic and wonderfully disruptive, this touch anticipates a whole world of inappropriate, irrational effects. It is doubt and playfulness tweaking the world of serious designs.

Wilder's love of disruption and unconventional effects reaches a high point in three of the 1928 volume's most ambitious plays, *The Angel That Troubled the Waters*, *Hast Thou Considered My Servant Job?* and *The Flight into Egypt*. Here, Wilder has attempted religious drama on a grand thematic scale—in scripts that are no longer than half a dozen pages apiece.

The plays were written about a year and a half before publication—and so represent *The Bridge* period. Although their quality varies considerably as they stage conflicts about faith, human pain, and the ironic aspects of existence, each play is outlandish and thoroughly out of step with literary naturalism. Wilder set himself the task, described in the foreword to the volume, of writing a kind of religious drama that deals with "human beings pushed to such an extreme that it resembles love." He felt a curiosity, "the French sense of a tireless awareness of thought," about the kinds of people whom he dealt with in the novels, people who came to an awareness of themselves and for whom words like "faith" and "hope" can have real significance. Ashamed of the language of Christian belief—words like "charity," Wilder tells us, have been ground down by didacticism—Wilder, almost like Hemingway, has to move away from the emptiness of these words and find some new way of discovering their meaning.

His manner of doing this in *The Angel That Troubled the Waters* is so overblown, stylized, and monumental that it seems more like a baroque painting come to life than a one-act play. A group of invalids is sitting beside the biblical pool at Bathesda awaiting the angel who will stir the waters and give them their cure. The ostensible conflict is between a newcomer who is not severely afflicted and another suffering man whose intense pain has caused him to throw himself into the pool before the angel has troubled the waters. The newcomer literally quotes the Marquesa's line in *The Bridge*—"Let me begin again." Troubled by "this fault that bears me down," he seems like another version of the Marquesa. The angel reminds him of a truth that has also been developed in *The Bridge*: "Without your wound where would your power be?" Only a "human being broken on the wheel of living" can understand and "serve" love. The newcomer, like Pio or the Marquesa or Esteban, must endure until his moment. Now if all this strikes the reader as stilted and sentimental, he should consider Wilder's ambitions. By no means a masterpiece, the little play nevertheless strives to carry forward one of the conceptions of a novel into a dramatic form; the play's almost preposterous use of space—"A vast gray hall with a hole in the ceiling open to the sky"—is an early attempt to bring the largeness of *The Bridge* and the backdrop of the Andes into the theater world. Wilder will succeed when he abandons such grandiose sets for something homelier; meanwhile, this is the beginning of an escape from the box stage.

Hast Thou Considered My Servant Job? is another not altogether successful attempt to break out of naturalistic form and verisimilitude. The piece is of interest because it reverses our expectations and also mixes trickery and spectacle with morality. Christ, not Satan, has been "going to and fro in the earth" in this spin-off on the Book of Job. Reversing the biblical Satan, he taunts the forces of evil by saying that Judas would not serve unless he was rewarded by Satan. Satan responds by handing Judas over for thirty-three years—in this time the servant of Satan has of course betrayed Christ, but he has also despaired of the powers of evil and hanged himself. As Satan is about to exult in the betrayal, "Suddenly the thirty pieces of silver are cast upward from the revolted hand of Judas." Judas, with "the black stains about his throat and the rope of suicide," curses Satan. Playing in almost every line with the biblical subtext. Wilder makes his piece into an attack on the smugness of modern pessimism and cynicism. We do not inhabit the worst of all possible worlds, and Satan's understanding of human nature is as simplistic as a Job's comforter or some cheery Bible-belt preacher. Seeking a place between 1920s-style cynicism and the pieties of his father's Puritan religion, Wilder finds it in the unpredictable character of Judas, Christ's "beloved son" who has been revolted by his own evil nature. That a way out of despair can be paradoxically found through despairing is of course Wilder's highly unorthodox solution to the problem of evil. Abandoning sense and stage logic, he opts for a stunning moment of awareness, Judas becomes an emblem of the way to a higher spirituality—a kind of salvation through dread and self-loathing, not unlike that proposed by modern existentialists.

The Flight into Egypt is by far the most successful and engaging of the

1928 one-act plays: in a few pages it manages to do all the things that earlier plays attempted; it also dispenses with pretentiousness, scales down effects, and adopts a contemporary idiom that is both charming and highly ironic. The protagonist is a donkey named Hepzibah, the animal who bore Christ and Mary in their flight. The plot is another of Wilder's journeys— this time a few minutes of tension with Herod's soldiers in pursuit. Hepzibah is no ordinary-talking, moralizing animal out of an exemplary tale or fable. Instead, Wilder has turned the Bible story into a collision between an extraordinary event and an ordinary creature; speaking in the tone and with the genial knowingness of a New York taxicab driver, the donkey becomes a humorous, complaining, helpful, and ever-curious example of the modern self as it encounters and tries to make sense of the world's glory and misery. During most of the flight Hepzibah is unaware of her burden: she stops to rest her legs and to emphasize a half dozen points about "the whole political situation" in Palestine. While philosophizing, the donkey touches on just about every Wilder theme we have encountered so far: this latest thinker is "at home in ideas of all sorts"—faith versus reason, fate and providence, the irony of destiny. Like Brother Juniper pondering the fates of the five victims, Hepzibah wonders about the slaughtered infants: "Even in faith we are supposed to use our reason. No one is contented to swallow hook, line and sinker, as the saying is. Now take these children that Herod is killing. Why were they born, since they must die so soon? Can any one answer that?" Such a display of old chestnuts scales down the ambitions of the play while paradoxically giving it resonance.

Wilder uses offhand language and a clumsy set to secure his effects. His stage consists of an old cyclorama from a dime museum: the Holy Land rolls by in the background as a highly stylized scene is played out before us. This abandonment of the realistic set for the conventions of the grammar-school play is Wilder's way of forcing the audience back to his language: the rudimentary set, stripped of his earlier pretenses, is a complement to the awkward, clumsy first-order questions of the average mind in its pursuit of meaning. The staging also creates an ironic contrast to the magnitude of the subject matter: abandoning the bizarre and exotic for the homely, Wilder ceases to overstate; the effect makes the little piece an unusual exploration of a religious theme. A talking donkey, clanking metal for Herod's army, the Tigris and Euphrates projected on the cyclorama, make for a small drama about the inappropriate and sometimes ridiculous nature of spiritual experience. Put in Hepzibah's terms, "It's a queer world where the survival of the Lord is dependent on donkeys."

The experiments in the 1931 plays published as *The Long Christmas Dinner and Other Plays in One Act* are a continuation and development of *The Flight into Egypt*. The three best of them are also journeys—through space and years. Thematically, Wilder seems to be offering us small occasions on which we may discover who we are.

The title play, *The Long Christmas Dinner*, lacks the charming comic touches of the small religious play about the flight, but it employs several stage techniques and a series of rising ironies to provide the audience with an even more arresting view of the strangeness of human life. The central conceit of the play—having generations of a family reveal their enduring concerns and sufferings at successive Christmas dinners—is perfectly fitted to Wilder's conception of human ambitions set against the terrifying backdrop of time. The dining room of the Bayards is the scene in which Wilder stages a concern that he explored in *The Cabala* and *The Bridge of San Luis Rey*: the awesome spectacle of men and women enmeshed in petty concerns and accelerating toward death. While his proscenium stage is conventional enough here, his reinvention of its resources is highly imaginative. Exit from stage left "is a strange garland trimmed with fruits and flowers": newborn children are brought through this. The black velvet on the opposite side of the stage indicates the door of death. Characters appear and disappear without any lengthy preliminaries—one character even takes a few steps toward the dark side and returns, recovered from alcoholism. Wilder's people sit down each year to an invisible turkey; they carry white wigs and shawls, which they put on to denote age. Time passes through the use of these stage devices and through the ironic repetitions of remarks, clichés, and greetings of the season. Each year people take wine for the occasion and comment on the weather, the church sermon, and the neighbors' health. Wilder also injects small but significant ironic changes in the family's fortunes: as they become more prosperous, they accumulate disease and conflict; as the house is expanded, its inhabitants scatter to other places; as the play ends, an elderly cousin, the last in the house on a Christmas day, reads a letter about a new generation in the East and then totters toward the dark portal.

The play is Wilder's first significant blending of experimental technique and American subject matter. Though universal and unprovincial in its themes, the small drama is nevertheless situated in an American town. The flavor and notation is midwestern, genteel, and Protestant; the Bayards are prosperous people whose native place grows from a small settlement to a large factory town. Wilder's people are correct, conventionally religious, and self-satisfied. But the placidity and correctness of their lives is periodically punctured by Roderick's drinking, his sister's loneliness and desperation, his grandson's rudeness, and the death of a young man in World War I. The swiftly dramatized agonies of the Bayards completely destroy the substance of Mike Gold's criticisms: Wilder, rather than being this critic's tightly controlled genteel chronicler of minor miseries, is a writer involved with the inexorable facts of living; his play is about desperation, decay, the endless cycle of talk and birth and death and suffering that all must endure. No "little lavendar tragedy," the play is instead a compressed presentation of all the large forces that sweep through human lives and carry them toward the dark portal. The cleverness of its technique makes its unadorned vision bearable and the rapidity of the one-act form is perhaps the most direct way of assaulting the audience with its own fund of fleeting pleasures and permanent fears.

Pullman Car Hiawatha is a more elaborate theatrical undertaking—a play that employs the machinery and strategy of experimentalism to maximum effect. Although less emotionally resonant and terrifying than *The Long Christmas Dinner*, it too manages to direct the audience to the absurd and sometimes tragic collision between our everyday lives and our ultimate destinies. But while it is also a play about time and decay, it is, in addition, a small drama that takes a group of riders to Chicago. Less matter-of-factly dreadful than *Christmas Dinner*, it lifts the audience by offering moments of pleasure, love, optimism and casual camaraderie. We arrive at a station, not at the death portal.

The play is a series of impressions given by a diverse group of travelers and also by the scenery through which they pass; fields and towns talk—as well as people, ghosts, and dead philosophers. The plot structure is loose and takes the form of the ordinary events and sensations of an overnight train trip: looking at places along the way, getting ready for bed, dreaming, waking up, getting off. During the night a young woman dies; a madwoman raves, characters lie awake and worry or fantasize, annoy each other, or mix their trivial concerns with their deepest desires and fears. The action rises as Wilder moves us from the inhabitants of the train to the creatures of the earth, to the planets and the realm of ideas and spiritual reality. When we have reached the most abstract realm of experience, we are returned to the everyday.

The play's stage technique is a startling leap forward for Wilder. The roots of experimentalism and stage artifice are in *The Flight into Egypt*, but here the development of staging makes the play into more than a charming tryout of strategies. At least four new approaches are used to produce emotional effect: the appearance of the stage manager, the use of characters who get a chance to "think," the development of characters as actors, and the use of literary quotations as both stage jokes and devices to enrich the theme. Together these ploys make a short play into a reflexive, complex, and witty modernist work.

Wilder's stage manager directs the characters' actions and assumes acting duties himself: part director and part character, he breaks down the naturalistic connections and causes the play to unfold in a way that directs us to texture and style. Like Pirandello's stage manager in *Six Characters in Search of an Author*, this director carries out his routine tasks—telling people when to speak, when to stop, where to stand—and at times is tempted into the action of the play itself. Wilder has softened the role of manager, made him less irascible and resistant to the drama before him than Pirandello's short-fused director: in so doing, he has created less stage furor and more community. *Pullman Car*'s manager becomes one of the first real American people/actors who give the audience a sense that the reality of a theater and the reality of their lives are intertwined. In gathering diverse elements together—"the whole solar system, please. Where's the tramp?—Where's the moon?"—the manager becomes a negotiator of the fantasies and mundane events of our lives. The word "please"—as well as all the cues and asides and stage directions—directs us to the acts of theater, to the fact that they are both conjured events and practical movements. Because of the stage manager, nothing happens in the play unless we watch the sheer physicality of its happening.

Supporting this strategy are Wilder's more general liberties with characters. Like Pirandello, he makes them self-conscious actors, often unsure of what they are doing and why. But Wilder is unlike Pirandello in *Six Characters* in at least two respects: his actor/characters do not lead him into subtle philosophical speculations, and his technique for revealing theme involves more fantasy. So it is that "Grover's Corners, Ohio" appears as a character: the guiding stage direction—"in a foolish voice as though he were reciting a piece at a Sunday School entertainment"—provides for even more exaggeration and artificiality. "The Field"—with gophers, mice, and bugs—speaks next; as the play builds to its climax, moving out of the earthly realm into the philosophical and theological, it introduces hours as philosophers who quote Plato, Aristotle, and Epictetus—and then the planets with their humming representing the music of the spheres; the archangels come next. After these we have two people, the Insane Woman and Harriet, the young wife, who tell about two of Wilder's abiding concerns: misunderstood suffering and the mistake of not having realized one's life. The Insane Woman is another of Wilder's hysterics—people strangely damaged by life who cry out in protest. "Use me. Give me something to do," she says; the line directs us back to the Marquesa in *The Bridge*. Harriet, the young wife who dies on the train, directs us forward to *Our Town*: after death she surveys the world, like Emily; as she looks back, she feels "I was angry and sullen. I never realized anything." Other characters who appear in this essentially plotless play include the archangels, Michael and Gabriel—in blue suits— the ghost of a German railroad worker killed in an accident, a worker in a lower berth who quotes Kipling, and a Pullman porter who has trouble thinking out loud according to the manager's cues. Surveying the realms of being—and keeping a steady eye on love, death, pleasure, and human diversity—Wilder brings his trainload to Chicago. "This train don't go no further," the porter says.

The Wilder imprint can also be found in his constant deployment of literature: mixing folk sayings, Bartlett-type quotations, and philosophical passages, he allows the words of others to do part of his work. No need to have his characters freshly discovering life's pleasure: "What is so rare as a day in June? Then, if ever, come perfect days." The old chestnut, quoted by "The Field," is dramatically a joke because of the speaker, but it still carries meaning. Similarly, Wilder avoids the pompous and pretentious by using "beautiful girls dressed like Elihu Vedder's Pleiades" to deliver lines of Plato, Aristotle, and Saint Augustine. Combining theater glitter and speculation about beauty and human passion, these figures are the typical creation of a writer who is more concerned with fusing realms of experience through experimentation than with any kind of plot logic. One of the most crowded small plays in American drama, *Pullman Car* is also pleasingly heavy with its writer's techniques.

A much simpler and perhaps greater work is *The Happy Journey to Trenton and Camden*. This one, another American trip, reveals its themes without the complex machinery of the experimentalist's techniques. The stage manager does no more than read the lines of minor characters "with little attempt at characterization." The stage experiment that disappears is replaced by a quiet, highly concentrated and unadorned presentation of the cycle of human pleasure and pain. As a dramatic plot, the *Journey* does no more than carry Ma Kirby, her husband, and children from their Newark house to the Camden house of Ma's married daughter, Beulah. Like *Pullman Car*, this play uses ordinary sights, trivial exchanges, and small occurrences to draw out large themes. But the *Journey* is stripped bare of fantastic elements and literary allusions. Confined to the mundane from start to finish, Wilder's people dignify the ordinary because they discover permanent truths about their world. Without condescending or sentimentalizing, Wilder treats a limited world and draws unlimited thematic capital from it. A car trip becomes an occasion for cosmic recognitions.

The play is so down-scaled in its techniques and so overtly undramatic in its subject matter that the onlooker almost forgets how tightly packed with meaning it is. Ma Kirby matter-of-factly delivers Wilder's themes in lines that are as plain as paint, but somehow never flat. Truisms and clichés are freshly polished and come out as forgotten realizations. Ma lives by an easily articulated code of decency, friendliness, love, and pride. She is the picture of petty-bourgeois, ungenteel health: unlike the characters in early plays and novels, she is unencumbered by the neuroses, fears, and guilts of better-bred people. She corrects children, only to be warm and loving with them; she respects conventions, but knows her own mind; she likes order and discipline, but knows that life is too complex to live by strict codes. Her only non-negotiable point is the goodness of God and the essential goodness of man. Wilder has transferred this theme, first encountered in *The Bridge*, into an American context: what was once a matter of Brother Juniper's theorizing is now a practical and abiding faith. The final recognition of the play—our understanding that daughter Beulah had a child that died at birth—is something already seen in *The Flight into Egypt* and *The Bridge*. The idea of loss and suffering is dealt with so unpretentiously that one cannot help but respect the victims: "God thought it best, dear. God thought it best. We don't understand why. We just go on, honey, doin' our business."

The next moment Ma is saying, "What are we giving the men to eat tonight?" While better minds offer fuller answers to the problem of human misery, Ma Kirby endures.

With such a vision, Wilder of course leaves himself open to the charge of provinciality and sentimentality. Can a writer produce a distinguished piece of theater when his protagonist and spokeswoman is someone who declares, "I live in the best street in the world because my husband and children live there"? How can a man steeped in Joyce and Proust and the classics lapse into park-bench philosophizing? If there is no irony in the portraits of the Kirbys, how can the modern audience, with tastes developed by Beckett and Strindberg, find resonance in this play? To begin with, Wilder's journey causes his people to wonder: it is anything but narrow. Arthur, the son, realizes in a few minutes, "What a lotta people there are in the world." No more than a line, this observation sets the family against the same kind of awesome backdrop we have seen in *Pullman Car Hiawatha*. As for sloppy sentimentality, one can only note that Wilder's people are too abrupt and matter-of-fact to wallow in emotions. A feeling may be unabashedly displayed, but Wilder's strategy is usually to follow it with some very ordinary fact or observation. Ma speculates on George Washington's veracity; Arthur's next line is about an Ohio license plate. Finally, this small play has a claim on contemporary audiences because of its homemade and courageous assembling of very familiar themes: without conceding to sophistication, conventional weltschmerz, or any attitude of the 1930s, it succeeds in being so old-fashioned as to be almost dateless. Although it lacks the bite and irony of Joyce handling the bourgeois mentality, it offers its own austere vision of the way things are for millions of people. Along with heavy championing of home and family, it is still a play about fears, struggles, and disasters.

During the late 1950s, Wilder conceived the ideas for two one-act play cycles—the first to be devoted to "the seven ages of man," the second covering "the seven deadly sins." Returning to the impulse of his youth—especially the tendency to envision great themes embodied in small forms—Wilder again made the mistake of miscalculating his ability to execute, polish, and conclude such projects. . . .

In 1958, two years after he had begun writing some new one-act plays, Wilder was reading about Joyce's *Dubliners* and thinking about the Joycean idea of moral history. It suddenly came to him that he too was trying to write a cycle of works about sin and the demands of the ethical life. Thereafter his small-scale dramas were drawn into an intellectual-moralistic scheme—something that now appears to be an exploration of the dark impulses of the Cold War period. Like a religious playwright turned loose in the age of McCarthyism, the U-2 incident, and bomb shelters, Wilder dramatized the American spiritual condition: that of a nation steeped in suppressed violence, filled with suspicions about "them," haunted by memories of World War

II and the Holocaust, and set on edge by technology and real and imagined espionage. The settings for such concerns were historical, mythical, and contemporary—the Italy of Saint Francis, the world of Apollo and the Fates, the suburban living room. The styles were to be no less varied: "My first intention had been to offer each play in the series as representing, also, a different mode of playwrighting: Grand Guignol, Chekhov, Noh play, etc., etc." The cycle remains in bits and pieces, a testament to Wilder's range and deep involvement with his country's moral climate.

Threats, tricks, betrayals, and violent encounters give thematic unity to "the seven deadly sins" plays. In a comic vein *The Drunken Sisters*, a completed work, explores gluttony: using the situation of *The Alcestiad*—how King Admetus's life was extended, how the Fates were tricked—Wilder devises a satyr play about the politics that shape lives. The Three Fates are set to cut the thread of King Admetus's life when Apollo the trickster appears in disguise as a kitchen boy and gets them drunk on wine that he claims to be carrying to Aphrodite. When they are drunk, he traps them in a wager that involves a riddle they cannot solve. His winning has saved the life of the king; their punishment is to be deprived, for a time, of their power. Ironically, the gluttony of the weird sisters has caused one life to be spared. The Greek story is employed to show that the most solemn outcomes—the sparing of Admetus, the sacrifice of Alcestis—are founded on the trickiness of the immortals. Rather than the use of Providence in *The Bridge of San Luis Rey*, we encounter the scheming of the postmodern era: the play is an exposé of how our world of trade-offs works.

Someone from Assisi is another play involving hidden identity. This time the secret involves the private sphere as it collides with public repute. Saint Francis, about to join Saint Clara and her sisters for a convent meal, is confronted by the local madwoman, his mistress before he embraced Lady Poverty. The play explores lust in the life of a great figure whose reputation has been built on abnegation. Francis was once the young man who sang profane French songs and celebrated a worldly mistress. As a lover of a different kind—the saint of brotherly love—he comes to the convent only to be recognized by poor crazed Mona, a fateful reminder of his own weakness. This discarded woman taught him his life's lesson—that because of the impermanence of living, one owns nothing. The Wilder of the 1920s plays has been deepened in his affirmations by the sheer complexity of existence: saints could found their identities on sins, and lust could produce great love.

The cycle continues in fragmented form with several drafts that are informed by Wilder's pessimistic view of his age. A play called *Bernice*—never produced on Bleecker Street—was meant to express the sin of pride. The plot involves the plans of a mysterious Mr. Walbeck (going under the name of Burgess) as he returns to his Chicago house after a prison term. Reestablished in the house that his wife left, provided with a household staff by his lawyer, Walbeck is prepared to assume a new, false identity. He soon meets Bernice, a maid who not only shares his secret but also lives with the same fate: she is a murderess who, like some figure in Conrad, has access to her employer's anguish. The two characters must decide whether to live alone and preserve their pride or reveal themselves to their children and face the world's scorn. Bernice suffers because hypocritical people don't accept the fact that crime is part of the human condition. She and Walbeck—and the world of conventional people—are probably better off with the proud fiction of their new lives, the lonely Chicago house and their pseudonyms. This small drama of concealment is about a destructive pride that Wilder has studied in *The Bridge*: like the Perichole, Walbeck is an isolated figure whose life is over, although his existence as a victim persists. "Would you advise me to kill off George Walbeck?" he asks. Can the guilty self be allowed to endure? Identity itself is a disgrace and a burden in *Bernice*.

Wilder's design in the cycle begins to come clear when a fragment called *The Wreck on the Five-Twenty-Five* is placed beside *Bernice*. This play, designated "sloth," is once again located in an American living room—and confronts the forces that are beating at the conventional life in one household. Intellectually rich, although dramatically rather muddled, the play is about concealed impulses, suppressed action, and the seething violence that lies below the crust of bourgeois culture. The scenes are a mixture of suburban conventionality and wild irrationalism. The Hawkins women—mother and daughter Minnie—chat about Mr. Hawkins's lateness. As they talk about the 5:25, routines and schedules, and changes, the play gathers thematic momentum. Men want change, Mrs. Hawkins says. Her husband reads Westerns for the excitement and once joked about the A-bomb to their minister: "Suppose the atomic bomb didn't fall, what would we do then?" Hawkins, we soon learn (through a telephone call to Mrs. Hawkins), is prowling outside his own home: soon he appears and talks wildly about wrecks, leaving his commuter routine, going to nearby Bennsville, and taking up a new life. Dostoyevskian in flavor, Hawkins's ranting is directed against the settled order of things: "Only a wreck could crack us open," he says. In search of a world elsewhere—something more than the commuter's view from the window of the 5:25—Hawkins feels "maybe things might look different through the window of another train." The "what if" motif—used in *Our Town* as Emily returns for her birthday—is here a gruesome experiment: what if a man tries to reject the design of his whole life? First of all, Hawkins seems like a madman; the cops find a gun on his person. But Wilder's intention is also seen in the sin of the play: the slothful world can't rouse itself to understand or accept the strange psychic energy that might be contained in each of us. Better not to be ourselves.

And yet Wilder's experiment with authenticity leads him in another direction as well. Part of the absurdity of human life comes from being conventional. There are several references to the way people look when seen through a window. Mrs. Hawkins says that people look silly when you can't hear them. Later on she remarks that her public aspect—the one she assumes on the street—would seem ridiculous to her husband. At another point Hawkins himself says, "[A]ll window glass is the same—you can't hear a word people say." Politics, he adds, is also a glass that separates us from hearing the truth. Altogether, the play is one of Wilder's most pessimistic examinations of civilization: despite its somewhat hackneyed references to life as a jail, it offers brilliant bursts of anxiety, resentment, and aggression that register Wilder's clear sense of the conflicts of the Silent Generation.

The most curious and unsettling fragment in "the seven deadly sins" cycle consists of a few drafts of *Wrath*. The concerns of these unfinished scenes set in postwar, middle-class America are—if dramatically unclear—at least thematically focused. The "play" consists of three versions of wrathful behavior—three short sketches. Draft 1 is about Mrs. Corbett and her son Rex, two affluent characters who inspect the world at large from their isolated vantage point. Both of them are cases, in that they suffer from bad dreams and anxieties; both are studies in the underground mind, the psyche that is closely in touch with violence. In just a few minutes Wilder manages to set the reader of this manuscript on edge. His characters are made to spring at us like recognized war criminals. (Be it noted that Wilder was thinking about the Adolf Eichmann trial at the time he was writing.) Mrs. Corbett is concerned with a night noise that awakened her and with a dream that the houseboy's wife had that night: the woman dreamed she was shooting Japanese. Soon Mrs. Corbett's son appears and starts to rail against the local housing project; it seems that Mr. Smith sold out, and the neighborhood will soon be like "a rabbit warren." Rex—in the tones of a hysteric of the Nazi era—says that "every house is packed with babies." Soon his language sounds like a clear adaptation of anti-Semitic propaganda: the poor are breeding like flies in a manure pile, he says. His solution is a nightmare in broad daylight that replicates the Holocaust: the community ought to send a wagon around on the first of the month to collect the babies.

Where Wilder was taking this material dramatically is unclear. Rex has had trouble with his wife; Mrs. Corbett is haunted; the houseboy's wife is on her way to confession. The jumble of elements doesn't come together—and yet the strong destructive theme colors the episodes and casts light on earlier work as well as on the cycle. The self as it has been damaged in time of war—whether the son in *The Skin of Our Teeth* or the murderous Uncle Charles in the filmscript *Shadow of a Doubt* (1943)—is one of the concerns of Wilder's later career. His exploration of the fascist mind in Uncle Charles—the killer of useless, fat widows, the madman visiting relatives in Santa Rosa—seems to lead in the direction of Rex. Both of them want to destroy "our town," the contemporary pluralistic society that Wilder celebrated so memorably in *The Happy Journey to Trenton and Camden*, among other midperiod works. Rex is an unsuccessful attempt to rework, update, and perfect an idea that dates from the war years.

The remaining *Wrath* fragments embody anxieties about the 1940s and 1950s but have almost no form. One, called "Ira," has a mother and son bantering about killing off the human race—and then going on to a discussion about getting rid of each other. The word *burden*—Walbeck's word in *Pride*—is used to describe the way they feel about each other. The other draft is an odd sketch about persecuted people who talk in a code language: an organization pretending to be about plant ecology has really come into being to protect its members against some vague political authorities who are capable of inflicting torture. The members use euphemistic dialogue to discuss their judges and the persecution that seems all too real. Whether or not they are suffering from paranoia is unclear. But what exists of the draft suggests that Wilder was reading Kafka and contemplating the uncertainties in *The Castle* and *The Trial*. "How to behave before your judges" is one of the issues that the organization in this version of *Wrath* discusses. The allusion to Kafka's "Before the Law" is fairly clear.

After the essentially grim explorations in "the seven deadly sins" cycle, "the seven ages of man" plays experiment with the ridiculous and playful rather than the malevolent aspects of consciousness. The two "seven ages" plays carry forward early themes, but do so in an almost uncategorizably charming, witty, and experimental form. Writing at the time when "the theater of the absurd" was a dominant force in the work of many important playwrights, Wilder shares the spirit of his age in his technique while dramatizing material that is all his own. Delicacy, subtlety, rich humor, and firm commitment to the humanist's position characterizes the late work. While compeers with great literary ambitions, like Beckett and Ionesco, explored the desperation of the human situation in bizarre forms—bums in *Waiting for Godot* waiting for nothing, men changing into rhinos in *Rhinoceros*—Wilder charted the American family's development in a deeply ironic, optimistic, and comic style. Building on the sly humor of *The Flight into Egypt* and the grim irony of *The Long Christmas Dinner*, he adds several new applications of irony, word play, and stage disjunction. In the manner of his exuberant, richly textured, and complex comedy, *The Skin of Our Teeth*, he builds comic effects: once again he uses Joyce's stream of consciousness and dreamlike effects to reproduce a world that we would otherwise not have access to—that of infancy and childhood. No myopic adult writing about childlike characters, he becomes a comic voyager willing to immerse himself in the impressions, fantasies, and impulses of a distant period in human development. Along with this Joycean frankness and sense of adventure— the impulse that led Joyce to begin *A Portrait of the Artist as a Young Man* with a child telling about a moo cow and the sensations of infancy—Wilder adds the stage dimension of the ridiculous; in the manner of the absurd playwrights, he uses full-grown men in baby carriages, adults who are parodies of maturity in their mechanical and ludicrous behavior, a whole array of clichés and misunderstanding for dialogue. While the plays of the 1930s were an essentially serious look at the family's destiny, these new works are infused with the comic-absurd spirit.

The concerns of the two later one-act plays seem to be foreshadowed in several journal entries from 1956. At that time Wilder was still trying to overcome the organizational difficulties of his Norton lectures on the American character. The focus of his book was to be disconnections, especially the ways that Americans are cut off from the social dependencies of Europeans and isolated in their own individualism. This theme, nothing new for the writer of *The Cabala* or *The Bridge*, was especially applicable to Emerson, Wilder's intellectual villain in the national letters: he argued that Emerson's spiritual happiness was separated from the happiness and woe of humanity. Emerson's "sufficiency"—always a pejorative term for Wilder—was an irrational and dangerous strain in American thought, an intellectual heirloom that Wilder was attempting to discard in his own late work. Wilder experimented with the idea of inserting transitional passages in the Norton lectures about a prototypical American character, one Tom Everage—an average, middle-class neurotic—troubled by his inability to connect his life with the world around him. A prisoner of fears, hatreds, and haunting memories, Tom was destined for a life of frustration—and perhaps violence. Wilder planted the seeds of his one-act cycle by referring to Tom's "infancy" as the period when the "frustrated emperor" was "crossed and obstructed at every turn." This Freudian allegory, combined with Wilder's own ideas of isolation, did not work in the lectures, but it enriched and shaped *Infancy* and *Childhood*—two plays about disconnectedness, isolation, and the situation of the lonely self. It also is clear that Wilder could siphon off the agony of the frustrated self—the predominant concern in "the seven deadly sins"—and turn isolation into a slapstick spectacle with pun-infested dialogue.

Infancy: A Comedy in One Act is an outlandish look at two babies' world of frustration and isolation. A counterpointed story like *The Bridge*, it tells about the infantile struggle of Tommy and Moe while presenting the more trivial struggles of Miss Millie Wilchick, Mrs. Baker, and Officer Avonzino. The scene is Central Park in the twenties, and the characters are deliberately caricatured types, reminiscent of figures from the early screen and vaudeville. Millie is a dim-witted baby nurse whose mind is filled with plots of dime-store romances; Officer Avonzino is part Keystone Cop—angry and equipped with billy club—and part Chico Marx with his shrewdness and his heavy Italian accent; Mrs. Boker is a Jewish mother whose precocious baby is driving her crazy. The babies are curious, aggressive, grasping, sexually aware monsters out of Freud. Tommy listens as Miss Millie quotes from a novel: "He drew her to him, pressing his eyes on hers." The infant mouths the words and immediately declares, "Wanta make a baybee!" He absorbs every adult concern, sniffs out every smell of food, and rages because he cannot obtain the pleasure that he imagines. Moe is another "genius" in a carriage—or one of the "ingeniouses" as Officer Avonzino calls him: he is skilled at manipulating his parents, watching their every move, and exploring the realms of sex and self-assertion. His father thinks he is dirty-minded; his mother acknowledges him as a master of domination. "I don't have to tell you what life with a baby is: (Looking around circumspectly.) It's war— *one long war*." Or as Officer Avonzino puts it, "All you babies want the whole world."

The play succeeds brilliantly in employing the comic mode for the purpose of exploring another dimension of our humanity. Often rationalized by creative writers, the world of childhood is a chaos of impulses that are not easily represented. Wilder focuses on the life force—the baby's rage to assert himself. This should be no surprise to the audiences familiar with Wilder's sanguine view of human potential: even the earliest plays assert the achievements of the human spirit, the drive to learn and progress. The journeys of the 1930s have now become the long stretch of the human life-span.

The second stage is *Childhood*, the only other play in the cycle that Wilder chose to publish. This play is more substantial and highly crafted than *Infancy*—a witty plot and a strong emotional appeal are added to the absurdist elements of the earlier work. Again, we are dealing with fantasies, dreams, and aggressive wishes. But this time, Wilder has shaped his play to show the movement out of infantile self-absorption. While *Infancy* explores isolation and rage, this small drama is about recognition of otherness; its theme is the growth of the child into the world of comprehension and tolerance. Three children and their parents are involved in this latest journey into knowledge: Wilder uses a game "which is a dream" to take his characters to the next plateau of recognition. Caroline, twelve; Dodie, ten; and Billee, eight, go on a "bus ride" and discover what their parents are like for the first time.

The plot line begins with the children's gruesome and funny world of play. "Hospital" and "orphans" are their two favorite games—the latter of course involving the pleasures of destroying their masters. Filled with resentment, the children express their loneliness and fear: parents go on trips to sick relatives and stay for years; they drink and scold and understand nothing. They never say or do anything "inneresting." They deserve to die as a punishment for being aliens. The parents, in turn, regard the children as strangers and interlopers. Occupied with their own routines and impatient with what they cannot understand, they too yearn for release. The father has a dream about a Mediterranean cruise where they are "somehow . . . alone." The early turning point in the development of the action comes when the father begins to reflect and asks "just once" to be "an invisible witness to one of my children's dreams."

From here the play takes off in a different direction—into a delightful realm of play, learning, and reconciliation. The imaginary bus ride allows the three children to interact with the driver (their father) and a veiled passenger (their mother). The main technique of this portion is the recycling of the children's basic concerns in the form of fantasy resolutions: whatever they have complained about or resented is dealt with and resolved by the bus driver. Drinking, loneliness, money problems, fear of death: each is treated with an offhanded word or two, which causes the children to move out of their world of isolated resentment into a shared existence. Of death the father says, "We don't think about that." Of drinking, he advises the eight-year-old Billee, "There'll be no liquor drinking on this bus. I hope that's understood." Of the battle to make ends meet: "Well, you know what a man's life is like, Mrs. Arizona. Fight. Struggle. Survive. Struggle. Survive. Always was." When the children decide to return home, the father's line is pure Wilder in its understated, ordinary, but emotionally charged quality— "I'll honor that ticket *at anytime*, and I'll be looking for you." Sentiment, to be sure, but the touch is so quick and deft that it never descends to sentimentality.

Wilder did not move much further with the "ages of man" project. The imaginative engine that produced non-naturalistic drama in several modes broke down in the early 1960s. Employing literature, history, and biblical motifs in the 1920s, popular American culture and the social life of ordinary people in the 1930s, social themes in the 1950s, Wilder finished his work in the 1960s as a one-act playwright by turning to smaller scenes and the psychic struggles of human development. From literature and art to society and self: the progress is away from the highly artificial, stylized, hothouse world of early plays about Childe Roland and Job.

Symbolist Dimensions of Thornton Wilder's Dramaturgy

PAUL LIFTON

Critics have compared Thornton Wilder's dramaturgical methods and aims with those of the expressionists,[1] the futurists,[2] Brecht,[3] and Pirandello,[4] and there is a valid basis for the comparison in each case, a certain sympathy of impulse or vision discernible in Wilder's playwriting technique or in his choice of themes and motifs. Relatively little attention, however, has been paid to the resemblances between his theater and that of the modern aesthetic movement with which it ultimately displays the strongest philosophical and thematic affinities—and, to a surprising extent, technical or stylistic ones as well—namely, French symbolism.[5] Wilder deviates from symbolist precepts and preferences in significant ways, it is true, and he can no more without qualification be labeled a symbolist than he can an expressionist or futurist or Brechtian. Nevertheless, the affinities are both striking and deep and deserve closer scrutiny.

They do not appear to be the result of sheer coincidence. Although it is unlikely that Wilder was intimately acquainted, at least at the time he was writing his major plays, with all the salient features of the symbolist theater aesthetics developed by Mallarmé, Maeterlinck, Lugné-Poë, and others, he unquestionably was familiar with the methods and most widely known works of some of the movement's leading poets and playwrights—and precursors. His mother, who was his closest confidante and most supportive critic during his youth, had tried her hand at translating some poems by the Belgian symbolist Emile Verhaeren (A. N. Wilder, 62), and she knew Maeterlinck's work as well (Harrison, 14). Wilder himself developed an enthusiasm early in his career for the poetry and criticism of Paul Valéry (A. N. Wilder, 38). One of his favorite instructors at Princeton, where he was awarded an M.A. in French in 1926, was Louis Cons, who lectured on, among others, Baudelaire and Verlaine.[6] Several references in Wilder's published writings show that he was familiar at an early date with Maeterlinck's work also, including at least one of the latter's theater essays,[7] and

This essay was written specifically for this volume and is published here for the first time by permission of the author.

when the Belgian playwright died, Wilder was one of a number of international literary figures who contributed eulogies to a volume titled *Hommage à Maurice Maeterlinck*.[8] Wilder's tribute indicates that he found the older dramatist's works intriguing and liberating when he first sought ways to combat the tyranny of the well-made realistic play.

Despite his knowledge of the movement's basic thrust, however, Wilder was not consciously attempting to write symbolist plays, as Maeterlinck was at first. The similarities between his theater and the symbolists' are due above all perhaps to the Neoplatonism that lies at the root of both his artistic vision and theirs. The symbolists' philosophical credo is most succinctly stated in the assertion by the sympathetic critic Albert Aurier that a symbolist work of art ought in the first place to be "Ideist, since its unique ideal will be to express the Idea."[9] One must understand, though, that for the symbolists the idea could be apprehended only by intuition or sudden insight—that is, by nonrational means—and not by reason, as Plato believed, and that the most effective medium for conveying it was not philosophical discourse but poetry. Wilder, for his part, although perhaps more strongly inclined toward rationalism than toward poetry—or at least equally inclined toward both—also propounded unequivocally Platonist views in his essays on the theater. He writes in his preface to the volume *Three Plays: Our Town, The Skin of Our Teeth, The Matchmaker* that "[i]t is through the theater's power to raise the exhibited individual action into the realm of idea and type and universal that it is able to evoke our belief."[10] Elsewhere he writes, "Modern taste shrinks from emphasizing the central idea that hides behind the fiction, but it exists there nevertheless, supplying the unity to fantasizing."[11]

As far as his dramatic writings are concerned, Wilder's Platonic—and even Neoplatonic—bias can perhaps most easily be seen in some of the early "three minute" plays for three characters (most of them written while the dramatist was still an undergraduate) that were published in the volume *The Angel That Troubled the Waters and Other Plays*. Simply in intending these closet playlets for performance in the "theatre of the mind," Wilder was acting in accordance with the Platonic preferences of Mallarmé and Maeterlinck, for whom the imagined performance was ultimately superior to any actual one. In terms of content the most explicitly Platonic of these brief dramas is the one titled *Centaurs*. The central thesis put forth in the playlet is that, in the words of the poet Shelley, who appears as a character in it, "the stuff of which masterpieces is made drifts about the world waiting to be clothed in words. It is a truth that Plato would have understood that the mere language, the words of a masterpiece, are the least of its offerings." According to the play, the *idea* of an unwritten poem by Shelley, "The Death of a Centaur," ultimately took form as Ibsen's *The Master Builder* (itself a favorite play of Mallarmé and other symbolists and one of the greatest successes of the early years of the Théâtre de l'Oeuvre).

118 ◆ PAUL LIFTON

It is probable that the entire Neoplatonic foundation of the play has more to do with the real Shelley's own Neoplatonic beliefs than with any symbolist influence or impulses on Wilder's part, but on the other hand, Neoplatonic concepts inform a number of the other "three minute" playlets wherein not the slightest mention of or allusion to Shelley is made. For example, a classic Neoplatonic conception of the individual is central to *And the Sea Shall Give up Its Dead*. Presenting the playwright's vision of the events following the final trumpet, the piece ends with the stripping of their identities from three drowned souls and their simultaneous fusion with the rest of creation in the "blaze of unicity" that follows the world's dissolution. The concept is reminiscent of the Button Moulder in *Peer Gynt*, except that here, as befits Doomsday, *all* individual souls, no matter what they may or may not have accomplished, are destined to be "melted down" into their primal material, which is even more basic than their idea or significant form. The vision of an essential "unicity" at the heart of creation gives this play a distinctly Neoplatonic, as opposed to simply Platonic, cast.

In fact, the founder of Neoplatonism, the philosopher Plotinus, held that the fundamental aim of the soul is to return to its source, of which it is merely an emanation. Thus, the peculiar outcome of Judgment Day presented in the piece—that is, the merging of all individual souls into one—can fairly be said to illustrate a basic tenet of Neoplatonist thought. Wilder apparently continued, moreover, to believe in the eventual extinction of the identity after death, if one can assume that the Stage Manager in *Our Town* is voicing the dramatist's own ruminations when, as he attempts to identify the "something eternal about every human being," he poses to the audience the rhetorical question, "[W]hat's left when memory's gone, and your identity, Mrs. Smith?"

Related to and springing from this underlying Neoplatonism is a theme central to Wilder's dramatic work and also encountered in the writings of Maeterlinck, the symbolist playwright par excellence, the theme that there is infinite, hidden wonder, to which most mortals are blind most of the time, in the smallest of earthly phenomena. Wilder's most explicit statement of this theme can be found in *Our Town*, of course, but it also permeates *Pullman Car Hiawatha*, *The Happy Journey to Trenton and Camden*, and *The Long Christmas Dinner*, as well as *The Matchmaker*. A few quotations from Maeterlinck's collection of mystical, inspirational, and theoretical essays, *The Treasure of the Humble*, should suffice to show his kinship with Wilder in this matter, a kinship already noted by Robert W. Corrigan in a 1961 article on the latter playwright (Corrigan, 167–173). First, referring to the "tragical" element in daily life, the Belgian dramatist writes. "Its province is . . . to reveal to us how truly wonderful is the mere act of living, and to throw light upon the existence of the soul, self-contained in the midst of ever-restless immensities."[12] The entire statement, without modification, could be taken as referring to *Our Town*, *The Happy Journey*, or *Pullman Car*

Hiawatha, especially the former play, with its recurrent references to the temporal, spatial, and populational immensities surrounding each individual life. All three plays could be considered perfect fulfillments of the desires expressed in another passage as well. Speaking of his disappointing experiences in the theater, Maeterlinck confesses, "I had gone thither hoping that the beauty, the grandeur and the earnestness of my humble day by day existence would, for one instant, be revealed to me, that I would be shown the I know not what presence, power, or God that is ever with me in my room" (Maeterlinck, 104). Mallarmé also, according to Haskell Block, conceived of the drama, like the other arts, as a vehicle first and foremost for revealing the "hidden wonder of the universe."[13]

To reveal this hidden wonder—that is, "to express the Idea" lurking behind ordinary phenomena—symbolist poets, artists, and dramatists tended in their own works to suggest or gradually evoke their meaning, rather than stating it directly or summarily, as one would do in addressing the rational mind. This gradual evocation of meaning is perhaps the single most important hallmark of the symbolist style. Wilder, on the other hand, is a generally straightforward writer, rejecting the vague and nebulous in favor of the direct and unambiguous. There are in the plays some notable exceptions to this tendency, however.

Again, some (but by no means all) of the most striking can be found in the "three minute" plays, especially the first one in the collection, titled *Nascuntur Poetae*. The playlet's central character is a child, who represents the soul of the poet in its prenatal condition, and the action consists of two conversations—one between the child and a woman wearing a chlamys that takes on the colors of the objects around her and the other between him and her "sister," a woman dressed in deep red. Each of the women prepares him for some aspect of earthly life, the woman in deep red by giving him a golden chain hung with pendants symbolizing the "dark and necessary gifts" attendant on the artistic life. The woman explains the meaning of each of the pendants in turn. One of these, a tongue of fire, is almost certainly a symbol of artistic creation itself, the divine "poetic frenzy" of the creative act (itself a Platonic conception, elucidated in the *Ion*). The "madness," however, is never explicitly named but instead merely suggested. The woman in deep red calls it only "a madness that in a better country has a better name." In reply, the boy pointedly remarks, "These are mysteries. Give them no names." To name an object was, for Mallarmé, "to banish the major part of the enjoyment derived from a poem, since this enjoyment consists in a process of gradual revelation."[14] The meanings of the other pendants too, which include a laurel leaf, a staff, and an unspecified object made of crystal (a ball?), are for the most part only suggested, and not directly stated. The fame or satisfaction symbolized by the laurel leaf is implied in the woman in deep red's reference to "pride and the shining of the eyes" and also in the ordinary symbolic associations of laurel. The crystal pendant symbolizes the gift/curse of heightened perception, but again the meaning of the symbol is not stated directly but merely implied in the woman's discussion of its contradictory qualities (it is "wonderful and terrible") and its attendant effects.

In the later plays too this sort of oblique revelation—or concealment—of meaning sometimes crops up, although it generally seems to be less of a mannerism than in symbolist writing, because Wilder usually provides realistic justifications for it. In *Our Town*, for instance, Simon Stimson's "troubles" are never identified, perhaps because the other characters "know the facts about everybody" in the town and need no reminders to jog their memories about so familiar a source of gossip. Also, when Mrs. Webb, before the wedding in act 2, expresses her regret that she has never discussed sex with Emily, her Victorian habits of speech prevent her from naming openly—or in euphemistic terms, for that matter—the topic she has failed to broach to her daughter.

In the less naturalistic third act, the technique is used even more liberally, although each instance of its use can still be justified on realistic, psychological grounds. First, the Stage Manager does not explicitly call the site of the action a cemetery until four paragraphs after he has begun speaking about it. He mentions its beauty and compares it implicitly with the more familiar and pretentious final resting places Woodlawn and Brooklyn. He never crudely or bluntly states the title of the third act either, contenting himself with telling the audience in act 2, "I reckon you can guess what that [the upcoming act] is about."

Of course, death, like sex, is a subject customarily swathed in euphemism, but it is not the only subject to which the Stage Manager is content merely to allude in his monologue. When he is faced with the task of explaining how the audience is to regard the dead they see on stage and how the dead themselves perceive things, he begins by saying, "We all know that *something* is eternal." Again, perhaps out of a spirit of broadminded tolerance or respect for religious diversity, he never explicitly *names* that thing. The speech would almost certainly collapse into banality if he did, but it is nonetheless significant that, in an effort to preserve a sense of the marvelousness of the world beyond the senses (itself a symbolist aim), the playwright is obliged to acknowledge implicitly the inadequacy of language—of names. The Stage Manager must convey the essence of what he has to say by means of a progressive elimination of incorrect conceptions of it. He observes that the eternal "something" "ain't houses and it ain't names, and it ain't earth, and it ain't even the stars." Significantly, according to Neoplatonist thinking, one way of beginning to arrive at an understanding of the nature of ultimate truth or reality is precisely this *via negativa*, this elimination of qualities or elements clearly *not* attributable to that reality,[15] the next step being the contemplation of those elements in the phenomenal world that *are* clearly *like* it. (For Plotinus, then, as for his symbolist descendants, truth may best be apprehended by an *indirect* approach.) Wilder may simply wish to avoid belaboring the obvious in this passage, but whatever the reason, the fact remains that he apparently, in this matter, shares Mallarmé's distaste for "naming an object" and employs an indisputably Neoplatonist technique for suggesting it instead.

On the other hand, Wilder is perhaps least like the symbolists, ironically, in his use of symbols. His plays are full of them, but they tend to refer to only one concept or general category of phenomena, instead of being polyvalent, as the symbolists' symbols were meant to be. Later in life, it is true, after he had composed all of his major plays, he asserted in a *Journal* entry that "a symbol is a lariat, formerly it has been sufficient that the lariat enwrap and bring to its knees a passing fancy, a fragment of a fragment of experience. There is something about the pressure on our minds today that demands that a symbol be a mode of stating the All—only so can it be a growing kinetic action of the mind. All symbols less than that are static metaphors. . . . It is these facile quasi-symbols that permit poets to flirt prettily with big ideas, and then draw back leaving them unexplored, unwrestled-with.[16] And in another entry of a few days later, carrying these same ideas a step further, he described "American Symbol-Making" in terms wholly consonant with (and in fact reiterating) orthodox symbolist theory. He wrote,

> [A]n American-made symbol . . . at the moment of its appearance in the *Dichter's* mind would be a way of "figuring" to himself the totality of experience. . . .
>
> The picture elements in the symbolic representation are not subject to [i.e., selected by] the conscious rational intelligence, and once present to the American are not so developed, *because* he, having freed himself from tradition, authority, inherited patterns of thinking, is in a position to recognize and trust images and concepts that associationally present themselves to his mind from feeling and intuition.
>
> The American symbol then is cosmological, extra-rational, and non-tendentious. (*Journals*, 218)

Without considering the references to the American mind, this passage sets forth a credo that no avowedly symbolist poet or critic would have wished to qualify or state any differently. Still, despite Wilder's enunciation in his *Journals* of such unequivocally symbolist views, in the plays themselves it is a very different matter. There the symbols are for the most part just such unambiguous, "static metaphors" as the dramatist here inveighs against. Moreover, they tend, especially in *The Skin of Our Teeth*, to be "public," in contrast to the "private" or obscure symbols generally employed by the symbolists.

There are a few exceptions, however, especially in the "three minute" plays. Most of the symbolism in *Nascuntur Poetae*, it is true, is univalent and unambiguous. The child is explicitly said to represent the poet's unborn soul and nothing else, the pendant representing a leaf of laurel is clearly an indication of fame or success, that in the shape of a staff signifies a life of wandering (whether spiritual or geographic), and so on. Nevertheless, the symbolic meaning of the two "sisters" is much more uncertain, although they are so abstract and so sharply contrasted in both their garments and their gifts that they cannot rightly be considered to be conventional characters, especially given the allegorical nature of the play as a whole. The color of the second woman's robe has a number of traditional symbolic associations—passion, fidelity, blood, love, shame—but there is no indication in the play as to which of these one is meant to regard as "correct." The chameleonic nature of the other woman's chlamys suggests that she represents the power of the senses to reflect or transmit images of reality to the mind, a power the poet or artist needs in extra measure. The suggestion is reinforced by the boy's statement that she has "poured on [his] eyes and ears and mouth the divine ointment," but the woman herself denigrates the "tumult of the senses" in her next line, and her costume might symbolize adaptability or mental flexibility as well.

The two women must be taken as symbols of contrasting or complementary but nameless spiritual agencies or influences. Their ethereal femininity lends the play a symbolist aura and links it with the artistic tradition of the symbolist painters Denis, Moreau, and Puvis de Chavannes—and indeed with the symbolist theatrical tradition as well, since Pelléas in Maeterlinck's *Pelléas and Mélisande* was originally played by an actress.[17]

An even vaguer symbolism than that found in these two "three minute" plays pervades the collection's title play, *The Angel That Troubled the Waters*. The central character is a physician who has come to the biblical pool at Bathesda in order to be eased of his burden of guilt and sin, the nature of which is never specified. The angel whose visitations are responsible for the cures for which the place is famous warns the physician away from the edge of the miraculous pool, however, saying that healing is not for him. His mission in life requires that he continue to bear his burden for the sake of his patients. The piece, like *Nascuntur Poetae*, is manifestly a parable, and everything in it—physician, angel, pool, and burden—possesses symbolic weight. Yet the range of possible specific meanings for these symbols is literally unlimited, thus adding to the mystery and vibrancy of the play as a whole.

Another early playlet, *Childe Roland to the Dark Tower Came* (inspired by Browning's poem), contains broadly suggestive symbols as well, including another pair of contrasted female characters—in this instance doorkeepers to the dark tower, which symbolizes death. Perhaps its most striking feature, however, is its use of a sentient setting, a marsh, which in effect constitutes a fourth character in the drama, an active, or at least reactive, observer. This anthropomorphizing and animation of the countryside not only foreshadows

Wilder's use of personified fields, towns, planets, and hours in *Pullman Car Hiawatha* but also harks back to the radical personifications of such symbolist poets as Verhaeren, de Regnier, and Moréas.[18]

Conspicuous (and less conspicuous) symbols also enrich the later, better-known, and more stageworthy plays, especially *The Skin of Our Teeth* and several of the one-act plays originally published in the same volume as *The Long Christmas Dinner*. Again, the majority, as befits symbols in works intended for the stage, are clear, unambiguous, and univalent. There is, however, at least one major symbol in several plays that is more broadly suggestive, although still not ultimately as ambiguous as the more uncompromising symbolists would prefer. That symbol is the journey, the central action of both *Pullman Car Hiawatha* and *The Happy Journey*. It has not gone unnoticed that the physical journeys in Wilder's writings frequently parallel inner voyages of spiritual discovery[19] (as they do in Strindberg's *To Damascus* plays and countless other works).

The pattern appears not only in *Pullman Car* and *The Happy Journey* but also in the "three minute" playlet *The Flight into Egypt*, in which a talking donkey carries the Holy Family to safety in Egypt without realizing, until it is almost too late, the nature of the burden she carries. The pattern can also be found in the novels *Heaven's My Destination* and *The Eighth Day* and in the later play *Childhood*, from the projected *Seven Ages of Man* cycle. In all cases the physical journey accompanies an increase in awareness, whether of the wonders of the universe, both physical and spiritual, as in *Pullman Car* and *The Happy Journey*, or of the needs and feelings and value of other people, as in *Childhood*, or of the interdependence of all human beings, or of the voyager's previously untapped potential. This variation in the specific object or nature of the increased awareness preserves some allusive richness for this pivotal, recurring symbol.

The archetypal nature of the central characters in *The Skin of Our Teeth* too gives them, as symbols, a greater resonance and depth than ordinary allegorical symbols, although George and Maggie Antrobus, Henry, and Sabina each "stands for" only one specific human type or set of impulses or values. In fact, although the play as a whole seems to lie at the opposite stylistic pole from symbolist dramatic norms, in its conception it is entirely consonant with the desires and theoretical injunctions of certain influential symbolist critics. First, Mallarmé wished the symbolist drama to relate not the stories of individual men and women or particular groups of them but rather *"la Passion de l'Homme"* (Block, 85), the universal story of the human race and its sufferings. A later critic, Albert Mockel, referred to the same ideal as *"l'histoire eternelle de l'Homme"* (Block, 113).[20] Yeats too, a second-generation symbolist, wished the actors in his plays to "greaten till they become all humanity."[21] Wilder's play might be said to have taken Mockel's statement literally as its starting point. Mallarmé, moreover, admired the vitality of popular melodrama and vaudeville, and so *Skin* is not so far from symbolist tastes and biases as it at first seems. It even has a nearly exact precursor in symbolist—or postsymbolist—writing, critic and poet Edouard Dujardin's "dramatic poem" *Le retour éternel*, in which the central character relives certain key events in human history. Like Wilder's play, Dujardin's, as its title implies, exhibits a cyclic structure.

More conventionally symbolist in style, though, are *Our Town* and some of the dramatist's other "minimalist" plays, with their de-emphasis of concrete phenomena on stage. In the first place, a reduction or elimination of stage scenery was an integral part of the symbolist theater aesthetic. Mallarmé was fascinated by the expressive potential of the utterly bare stage (Styan, 92),[22] and Lugné-Poë agreed with him that the best setting for a symbolist play was one that boasted *"Pas de décor, ou peu"* (Block, 106). In 1891 critic Pierre Ouillard wrote, "The word creates the decor along with the rest. . . . The decor ought to be a simple ornamental fiction that completes the illusion by analogies of colors and lines with the drama. Most of the time a backdrop and some movable draperies will be sufficient" (quoted in Robichez, 188; my translation). The trellises in *Our Town* are neither more nor less than "simple ornamental fictions." Another symbolist critic, Charles Morice, wrote in 1893 that "it is poverty . . . that creates true opulence, that of the spirit" (quoted in Robichez; my translation). Yeats, finally, wrote after a performance in Lady Cunard's London drawing room of his play *At the Hawk's Well*, "My blunder has been that I did not discover in my youth that my theatre must be the ancient theatre that can be made by unrolling a carpet or marking out a place with a stick. . . . It has been a great gain to get rid of scenery, to substitute for a crude landscape painted upon canvas three performers who, sitting before the wall or a patterned screen, describe landscape or event" (quoted in Styan, 68–69).

This emphasis on material poverty as a concomitant of spiritual riches has its foundation, of course, in Platonic principles—especially in the theater, since the absence or reduction of material phenomena on stage leaves the spectator nothing to contemplate but the ideas of those and of all phenomena. Moreover, Mallarmé, in a famous phrase, speaks of the idea in terms of absence. He notes that his task as a poet, if he is describing a flower, is to evoke *"l'absente de tous bouquet,"*[23] the "absent one from every bouquet," the universal flower corresponding to none on earth. The phrase is on one level a superbly apt description of Mrs. Gibbs's heliotrope.

Further, both Wilder and the symbolists conceived of the material impoverishment of the stage as serving another, more practical purpose besides the Platonic one: to impel the spectator toward a more active involvement in the play. Mallarmé addressed his projected dramatic poem *Igitur* "to the Intelligence of the reader which stages things itself."[24] Earlier Baudelaire had gone further, observing that in all the arts—music, painting, and imaginative writing—"there is always a lacuna completed by the auditor's imagination."[25] Wilder too actively sought by means of his minimalist techniques to involve the spectator's imagination in the cocreation of the dramatic reality. In a preface to *Our Town* published after the play opened in New York, he writes, justifying his decision to require that the play be staged without scenery, "The spectator through lending his imagination to the action restages it inside his own head."[26]

Actually, the idea of writing plays requiring a scenery-free stage came to Wilder from a source other than symbolist writings or accounts of symbolist productions. According to his biographer Harrison, Wilder first conceived of the idea after he read an account of the staging of André Obey's plays by Michel Saint-Denis at the Théâtre du Vieux Colombier (Harrison, 152), and his acquaintance with the minimalist style for which that theater was famous dates from an even earlier period, since, as another source reports, he saw a production by the Vieux Colombier's Compagnie des Quinze, directed by its founder, Jacques Copeau, during at least one of the group's American tours—in 1917–18 or 1918–19.[27] Copeau's famous *tréteau nu* itself, however, has its roots in the symbolist aesthetic. The French director was strongly influenced by the ideas of both Appia and Craig (Styan, 91),[28] whose designs are generally classified as symbolist in style and inspiration, and his reverence for the dramatic text is more than a little reminiscent of the attitude of Mallarmé and his disciples.

Along with a reduction of decor, the symbolists advocated and practiced in their plays a reduction or elimination of dramatic incident or intrigue and even, at moments, of spoken dialogue. The element of anecdote in Wilder's plays, especially *Our Town*, *The Happy Journey*, *Childhood*, *Infancy*, and *Pullman Car Hiawatha*, is negligible, and although in one essay the playwright, arguing against Maeterlinck, asserts that drama as a representation before an audience necessarily involves forward movement ("Some Thoughts," 122), many of his own plays exhibit only cyclic movement at best. Moreover, the patiently expectant immobility of the dead in act 3 of *Our Town* resembles the somewhat tenser, more fearful expectancy of the waiting characters in Maeterlinck's *The Intruder* and *The Blind*.

The temporary elimination of dialogue in suspenseful, enigmatic silences, which help to underscore the atmosphere of anticipation, adds a further Maeterlinckian tinge to the same act of Wilder's play. Maeterlinck described the inexplicable, cosmic silence he regarded as "the source of the undercurrents of our life" (Maeterlinck, 11–12), an enveloping presence in everyday existence, in the following terms (replete with personification): "[L]et one of us but knock, with trembling fingers, at the door of the abyss, it is always by the same attentive silence that this door will be opened" (Maeterlinck, 11–12). Mysterious, unfathomable silences similar to those in Maeterlinck's (and, of course, Chekhov's) major plays are even more abundant in the first act of Wilder's play as well. After remarking that the morning star "always gets wonderful bright the minute before it has to go," the Stage Manager "stares at it for a moment, then goes upstage." When later that night the ladies returning from choir practice notice the moonlight falling all about them, they become "silent a moment, gazing up at the moon." When Dr. and Mrs. Gibbs stroll through their garden a few minutes later, they too fall silent for a short time as they smell the heliotrope in the moonlight. In fact, the playwright's beloved and admired former mentor Charles Wager was most deeply moved by the silences when he read the play.[29]

In symbolist aesthetics silence was not only the temporal counterpart of the bare stage, a manifestation of the void that contains the infinite (a favorite notion of Mallarmé), but also a component in the verbal "musicality" that symbolist poets and dramatists, influenced by Wagner, sought to achieve. Wilder incorporates a whimsical example of this verbal musicality into *Pullman Car Hiawatha*. At two points in the play, the personifications of the towns and fields the car has passed and of the appropriate planets and hours of the night, as well as the human characters connected with its journey, all murmur their individual mottoes or nonverbal sounds, while the Stage Manager adjusts the dynamics or tempo of their murmurings, conducting them "as the director of an orchestra would." The fact that the "music" he conducts is primarily verbal, moreover, even brings the passage into line with specifically symbolist, as opposed to Wagnerian, biases, since Mallarmé and his followers felt that poetry—the Word—was meant to be the dominant art in the *Gesamtkunstwerk*, whereas Wagner, naturally, felt it was music.

All these symbolist features of Wilder's plays do not, to reiterate, necessarily make him a thoroughgoing symbolist playwright. As stated at the outset, his dramaturgy shows affinities with a multitude of modern (and ancient) artistic movements and with the work of a number of individual playwrights. Even this aspect of his theater, however, has precedents in symbolist theory, if not in symbolist practices. Yeats consciously sought to achieve a playwriting style "that remembers many masters, that it may escape contemporary suggestion" (quoted in Styan, 64). Wilder's adoption and refinement of such a style allowed him to do one thing of which Mallarmé could only dream—namely, create a drama that is both popular and, to a high degree, symbolist.

Notes

1. See A. R. Fulton, "Expressionism—Twenty Years After," *Sewanee Review* 52 (Summer 1944): 398–413; Tom F. Driver, *Romantic Quest and Modern Query: A History of the Modern Theatre* (New York: Delacorte Press, 1970), 339; Walter H. Sokel, *The Writer in Extremis: Expressionism in Twentieth-Century German Literature* (Stanford, Calif.: Stanford University Press, 1959), 1; Malcolm Goldstein, *The Art of Thornton Wilder* (Lincoln: University of Nebraska Press, 1965), 75–76; and J. L. Styan, *Expressionism and Epic Theatre*, vol. 3 of

Modern Drama in Theory and Practice (Cambridge, England: Cambridge University Press, 1981), 115–17, 165.

2. See Michael Kirby, *Futurist Performance* (New York: E. P. Dutton, 1971), 67–68, and Oscar G. Brockett and Robert R. Findlay, *Century of Innovation: A History of European and American Theatre and Drama since 1870* (Englewood Cliffs, N.J.: Prentice Hall, 1973), 530, 533.

3. See Douglas Charles Wixson, Jr., "The Dramatic Techniques of Thornton Wilder and Bertolt Brecht: A Study in Comparison," *Modern Drama* 15, no. 2 (September 1972): 112–24; M. C. Kuner, *Thornton Wilder: The Bright and the Dark* (New York: Crowell, 1972), 104, 125, 138; Amos Niven Wilder (quoting a speech by Franz H. Link), *Thornton Wilder and His Public* (Philadelphia: Fortress Press, 1980), 70–71, 77 (hereafter cited in text as A. N. Wilder); Helmut Papejewski, *Thornton Wilder*, trans. John Conway (New York: Frederick Ungar, 1968), 96; and Horst Oppel, "Thornton Wilder in Deutschland: Wirkung and Wertung seines Werkes im deutschen Sprachraum," *Abhandlungen der Klasse der Literatur/ Akademie der Wissenschaften und der Literatur*, Jg. 1976/77, no. 3 (Mainz, 1977): 1–31 (discussed in A. N. Wilder, 17).

4. See, for example, Kuner, 137–38, 148; Gilbert A. Harrison, *The Enthusiast: A Life of Thornton Wilder* (New York: Ticknor & Fields, 1983), 186 (hereafter cited in text); and John Modic, "The Eclectic Mr. Wilder," *Ball State Teachers College Forum* 1 (Winter 1961): 55–61.

5. Some exceptions include Robert W. Corrigan, who discusses one important theme found in both Wilder's drama and Maeterlinck's in "Thornton Wilder and the Tragic Sense of Life," *Educational Theatre Journal* 13 (October 1961): 172 (hereafter cited in text), and Rex Burbank, who in his study *Thornton Wilder* (New York: Twayne Publishers, 1961), 35, 41, mentions Maeterlinck briefly as a kindred (antinaturalistic) spirit to Wilder but goes into no further details.

6. Linda Simon, *Thornton Wilder: His World* (Garden City, N.Y.: Doubleday, 1979), 42.

7. See, for instance, Thornton Wilder, "The Turn of the Year," *Theatre Arts Monthly* 9, no. 3 (March 1925): 152, and "Some Thoughts on Playwriting," in *The Intent of the Artist*, ed. Augusto Centeno (Princeton, N.J.: Princeton University Press, 1941), reprinted in Thornton Wilder, *"American Characteristics" and Other Essays*, ed. Donald Gallup (New York: Harper & Row, 1979), 122.

8. *Hommage à Maurice Maeterlinck* (Brussels: Brochure-Program de L'Institut National Belge de Radiodiffusion, 1949), 78–79.

9. Albert Aurier, "Le Symbolisme en Peinture: Paul Gauguin," *Mercure de France*, sér. moderne 11 (Mars. 1891), 162. My translation.

10. Thornton Wilder, preface to *Three Plays: Our Town, The Skin of Our Teeth, The Matchmaker* (New York: Harper & Bros., 1957), reprinted in *"American Characteristics,"* 108.

11. Thornton Wilder, "Some Thoughts on Playwriting," reprinted in *"American Characteristics,"* 118; hereafter cited in text as "Some Thoughts."

12. Maurice Maeterlinck, *The Treasure of the Humble*, trans. Alfred Sutro (New York: Dodd, Mead, 1900), 97–98; hereafter cited in text.

13. Haskell M. Block, *Mallarmé and the Symbolist Drama* (Detroit: Wayne State University Press, 1963), 102; hereafter cited in text.

14. Quoted in Charles Chadwick, *Symbolism: The Critical Idiom* (London: Methuen, 1971), 16:2. Author's translation from Mallarmé's *Oeuvres complètes*.

15. W. T. Jones, *A History of Western Philosophy* (New York: Harcourt, Brace, 1952), 299–300.

16. Thornton Wilder, *The Journals of Thornton Wilder, 1939–1961*, ed. Donald Gallup (New Haven, Conn.: Yale University Press, 1985), 215; hereafter cited in text as *Journals*.

17.   Gertrude R. Jasper, *Adventure in the Theatre: Lugné-Poë and the Théâtre de l'Oeuvre to 1899* (New Brunswick, N.J.: Rutgers University Press, 1947), 98n.

18.   For example, in Verhaeren's "The Mill" and "The Factories," de Regnier's "Town of France," and Moréas's "A Young Girl Speaks." See also Kenneth Cornell, *The Symbolist Movement* (New Haven, Conn.: Yale University Press, 1951), 71.

19.   Mark Evan Littman, "Theme and Structure in the Plays of Thornton Wilder," Ph.D. diss., Northwestern University, 1969, 45, 75n.

20.   Anna Balakian, in her study *The Symbolist Movement: A Critical Appraisal* (New York: New York University Press, 1977), 9–11, stresses the cosmopolitan, international character of the movement—its "non-temporal, non-sectarian, non-geographic, and non-national" focus—even while it was centered in France.

21.   Quoted in J. L. Styan, *Symbolism, Surrealism, and the Absurd*, vol. 2 of *Modern Drama in Theory and Practice* (Cambridge, England: Cambridge University Press, 1981), 64; hereafter cited in text.

22.   See too Jacques Robichez, *Le symbolisme au théâtre* (Paris: L'arche, 1957), 44; hereafter cited in text.

23.   Stéphane Mallarmé, "Crise de vers," *Divagations* (Paris: Fasquelle, Club français du livre, 1961), 213; quoted in Chadwick, 3–4.

24.   Stéphane Mallarmé, *Selected Poetry and Prose*, ed. Mary Ann Caws (New York: New Directions, 1982), 91.

25.   Charles Baudelaire, "Richard Wagner et Tannhauser," *Oeuvres complètes*, Édition établie et annotée per Y. G. LeDantec; revisée, completée, et presentée par Claude Pichois (Paris: Gallimard, Pleiade, 1966), 1210–11. My translation.

26.   Thornton Wilder, preface to *Our Town*, in *"American Characteristics,"* 101.

27.   Richard H. Goldstone, *Thornton Wilder: An Intimate Portrait* (New York: Saturday Review Press/E. P. Dutton, 1975), 199n.

28.   See too John Rudlin, *Jacques Copeau*, Directors in Perspective Series (Cambridge, England: Cambridge University Press, 1986), 2, 4, 36–39, 58–59.

29.   Harrison, 180, quotes letter from Wager to Wilder.

"Preparing the Way for Them": Wilder and the Next Generations

Donald Haberman

> I should be very happy if, in the future, some author should feel . . . indebted
> to any work of mine.[1]

Thornton Wilder probably speaks for every writer when he hopes some work of his might prove useful to a writer who comes after. One of the signs of vitality of writing is its appearance in some new shape or with a new meaning in subsequent writing. Certainly, though, every writer wishes first for his work a continuing life of its own, and in the case of plays the life is obviously in performance.

But if Wilder speaks the wish of all writers, he continues with a modesty and an expression of disappointment with himself, whatever truth might be concealed therein, that are especially characteristic of him:

> I hope I have played a part in preparing the way for them [future writers]. . . .
> I am not an innovator, but a rediscoverer of forgotten goods. ("Preface," xiv)

Wilder's view of his role in the continuing history of the stage was as a kind of John the Baptist for the real thing that might come after. He dismissed any definition of himself as original; like most thoughtful playwrights, he saw himself as returning to the sources of traditional theater life.

Now, more than 15 years after his death and 50 years after the premiere of *Our Town*, though not so long as survival for a writer is measured, some of the ways Wilder's writing for the stage has a continuing life can be observed. Wilder wrote relatively few plays. His reputation depends on three short plays, *The Happy Journey to Trenton and Camden*, *Pullman Car Hiawatha*, and *The Long Christmas Dinner*, and three full-length plays, *Our Town*, *The Matchmaker*, and *The Skin of Our Teeth*. But it is not unusual for only three or four plays of even playwrights more prolific, say, Pirandello, Cocteau, or Tennessee Williams, to be all that are performed on the international stage.

This essay was written specifically for this volume and is published here for the first time by permission of the author.

Our Town was a success from the beginning. *The Merchant of Yonkers* did not catch on until its revision as *The Matchmaker*; its transformation into *Hello, Dolly!* was even more popular. Though *The Skin of Our Teeth* opened in New York in 1942, during the period after the World War II it became Wilder's most important play.

The American government thought of *The Skin of Our Teeth* as sufficiently representative to send a production by the American National Theater and Academy to the *Salut à la France* in Paris in 1955 with Helen Hayes as Mrs. Antrobus and Mary Martin as Sabina. Another production in 1961 with Helen Hayes was sent abroad again by the government.

These official productions with famous stars attracted attention and gave the play greater recognition. But as Wilder himself acknowledged with some pride, it was on the Continent, especially in the German-speaking world, that *The Skin of Our Teeth* had the most astonishing and profound effect. The play directly addressed an audience literally reconstructing itself. It offered the idea of a future in a world that had survived destruction and all too easily might be content with chaos and despair. For the audiences all over Germany, the "meaning" was first. And German interest and commitment to Wilder survived those unhappy years; today his work in Germany is still the object of sustained and continuing academic consideration.

Those in Germany who were committed to the theater saw in Wilder's play more than emotional or spiritual encouragement. *The Skin of Our Teeth* and to a lesser extent *Our Town* gave evidence, both in particulars and in general, that a play with an unusual form that took into account new attitudes toward time, language, the definition of mankind, and the theater itself need not be relegated to experimental theaters with small fervent audiences or perhaps to publication only where it would scarcely be read by anyone. Such a play might attract and compel the crowd.

Bertolt Brecht, despite his apparently expressing the belief that Wilder had stolen from him the actors' address to the audience and the self-conscious use of the stage in *Our Town*, as well as the idea for a novel about Julius Caesar, thought Wilder would be the ideal translator of his *The Good Woman of Setzuan*, partly because Brecht believed that Wilder could influence the American audience in his favor.[2] Brecht did not see the relationship between his plays and Wilder's only with accusatory anger. *The Skin of Our Teeth* was the first American play he selected to join his own in the repertory of what would become the Berliner Ensemble. For a while, at least, he had some difficulty finding other American plays that shared his notions of theatrical expression.

The two other important German-language writers for the stage in the second half of the twentieth century are Swiss: Max Frisch and Friedrich Dürrenmatt. Both have expressed a debt to Wilder.

Frisch credits Wilder as "the man who re-awoke my youthful love for the theater after it had lain dormant for a full decade,"[3] presumably including the war years. Two of his earliest plays, *Now They Are Singing Again* (1945) and *The Great Wall of China* (1946), reveal the debt to Wilder in their episodic staging—the idea of the Dead, the bringing together of historical characters who coexist in the mind if not in historical time and place—and in their expression of the possibility of human survival. Both premiered in the Zurich Schauspielhaus, where Wilder's plays were seen by Frisch.

Although the two playwrights met, it was by Frisch's account not a success, largely because a young German turned the direction of conversation to the question of the effect of the barren environment of "narrow-minded Switzerland" on the "creative person." Vexed, Frisch protested too much; Wilder remained silent. To provide a more successful defense, Frisch slyly and not so casually reports that the man who introduced them "does not neglect to mention that I come from Zurich (where Wilder incidentally wrote *Our Town*)." He dramatically expresses his admiration for the play and his national dignity both at once.

Dürrenmatt, to illustrate his observations about scenery and place on the modern stage, refers to the "fine play" *Our Town* and to *The Skin of Our Teeth*. Scenery supports the representation of place on the stage, but it does not describe it, and abstraction in modern scenic design is a failure. Wilder's success is in "immaterializing the scenery" through the use of a few everyday objects: the chairs, tables, and ladders of *Our Town*. And in *The Skin of Our Teeth*, through immaterializing "the dramatic place," where the play actually happens, by confusing time and the stages of civilization.[4]

Dürrenmatt knows as well as anyone that, in the European theater anyway, Wilder in 1938 was not unique. In fact, he considers Wilder's achievement, quoting Frisch, as "making poetry with the stage," a possibility realized by playwrights throughout the history of the theater. Dürrenmatt uses the example of Frisch not only to describe what Frisch has done but also to objectify his observations about his own work. Without insisting on a conscious, specific influence, he identifies Frisch's experiments with indefiniteness of place, which continued past his early plays where the influence of Wilder is obvious, as well as Samuel Beckett's ("no man knows where to wait for Godot") with Wilder in general. Wilder's plays have an authority for Dürrenmatt because they are well known: "Living theater demands that a piece be played."

Dürrenmatt cites the turning to the audience by the characters in *Our Town* and addressing it directly as adding "the epic element of description" to the drama. He cites Shakespeare's and Goethe's plays as examples from the past of epic drama, by which he means giving up condensing "everything into a certain time . . . in favor of an episodic form." Now *epic* is certainly a term most usually associated with Brecht's drama, but in Dürrenmatt's explanation Brecht's name is nowhere to be found, only Johann Nestroy, the Viennese playwright who is the major source for Wilder's *The Merchant of Yonkers* and its later versions, Shakespeare, Goethe, and Wilder. Partly his choice is based on their popularity with audiences. What is significant here is the accuracy of Wilder's importance to Dürrenmatt, not justice for Brecht.

Frisch also wrote of Wilder's use of direct address by the actor to the audience, citing Sabina's appeal for the theater seats to use as fuel for the fire to save mankind from the Ice Age. It is an attempt to put the play on the same level as the audience. The effect of surprise is ephemeral, as Wilder knew, [5] because he brings down the curtain immediately after it. After wondering whether the playwright sacrifices the separateness of his art from the real world—"To be fashionable? In despair?"—Frisch concluded, "Perhaps it was not pure chance that made me use Sabina. . . . Perhaps there is nothing literature can do when it recognizes its impotence, demonstrates its impotence, but go under with a final cry of warning." Wilder's didacticism is so often thought to be preaching an absolute and universal salvation. Here Frisch, with obvious if wistful approval and identification, sees only recognition and warning in Wilder's play. For so political a playwright as Frisch, the acknowledgment of this limitation of literature to bear witness, to warn, is an important reminder of Wilder's aims. Except for those who are unsympathetic to Wilder, at his most successful he maintained active hope, but he resisted falsifying reality.

Between them Dürrenmatt and Frisch describe the bases for Wilder's influence on the stage at the end of the war. He was for many a source of encouragement on a very personal level. He called attention to the need to recover the poetry of stage time and place from calcified realism. He broke the stage illusion. And most surprising, perhaps, for those who have been deceived by the sentimentality encrusted on the plays as a result of misguided productions and false memory, Wilder presented a realistic human image on the stage, free from despairing necessity.

For me to try to prove the precise nature of Wilder's influence on particular playwrights since the 1950s would be both foolish and futile. Any writer worth noticing speaks in his or her own distinctive voice. Even when one writer generously acknowledges his or her relationship to another, my interest is not to diminish the writer's originality by pointing out Wilder's real presence. But a sampling of some plays for which Wilder, through his example, may have prepared the attitudes of theater professionals and audiences, as well as encouraging the playwrights themselves, is useful to gauge Wilder's place in recent theater history.

The British have never been enthusiastic about Wilder, but Laurence Olivier directed a production of *The Skin of Our Teeth* in 1945 for London with Vivien Leigh as Sabina. When Olivier and Leigh toured Australia and New Zealand with it in 1948, he played Antrobus himself. From all reports it is difficult to distinguish Olivier's enthusiasm for *The Skin of Our Teeth* from his enthusiastic friendship with Wilder. The audiences perhaps were at least as interested in the starring actors of Olivier's productions as in the play. Despite its success, the work of Olivier is no measure of Wilder's effectiveness on the British stage.

More recently Tom Stoppard, despite the popularity of *The Matchmaker* and even greater renown of *Hello, Dolly!*, did his own version of one of Wilder's sources, Nestroy's *Einen Jux will er sich machen*, as *On the Razzle*. Though he acknowledges Wilder,[6] his own version of Nestroy is closer to the original than it is to Wilder (or than Wilder is to the original). Though Wilder might have brought Stoppard's attention to Nestroy and despite some similarities between their attitudes toward the idea of the stage, the relationship between the two is tenuous.

Caryll Churchill seems a more likely follower of Wilder's innovations. *Fen* is a kind of grimmer *Our Town*, dramatizing the life of a variety of characters in a community from a particular perspective. The cartoonlike aspect of *Cloud-9* and the mixing of characters from disparate times and places in *Top Girls* look very much like *The Skin of Our Teeth*. Churchill's plays may resemble the poetic theater (and one of its descendants, absurdist drama) often identified with Paris between the wars. But Churchill is more political in her aims than the playwrights of poetic drama; like Wilder, she has little interest in the intimate interaction between art and life. (In contrast, for example, though their stage techniques are sometimes thought of with Wilder's, Stoppard and also the American Arthur Kopit are closer in spirit to the self-conscious theatricality of the poetic theater.) Dürrenmatt recognized Wilder's difference: the bare stage does not mean "black curtains," or at the other extreme, "threadbare poverty." In his "Author's Suggestions for Staging the Play" *The Skin of Our Teeth*, Wilder wrote scornfully, "I have never seen a cyclorama that did not suggest 'beauty' of the poetic drama type." He also rejected "poverty": "I do not mean that it [the bare stage] should be dismal or dull."[7]

Tennessee Williams, though his comments on Wilder generally are condescending and testy, is probably the first major American playwright to see opportunities for himself in Wilder's experiments. He called his first success, *The Glass Menagerie*, a memory play, a phrase often applied to *Our Town*, because Wilder found a way to dramatize the past from the perspective of the present. In his production notes Williams called attention to its "unconventional techniques" replacing "the exhausted theatre of realistic conventions," supporting essential "poetic imagination," and rejecting the "unimportance of the photographic in art."[8] Whether consciously or not Williams echoes Wilder's words in his various explanations of his stagecraft.[9] Tom is like Wilder's Stage Manager too, in and out of the story, playing his part as well as commenting on the events.

Camino Real, despite its never attracting the affection of audiences, had a special place for Williams and has certainly proved attractive to editors of anthologies intended for the classroom. From some perspectives it can appear to be a version of *The Skin of Our Teeth*. The place is anywhere, though it has a specific atmosphere. The characters, largely from literature, are brought together arbitrarily. There is no developing story. The situation is largely hopeful waiting. Gutman is like Wilder's Stage Manager in *Our Town*. Even the concluding hopeful survival, despite Kilroy's setback with Esmeralda, is like Wilder. The suffering of the characters, despite their superficial colorfulness and eccentricity, is the pain of everybody. Its very weaknesses— sentimentality and philosophical self-importance—are those thought of (wrongly) as Wilder's and serve to point up Wilder's superior mastery.

In the great outpouring of American plays since the 1960s, many of the writers have shown themselves to a greater or lesser degree as Wilder's heirs. Even if some of these writers could be totally unaware of Wilder, their plays have a family resemblance to his. (Actually, it is unimaginable that an American playwright after World War II could be ignorant of Wilder's plays. Recently, for example, the television reviewer for the *New York Times* described the use of the bare stage in an adaptation of Willa Cather's *O, Pioneers!* as "a gracious bow to Thornton Wilder's 'Our Town,' " assuming every reader would recognize at once the style of production. Comically, the production used a cyclorama.)

A. R. Gurney, Jr.'s *The Dining Room* makes use of a situation and occasion like those in *The Long Christmas Dinner*. The generalized occasion of dinner in both plays presents the changing American experience through several generations. The actors never become the characters, but assume a variety of roles as the situation demands.

The Wayside Motor Inn, at the beginning of Gurney's career, is like *Pullman Car Hiawatha* in showing a number of people at some crucial time in their lives, all sharing the same location, one associated with movement, a motel, a similar but more up-to-date place than a sleeping car on a train. These plays, like others of Gurney's, seem close to Wilder's in tone also.

Very different in tone, *The Basic Training of Pavlo Hummel*, by David Rabe, is a memory play that begins with Pavlo's death. The effect, like that of the third act of *Our Town*, is to endow Pavlo's small life with value. The events of his army experience, like Wilder's use of a single repeated event, fluidly dramatize his life. Pavlo is like one of Wilder's ordinary Americans who can tell us something important about who we are. The play is obviously angrier than anything of Wilder's, but like Emily who must return to her birthday, Pavlo "gotta get that stuff [he howls *shit*] outa you, man." The audience is left with the final injunction: "Lift your heads and lift 'em high . . . Pavlo Hummel . . . passin' by."[10] Even the irony cannot deny Pavlo's human dignity, and the harshness of manner does not disguise the resemblance of Rabe's conclusion to Wilder's.

A single shared ordinary experience like the dining room or the pullman car, dramatized to reveal an entire life, serves a number of playwrights. Waiting on line, for what is never established, is the occasion of Israel Horovitz's *Line*. Murray Schisgal presents a more sweeping picture of modern life through the dreariness of clerical office work in *The Typists*. As in *The Long Christmas Dinner*, the two typists move through almost an entire life. Both these plays seem more hopeless than Rabe's, but even they are ambiguously grim. Arnall cries at the end of *Line*, "I never wanted first. But I'm first. And I like it, Molly. First is good!"[11] Though the play establishes any such victory as vain, who can deny winning (something) is generally better than losing? The play does not allow the alternative of refusing to wait. The typists as they exit give "a friendly good-bye just the same,"[12] and Paul, though at first forlorn, picks up his crumpled cards before he leaves. Whether the conclusion is one more expression of deadening routine and habit or the survival of some minimal sense of human correctness is unclear. Both Horovitz and Schisgal, like Wilder, in the face of desolation cling to some shred of expectation.

Ed Bullins in *The Taking of Miss Janie* dramatizes racial collision. The scene is an almost bare "depiction of cheap living spaces" in "Los Angeles, San Francisco, Manhattan, Boston, etc."[13] This is far from Wilder's playful middle class, but it is Wilder's "immaterialized" space. The characters speak to the audience—or at least to some middle distance, probably somewhere in the auditorium. There are slide projections (*The Skin of Our Teeth*); it is a memory play, beginning at the end, after the "rape," not death this time. The play takes place during a party, which covers some extended time. In general intent too the play is not unlike Wilder's: a dramatization of *why* Monty "raped" Miss Janie. There is no program to cure America's racial anguish; it is a view of the way we are in the racial part of our living. Some of Bullins's audience do discover a call for some kind of particular action that is at least implied; Wilder was familiar with this limited understanding of his work too.

Edward Albee has credited Wilder with suggesting he write plays. His early success *The American Dream* is a kind of updated sour *Our Town*. The dramatic action is the everyday events of family living; the language is like the ordinary speech of everybody in Wilder's plays, whose meaning is something more and different from what it apparently is saying. Almost parodying *Our Town*'s Stage Manager and Sabina in *The Skin of Our Teeth*, Grandma arbitrarily stops the play: (*Interrupting . . . to audience*) "Well, I guess that just about wraps it up. I mean for better or worse, this is a comedy, and I don't think we'd better go any further. No, definitely not. So, let's leave things as they are right now . . . while everybody's happy. . . . Good night, dears."[14]

David Henry Hwang's use of Chinese theatrical techniques in his early plays and more recently in *M Butterfly* can perhaps be explained personally and ethnically by his being an American descendant of Chinese immigrants. Wilder was there ahead of him, making use of what he had seen in a performance of the Chinese actor Mei Lan-fang to bring to life the Americans of Grover's Corners. It is possible to imagine his delight at the surprises and ironies in this happy rediscovery of a strange (to the West) theatrical style.

To mark the occasion of *Our Town*'s fiftieth anniversary and to celebrate a production of the play by the Long Wharf Theater in New Haven, Lanford Wilson[15] and Mel Gussow[16] wrote about the play in tandem for the Sunday *New York Times*. Like Dürrenmatt, Gussow, though not wanting to "carry the comparison too far," put Wilder in company with Beckett and James Joyce. He suggested that Sam Shepard and David Mamet, "in terms of finding the extraordinary within the most ordinary situations," are two playwrights "deeply, although perhaps subliminally, affected by Wilder's work." He acknowledged that *Our Town* is still "a pioneering work of experimental theater" and concludes that "it is a play of enduring authenticity and austerity." The Long Wharf production, followed by Lincoln Center's, is proof that even for audiences who thought the play was all too familiar, it could still exert its power. It continues to have a life of its own apart from its effect on the work of others; as Wilson wrote, "*Our Town* will still play."

About himself Wilson wrote, "I didn't think I had been influenced by 'Our Town' specifically. . . . I was shocked when I reread the play. The Stage Manager's opening speech was completely stolen from Matt's first speech in my play 'Talley's Folly.' I could sue. And it was totally unconscious. That's being influenced." Wilson's explanation of the nature of the influence of Wilder probably fits most of the playwrights who have some kinship with him.

From the mid-1970s a more radical appearance of *Our Town* took place in *Route 1 and 9 (The Last Act)* by the Wooster Group, an experimental collaborative theater. Wilder's play was "deconstructed" and juxtaposed on a Pigmeat Markham comedy routine. Scenes from a parody of an Encyclopaedia Britannica lecture film on *Our Town* and some scenes from the play itself were played on a row of television monitors while the Markham routine was acted out by live actors on the playing space. The attitude toward Wilder was ambivalent; it recognized his fight against the restrictions of realism, but it also identified him with repressive white middle-class ideology. But one of the work's creators admitted that *Our Town* resisted destruction. David Savran in his book-length study of the Wooster Group, attempting to evaluate the use of Wilder objectively, wrote, "Ironically, during a period of retrenchment in the 1980s, in the midst of a revival of realistic playwriting, Wilder's [hope that he had helped to prepare the way for a new drama] has been fulfilled less conspicuously by new dramaturgy than new performance, and most powerfully perhaps, by a work that uses his own script as a starting point."[17]

If these suggestions of evidence in what I hope is a representative sampling of Wilder's continuing life on the stage in the work of others seem to lack coherence or a clear pattern, that may be one of the useful conclusions.

There is no one style in the modern and postmodern theaters; variety and rich individuality are among its characteristic qualities. Thornton Wilder's experimental theatricalism, characterization, and language are flexible and adaptable precisely because, as he claimed, he was a "rediscoverer." His experiments in the theater were a return to its beginnings. His influence is not limited to a single ideology or aesthetic view. He keeps peculiar company and shows up in strange places, where his good manners surprisingly are not out of date or out of place, but do what good manners are supposed to do, make human dialogue easier. Other playwrights hear him and respond.

Notes

1. Thornton Wilder, "Preface," *Three Plays* (New York: Harper & Bros., 1957), xiv; hereafter cited in text as "Preface."

2. Eric Bentley, *The Brecht Memoir* (New York: PAJ Publications, 1985), 40–41, discusses Brecht's "paranoid suspicions." James K. Lyon, *Bertolt Brecht's American Cicerone* (Bonn: Bouvier, 1978), provides facts about *The Good Woman of Setzuan* and *The Skin of Our Teeth*. D. C. Wixson, "The Dramatic Techniques of Thornton Wilder and Bertolt Brecht: A Study in Comparison," *Modern Drama* 15 (September 1972), 112–24, examines the similarities between Wilder's and Brecht's plays, and although he is unwilling to assert unequivocally that Wilder imitated Brecht, he appears to think so.

3. Max Frisch, *Sketchbook, 1946–1949*, trans. Geoffrey Skelton (New York: Harcourt Brace Jovanovich, 1977), 228–30.

4. Friedrich Dürrenmatt, *Problems of the Theatre*, trans. Gerhard Nellhaus (New York: Grove Press, 1958), 7–39.

5. Thornton Wilder, *The Journals of Thornton Wilder, 1939–1961*, ed. Donald Gallup (New York: Harper & Row, 1979), 22.

6. Tom Stoppard, preface to *On the Razzle* (London: Faber & Faber, 1981), 8.

7. Thornton Wilder, "Author's Suggestions for Staging the Play." Yale Library Collection of American Literature.

8. Tennessee Williams, "Production Notes," *The Glass Menagerie* (New York: New Directions, 1970), 7–10.

9. Thornton Wilder, "Preface," *Three Plays* (New York: Harper & Bros., 1957), vii–xiv, and *American Characteristics and Other Essays*, Ed. Donald Gallup (New York: Harper & Row, 1979).

10. David Rabe, *The Basic Training of Pavlo Hummell*, in Ted Hoffman, ed., *Famous American Plays of the 1970s* (New York: Dell, 1981), 115–16.

11. Israel Horovitz, *Line*, in *First Season* (New York: Random House, 1968), 68.

12. Murray Schisgal, *The Typists and The Tiger* (New York: Coward-McCann, 1963), 72.

13. Ed Bullins, *The Taking of Miss Janie*, in Ted Hoffman, ed., *Famous American Plays of the 1970s* (New York: Dell, 1981), 200.

14. Edward Albee, *The American Dream and The Zoo Story* (New York: NAL Signet, 1963), 127.

15. Lanford Wilson, " 'Our Town' and Our Towns," *New York Times*, 20 December 1987, sec. 2, p. 36.

16. Mel Gussow, "A Theatrical Vision Endures," *New York Times*, 20 December 1987, sec. 2, p. 36.

17. David Savran, *The Wooster Group, 1975–1985* (Ann Arbor, Michigan: UMI, 1986), 18.

ESSAYS AND JOURNALS

◆

Review of *American Characteristics and Other Essays*

MEGAN MARSHALL

When Thornton Wilder died in 1975 at the age of 78, he was best known as a novelist and playwright. After all, he had won Pultizer Prizes in both fields early in life—for *The Bridge of San Luis Rey* at 30, and for *Our Town* 10 years later—and kept right on going with *The Skin of Our Teeth* (1942), *The Matchmaker* (1954), *The Eighth Day* (a National Book Award winner in 1967), and *Theophilus North* (1973). Yet, perhaps surprisingly, the creator of *Our Town* (who can forget that nostalgic picture of small town life?) was also an able literary scholar, something of an expert on the modern period, who recorded his thoughts in enough articles and essays to fill a respectable volume.

During the same years that produced *Our Town*, Wilder made his living as an English teacher, first at New Jersey's Lawrenceville Prep, and later at the University of Chicago. And Wilder wasn't just putting in time—he cared about students and worked hard to make the University of Chicago the thriving center for the study of literature it was in the 1930s. Wilder himself enjoyed touring the country to lecture on a wide assortment of literary and philosophical topics. When the success of *Our Town* convinced him he could make a living as a dramatist, he gave up teaching but continued to lecture (the actor in him loved standing up in front of a crowd) and to study and write about the works of his favorite authors, primarily Goethe, Joyce, Gertrude Stein, and the Spanish playwright Lope de Vega.

In *American Characteristics and Other Essays* Donald Gallup has collected just about all the documents of Wilder's scholarly self, lecture notes, brief articles and introductions written between 1930 and 1960, plus a charming foreword by Wilder's sister, Isabel, which places each of the pieces in Wilder's personal history. It would be safe to say that Wilder never intended these essays to be collected—there is much repetition of ideas, even of passages, from one essay to the next. Several of the never-before-published essays might best have been left that way (these reveal Wilder's confessed difficulty in

From *The New Republic*, 5, 12 January 1980, 32–34. Reprinted by permission of *The New Republic*, © 1980, The New Republic Inc.

"putting down one declarative sentence after another" in stilted or scatter-shot organization). And, to get the carping over with, Wilder's "big" ideas are few, and derived mainly from his reading of Gertrude Stein and the classics. But what the essays do offer—and this should not be dismissed—is a personal view of literature from a writer whose intuitive understanding of human nature supports all his great works, whether dramatic, fictive, or critical.

First, the ideas. The three essays on "American Characteristics," taken from Wilder's 1950 Norton lectures on Melville, Thoreau, and Emily Dickinson, set out most of the themes that appear in the rest of the volume. Wilder's effort here is to define American literary classics which, he says, can only be understood as the works of the prototypical American, the loner. Wilder's American has retained the separatist spirit that brought the first colonies from Europe: he is a "nomad in relation to place, disattached in relation to time, lonely in relation to society and insubmissive to circumstance, destiny or God." (Sweeping statements like this are Wilder's strong suit; he rarely crosses the line from eloquence to bombast.)

The American isolation, says Wilder, fuels a creative spirit. Because he is disattached, lonely, and insubmissive, the American cannot define himself as the European does, by his neighborhood, the things and people around him. (Readers of Gertrude Stein will recognize her imprint here.) But this prototypical American will discover the need to "invent what it is to be an American" in writing, painting, music. These twin impulses, to separate and to create, are what took Thoreau to Walden and Melville to sea—and made them write.

But most important to Wilder is the kind of creativity the American character engenders. In writing, for example, the rootless American will be much less concerned with scene-setting and characterization than with the larger questions of epistemology and ontology. Thoreau went to Walden not to write a nature study but to, in his words, "meet the facts of life." And Melville managed to transform a sailor's yarn into an epic confrontation between good and evil, innocence and experience, meaning and meaninglessness. Even house-bound Emily Dickinson managed, in her verse, to "love the particular while living in the universal."

Of course Wilder would find the theater ideally suited to presenting the larger truths, the particular universalized, and his essays on drama mainly explore this idea. "Each actor before us is indubitably a living, breathing 'one'; yet [a play] tends and strains to exhibit a general truth," he writes in the introduction to his own *Three Plays*. And it is astonishing to discover just how much *Our Town* is rooted in theory: Wilder's notions of the lonely, self-inventing American and of the truth-telling capacity of the theater come together in *Our Town*. His famous innovations—eliminating props, simplifying stage sets and costuming—were all intended to emphasize the universal, enduring aspects of a particular American family, as he says, "to find a value above all price for the smallest events in our daily life."

But what is best about these essays is not Wilder's theory of drama, nor his notion of the American loner—an outmoded ideal sustained these days mostly by graduate students and politicians. Wilder's gift, ironically, is not for naming universals, but for understanding the *particular* problems of the authors he studied—problems which, not accidentally, mirror his own.

Thornton Wilder was the second son of a newspaper-editor-turned-diplomat, and spent his boyhood between homes and boarding schools in Wisconsin, China, and California. On top of this rather traumatic childhood, Thornton must have been haunted by the recollection of his identical twin brother who died at birth. Thornton's father Amos was, by all accounts, a tyrant, reappearing after stays in the Far East to demand recitations of homework assignments from his children. He was dead set against Thornton's writing career and secured the Lawrenceville teaching job for him in an effort to head it off. In fact, Amos Wilder decided everything for his son, not just his first job, but which colleges to attend, what countries to travel to, everything. When his father died in Thornton's 39th year, the son confided to close friends that he was more than a little relieved.

Small wonder, considering this domineering father, that young Thornton was something of a mama's boy. His mother, after all, provided the cheesecloth costumes for Thorntie's early dramatic projects with his brothers and sisters, and scrimped to send her son to the theater. After his father's death, Thornton built a large house in Connecticut for his mother and unmarried sister Isabel which he shared with them as a bachelor for the rest of his life.

Wilder is at his best when writing about familiar subjects: because it draws on his firsthand knowledge of single women and dominated children, his essay on Emily Dickinson is the most insightful of the collection. Wilder acknowledges the traditional explanation for Dickinson's homely verse style—the protestant hymn stanza—but goes deeper. He claims Emily never outgrew a need to attract her emotionally distant father's attention (a father whose soul she described as "pure and terrible") with clever remarks which quite early took the form of coy verses. But the best of her verses are, of course, not merely coy. They contain something "terrible" of their own, among other things, an obsession with death that "confirms a sense of how deep a wound she received [from her father]." The countless poems on mourning and loss disguise her longing for other people to die in retaliation for what she had suffered.

Wilder also takes us into the private lives of Thoreau, Stein, and George Bernard Shaw—all writers who "have spent their childhood under a senseless and immitigable tyranny." Stein's life was closest to Wilder's: she too had lost a twin at birth, and suffered under a dominating father and older brother.

Wilder also writes convincingly of Thoreau's failure at finding a true friend and lover. Although Shaw experienced political rather than familial tyranny (growing up in a repressive Ireland), Wilder clearly identified with the problem it brought on Shaw: a ruinous need to please audiences with his work rather than himself.

Wilder's obsession with the parental relation extends beyond the biographical passages even into the theoretical ones. Again and again his theories are phrased in terms of the family, as when explaining the loner in "American Characteristics" he writes: "In America the family is the nexus of an unusually powerful ambivalence. On the one hand the child strains to break away and lead his own life. On the other hand [he] is exceptionally aware of the multitude of the human race." He goes on to talk about the child's loneliness in the face of this choice. Wilder next turns fierce in "Culture in a Democracy" as he denounces his father in what he terms the "Feudal Fiction" which he believed infected all literature of the past: "God was a King and a Father; so all kings and fathers participated—by metaphor—in an element of divinity. God was above; and kings and fathers were above—and everybody else was *low*." This is the tormented son speaking. Even the most abstract statements—"Didacticism is an attempt at the coercion of another's free mind even though one knows that in these matters beyond logic, beauty is the only persuasion"—recalls the Wilder family triangle. The father who constantly made extra homework for his children is coercing Didacticism; and the more sensitive mother who encouraged Thornton's artistic efforts from the start is Beauty.

The reader of *American Characteristics* will find much that is missing from many a more considered volume of criticism. There is the refreshing straightforwardness of the creative artist considering his craft: in the midst of disquisition on the style of *Finnegans Wake*, Wilder asks, "do all books hence forward have to be written like this?" There is the smart aleck humor of the playwright taking potshots at his colleagues: on the derivative Shaw, "he could only think by ricochet." And there is the eloquence we recognize as the novelist's: on the letters of Madame de Sévigné, "Time after time the letter rises beyond the understanding of the daughter and becomes an *aria* where the overloaded heart sings to itself for the sheer comfort of its felicity, sings perhaps to the daughter she might have been." But above all we get to know Thornton Wilder, the loner who spent his childhood hither and yon, who never did find his mate, but who still managed to break out of his loneliness by recognizing his kinship with other great American writers with whom, through this book, he takes his place.

Global Villager: *The Journals of Thornton Wilder, 1939–1961*

HARRY LEVIN

In 1949 the bicentennial of Goethe's birth was celebrated by an international symposium at Aspen, Colorado. What other American man of letters at the time, if not Thornton Wilder, could have met so well that cosmopolitan occasion? His topic was the Goethean ideal of world literature, which he proceeded to demonstrate by translating the German and Spanish addresses of Albert Schweitzer and José Ortega y Gasset. Wilder had attended a German school in China, when his father was serving as consul there. Later on, after graduating from Yale, he had spent a year of classical studies at the American Academy in Rome. Nicolà Chiaromonte characterized him as "the only contemporary American writer who is literate in the European sense, . . . the humanistic sense." Some of his compatriots regarded Wilder as being all too literary, too widely traveled and highly cultivated, for his own good as a writer. On that score he was stridently attacked, despite his popularity and geniality, from two very different points of view.

The first attack came as a polemical review of *The Woman of Andros* (1930) by a communist hatchet man, Michael Gold. From the immediate standpoint of relevance to the class struggle, this novel seemed to him unduly slight, unconscionably precious, and inhibited by the genteel tradition. Like its predecessors, the quasi-Proustian *Cabala* (1926) and the Pulitzer Prize–winning *Bridge of San Luis Rey* (1927), it dealt with exotic settings, religious subtleties, and feelings—symbolized by the broken bridge—of unrequited love. Wilder's good-humored response to the attack took the form of a picaresque sally into the Depression, *Heaven's My Destination* (1935), caricaturing his own high-mindedness through the divagations of an evangelical traveling salesman, not excluding the proverbial misadventure with a farmer's daughter. Turning toward the theater, Wilder became more and more involved with domestic and quotidian themes. Except in his historical pastiche, *The Ides of March* (1948), with its simulated letters from Caesar, Cicero, and Catullus, he managed to live down the smell of the lamp.

The second attack on Wilder purported to be an exposure. He was

From *New York Review of Books*, 21 November 1985, 31–34. Reprinted by permission of the author.

accused by two Joycean devotees, Joseph Campbell and Henry Morton Robinson, of having plagiarized from *Finnegans Wake* in his cosmic comedy, *The Skin of Our Teeth* (1942). Wilder, a far more perceptive reader of Joyce than his accusers, had made no secret of his devotion. Perhaps his Roman training had instilled in him a palimpsestic approach to literature. The most vivid character in *The Bridge of San Luis Rey* is modeled on Madame de Sévigné, while his English title, *The Woman of Andros*, acknowledges its Latin source in the *Andria* of Terence. If *The Matchmaker* (revised by Wilder from his *Merchant of Yonkers*) was originally derived from J. N. Nestroy's *Einen Jux will er sich machen*, that Viennese extravaganza had in turn been based upon the Victorian farce of John Oxenford, *A Day Well Spent*—in a cumulative process of transposition that would later adapt to music and reach the screen with *Hello, Dolly!*

Today we are more conscious of, and less self-conscious about, what has come to be known as intertextuality. Wilder was hardly less preoccupied than Joyce had been with the *da capo* recurrence of things, thematic as well as textual. Both of them, after harking back to prehistoric monsters and tribal bards, looked ahead through war years toward survival. Both embodied their universals in a family pattern, varying as the Earwickers of Dublin did from the Antrobuses of suburban New Jersey. But drama, much more readily than prose fiction, can generalize about the human race. By striking the box set and opening the stage, Wilder rejected naturalism and revived the morality play: *Everyman*, *Mankind*. As for womankind, he argued, on stage all could be represented by one, "a timeless individualized Symbol." Sabina could be maid-of-all-work, beauty queen, reincarnation of Lilith, the eternal Other Woman, and also Tallulah Bankhead creating the part while rebelling against it in lines supplied by the playwright.

"The supranational subject is mine—" he noted in self-appraisal, "the individual in the all-time." And yet, in order to be individualized, the subject had to be localized. In *Our Town* (1938) we were told about a letter addressed to "Jane Crofut; the Crofut Farm; Grover's Corners; Sutton County; New Hampshire; United States of America; Continent of North America; Western Hemisphere; the Earth; the Solar System; the Universe; the Mind of God." Here Wilder may again have been borrowing from Joyce, for Stephen Dedalus similarly orientates himself in *A Portrait of the Artist as a Young Man*. But Stephen was echoing a traditional schoolboy formula, after all, and the variance means more to us than the parallel between his Dublin and Jane's Grover's Corners. Wilder's allegory of life cycles is fleshed out in the local colors of Main Street. Generalities are vernacularized through his Middle American dialogue. Indeed this fastidious stylist, not unlike Flaubert, had an especially sensitive ear for the *cliché juste*.

But Wilder remained, with Goethe, ever curious about the telescopic view, about man's place in nature and in history. Hence it is not surprising if we remember him—warmly—in paradoxical images: as the homespun classicist, the backslapping aesthete, the familial bachelor, the gregarious recluse, the folksy citizen of the world. Equally at ease in the classroom and backstage, he acted out the American dilemma of society and solitude: in his case, of innumerable friendships ranging from Gene Tunney to Gertrude Stein and periodic withdrawals to undisclosed retreats, where much of his creative work was accomplished in the utmost privacy. He was a personality in the sense that Henry James was and that William Faulkner, apart from his writing, was not. In the sense that Hemingway and Fitzgerald were strained and egocentric personalities, his was a mellow and generous temperament. The fact that he was haunted by the ghost of a stillborn twin brother might have had something to do with his psychic duality.

That personal identification with otherness inclined him to be something of an actor, and consequently he was more in his element as a dramatist than as a novelist. He was also somewhat inclined by descent and conscience to play the preacher, while doctrinally more attuned to Kierkegaard than to Calvin. Moreover, he had started out in, and often reverted to, the role of a teacher. It was therefore not surprising when his own persona, charged with so many interests and ideas, tended to outshine his dramatis personae. Much of this went into his prolific and many-sided correspondence, which unquestionably deserves to be collected and published. It is fortunate that voluminous journals, kept by him off and on for more than fifty years, have been preserved among his papers and manuscripts in the Beinecke Library at Yale. A central selection from them has now appeared under the authoritative editorship of Donald Gallup, who is both Wilder's literary executor and the leading bibliographer of modern American literature.

Mr. Gallup has given us "rather more than one-third" of the material spanning a twenty-two-year period in Wilder's later life. The unifying principle among these thoughtful jottings, dated mostly from hotel rooms in both hemispheres, seems manifest in an entry from 1940: "Now that I am thinking of becoming a critic. . . ." Not that the critical diarist has abandoned his imaginative undertakings, though the record is missing between 1941 and 1948—an interval that witnessed the emergence of *The Skin of Our Teeth* and *The Ides of March*, and included Wilder's three-year wartime service in the United States Military Intelligence. The diaries teem with embryonic projects, few of which were carried through gestation. The main completed exception was *The Alcestiad*, a Wilderesque reworking of the resurrection myth still best remembered through Euripides' *Alcestis*. After years of interrupted tinkering, it became the least successful of Wilder's works, both as a play and afterward as an opera libretto.

The perpetual work-in-progress to which these notes return most frequently, and from which two finished scenes are appended to Gallup's book, is *The Emporium*. The notion of Americanizing Kafka by dramatizing his alluring and off-putting Castle as a metropolitan department store, and by turning his bewildered protagonist into a Horatio Alger hero—this was one of Wilder's more engaging premises. But inspiration was always much easier for him than realization. Mocking the conventions and planning the surprises made it all the harder. He was worried by his happy endings and held up by his last acts. The pageantlike conclusion to *The Skin of Our Teeth* was contrived and anticlimactic; *The Bridge of San Luis Rey* had the peculiar advantage of beginning with the catastrophe and then looking backward to explore the meaning of its five victims' lives. Wilder's journals, like James's prefaces, take us into the writer's confidence, confront us with his technical problems, and suggest angles for their solution.

There are some lively comments on fellow dramatists—O'Neill, Claudel, Anouilh, Büchner, the Greeks—along with occasional discussions of the other arts, notably music and film; but the volume's most sustained and valuable contribution lies in its series of observations on major novelists. These knowledgeable insights can be sharply aphoristic. Thus Thomas Mann, though respectfully cited, is termed "that ponderously signpost-planting author." André Gide's outlook is skeptically described as "the sincere desire to be sincere of one who cannot be so." Discriminating admiration for James is qualified by this stricture: "Never was there a greater fuss-budget of a novelist, continually intruding his view of the case precisely under the pretense of withholding it." And, though Wilder gradually learned to appreciate Faulkner, he maintained a temperamental and cultural distance: "It is as though we were hearing the fall of the House of Atreus told by a voice that was feverish and shrill, scandal-mongering-nosey, and a little prurient."

The pungency of such remarks, set down by a fellow craftsman and not primarily for publication, is warranted by their professionalism. Further animadversions throw unaccustomed light upon novels by Cervantes, Stendhal, Dickens, Gogol, Tolstoy, Camus, and Genet. But Wilder's criticism was increasingly focused upon the classics of the American Renaissance, which he had undertaken to reconsider as Charles Eliot Norton Professor of Poetry at Harvard in 1950–1951. Many of the pages in his journals are taken up with preliminary sketches for the six public lectures or with afterthoughts and outlines for the book that was to be organized around them.[1] The assignment, which he characteristically viewed as an opportunity to deliver "lay sermons," stimulated his flair for comparing national characteristics and his quest for psychological archetypes. On the premise that "the central figure of the superior works of our literature is Everyman," he typified the difference between our culture and all others in a personification named Tom Everage—that everyday average man, so unlike Thornton Wilder.

He was at his best in treating authors as individuals, who faced their common task—and his—of "American Symbol-Making." Under his trenchant analysis Poe and Whitman stand out; Emerson subsides into "odd doubletalk," Thoreau into "idiosyncratic exaggeration"; and Melville gets ship-wrecked before and after his unique triumph in *Moby-Dick*. Hawthorne is most severely judged, perhaps because he comes closest to Wilder as a fabulist and moralist.

> For Hawthorne, the basic sin which he claims to hold before our eyes is: resorting to the head rather than to the heart. Yet an obsession on his part is that sex is sin. But sex is nearer the heart than the head, and N.H. is at once entangled iri a series of contradictions which make havoc throughout his book [*The Scarlet Letter*].

Hester Prynne is unfavorably contrasted with Anna Karenina and Goethe's Gretchen:

> Gretchen [in *Faust*] and Anna Karenina are broken by society and by their lovers but not by their poets; Hester is disavowed by her creator, who reserves for her only the cold justification that—had she been less "impure"—she might have launched a crusade for bettering the world's understanding of women.

As an auditor of Wilder's Norton Lectures, I can attest that they were polished performances, all but ready for publication as first presented. But, having fallen dangerously "in love with the Norton book," he went on elaborating drafts, prolonging revisions, and accumulating reservations until it turned into an albatross. He would produce no "writing of the category imaginative narration" for sixteen years. Nor could it be claimed that his two septuagenarian novels, *The Eighth Day* (1967) and *Theophilus North* (1973), lived up to his earlier achievement.

"That didactic-expository year at Harvard," he would explain to himself, ". . . brought into focus those modes of thinking that are disturbingly incompatible with what I gropingly call symbolization." Yet, when he responded to that call from Cambridge, he had already been deeply immersed in two abstruse hobbies involving scholarly research. One was his "compulsive infatuation" with the exegesis of *Finnegans Wake*, a "narcotic" inducing the illusion of an ersatz creativity, which he would subsequently renounce. As if this were not demanding enough, the other hobby was not simply the baroque Spanish drama of Lope de Vega; it was, more specifically, the problem of dating his 450 extant plays, and thereby charting his chronological development. "Fun, fun, fun," Wilder chortles, at the prospect of putting together a learned article; but the 1198 journal pages of notes on Lope remain unpublished. At all events, they show—as do the Joycean marginalia—how easily the artist in Wilder could be sidetracked, even before the roadblock of "the Nortons."

He had reached the point where personality flourished at the expense of artistic practice. Given his generosity as well as his curiosity, he could offer little resistance to the social distractions coming his way: testimonial dinners, honorary degrees, polyglot speeches, UNESCO conferences, trips to Hollywood, unremitting other travels in the US and abroad, lunch with *Bundeskanzler* Adenauer and dinner with mystagogic Gurdjieff—not to mention the unstinted and unrecorded attention he gave to friends everywhere. In setting his career into perspective, these journals can be usefully supplemented by the sympathetic biography of Gilbert A. Harrison. . . .

[In writing *The Enthusiast*] Mr. Harrison had access to Wilder's journals, and has included tantalizing excerpts from them that have not been reproduced in the Gallup edition.[2] These omissions seem to result from an editorial policy which excludes "most passages of introspection and self-analysis." Yet such passages would constitute the core of the most interesting writers' journals, and Wilder as a reader would probably have been most interested in them. Consider, for example, five pages printed by Harrison under Wilder's heading, "A Look-Around My Situation," *written* at Saint-Jean-de-Luz in the spring of his climacteric year, 1950. Gallup's one-page extract covers merely his itinerary and agenda. But this was arrived at, in context, through painful self-searching, a recoil from the sociable whirl, and a statement about the author's "removedness from the writings." Surely the final paragraph ought to be quoted:

> One last word: The disarray in my psychic life which was perhaps caused by the uprooting which was the war and which has been so advanced by the even deeper immersion in the "false positions" I have recounted, have [sic] one still more harmful result. All these activities have been *flights from seriousness*. I am deep in *dilettantism*. Even my apparent preoccupation with deeply serious matters, e.g., the reading of Kierkegaard, is superficial and doubly superficial because it pretends to be searching. Gradually, gradually I must resume my, my own meditation on the only things that can reawaken any writing I have to do. I must gaze directly at the boundless misery of the human situation, collective and individual.

It should be clear that there is nothing at all discreditable in this momentary confession. Nor should it be held against Wilder that he never actually succeeded in carrying out this uneasy resolve. On the contrary, and regardless of any outcome, his self-doubts do great credit to the virtues that he possessed in abundance: modesty, conscientiousness, and high standards. His dissatisfaction with dilettantism (dilettantism in depth?) bespeaks the professional. If he worried so over his departures from seriousness, he must have been a truly serious man. Cheerfulness kept breaking in, and his ebullient manner made it all too easy for his contemporaries to set him down as an incorrigible optimist—or, in Mr. Harrison's ambiguous epithet, an enthusiast. But, though he commented knowingly on *Don Quixote*, he was not quixotic himself. Ultimately he never allowed his bookish idealism or his comic ingenuity to derange his oceanic awe before the tragic realities that bound our daily existence.

Notes

[This essay's title was incorrectly printed as "Global Villagers" in its original publication.—Ed.]

1. It was never completed. Three of the lectures were published in the *Atlantic Monthly* (1952) and, with some revision, in Wilder's posthumous collection, *American Characteristics and Other Essays* (1979).

2. There are a few small discrepancies where the same passages have been transcribed by both Gallup and Harrison.

Index